Making It in Broadcasting

Making It in

Broadcasting

AN INSIDER'S GUIDE TO
CAREER OPPORTUNITIES

Leonard Mogel

COLLIER BOOKS
MACMILLAN PUBLISHING COMPANY
NEW YORK

MAXWELL MACMILLAN CANADA
TORONTO

MAXWELL MACMILLAN INTERNATIONAL
NEW YORK   OXFORD   SINGAPORE   SYDNEY

Collier Books
Macmillan Publishing Company
866 Third Avenue
New York, NY 10022

Maxwell Macmillan Canada, Inc.
1200 Eglinton Avenue East
Suite 200
Don Mills, Ontario M3C 3N1

Macmillan Publishing Company is part of the Maxwell Communication Group of Companies.

Library of Congress Cataloging-in-Publication Data
Mogel, Leonard.
Making it in broadcasting: an insider's guide to career opportunities / [Leonard Mogel].
p.   cm.
Includes bibliographical references and index.
ISBN 0-02-034553-4
1. Broadcast advertising—United States. 2. Television advertising—Vocational guidance—United States. 3. Radio advertising—Vocational guidance—United States. I. Title.
HF6146.B74M63   1994
659.14'023'73—dc20   93-9012
CIP

Macmillan books are available at special discounts for bulk purchases for sales promotions, premiums, fund-raising, or educational use. For details, contact:

Special Sales Director
Macmillan Publishing Company
866 Third Avenue
New York, NY 10022

First Collier Books Edition 1994

10   9   8   7   6   5   4   3   2   1

Printed in the United States of America

To my loving sisters, Gracye Weisbrot, Frances Strassner, and Florence Fisher, and to my dear brother, David Mogel

CONTENTS

PART VI   PURSUING A CAREER IN BROADCASTING

ACKNOWLEDGMENTS

Appreciation goes to my wife, Ann Mogel, for her patience, encouragement, and major contribution to this project. My sincere thanks to my editor, Natalie Chapman, for her consummate editing of this book, and to Nancy Cooperman for her splendid cooperation.

I wish to express my gratitude to all the people who enhanced this book by agreeing to be interviewed: Mel Tolkin, Amy Coe, Leah Sanders, Bruce Sidran, Anna Carr, Ellen Hulleberg, and George Nicholaw and Bob Sims of KNX radio.

I may miss a few names, but my sincere appreciation for their cooperation goes to: Roger Bumstead; Joe Tiernan and Vernon Stone of the RTNDA; Larry Stewart of the *Los Angeles Times*; Louisa Nielsen of the Broadcast Education Association; Steve Haworth and Alyssa Levy of CNN; Ken Moffett and John Krieger of NABET; Jack Loftus of Nielsen Media Research; Donald West of *Broadcasting & Cable*; the National Association of Broadcasters; and the AEJMC.

Making It in Broadcasting

PART I

Introduction to Television

Courtesy CNN

CHAPTER 1

A Brief History
of Television

FROM TUBE TO SATELLITE IN HALF A CENTURY

Fifty years ago, TV reached a few thousand homes over a postage-stamp–size set. In 1993, a billion people around the world watched the Super Bowl, many on wall-size screens. Who can project what the next fifty years will bring to this dynamic medium?

A series of inventions in the latter part of the nineteenth and early twentieth centuries led, in the 1940s, to a television broadcasting system. It all started in 1884 with the first patent for a rudimentary television process given to a German inventor, Paul Nipkow. In the early part of the twentieth century, the invention of the first electron tube by the English physicist J. A. Fleming and the invention of wireless telegraphy by an American, Lee De Forest, were giant steps in modern TV research.

Other dramatic developments followed, the foremost being the iconoscope camera tube, which was patented in 1923 by V. K. Zworykin, a Russian immigrant to the United States. At the same time, Philo T. Farnsworth, an American engineer, was working independently toward an electronic scanning system along somewhat the same lines as Zworykin's iconoscope.

During the 1930s, RCA actively pursued experiments in TV research, although the Germans were first with a broadcasting service in 1935, courtesy of Adolf Hitler. On April 30, 1939, at the opening of the New York World's Fair, NBC held a public demonstration of TV and announced that it was ready to begin broadcasting for two hours per week.

By mid-1940, the Columbia Broadcasting System and the Dumont network had joined NBC. Allen B. Du Mont had earlier developed the kinescope tube and marketed the first modern home TV receiver in 1939; however, World War II brought nearly all activity to a halt as electronics factories were converted to wartime production.

At the end of the war, there were only 7,000 TV receivers in the United States. Only five cities had stations: New York, Philadelphia, Chicago, Los Angeles and of all places, Schenectady, NY. In 1949, however, one million TV receivers were already in use. By 1951 that number had jumped exponentially to ten million sets, and by 1959 soared to fifty million.

Although the first practical demonstration of color took place in 1928, the widespread purchase of color receivers did not begin in the U.S. until 1964.

The first step in live global communications via outer space came on July 10, 1962, when the National Aeronautics and Space Administration (NASA) launched the Telstar I satellite. The first transatlantic broadcast was of Vice President Lyndon B. Johnson and other officials speaking in Washington, D.C. From there the program went over telephone wire to AT&T's facility in Andover, Maine. It was then relayed to Telstar I, somewhere in space, which passed the message to a station in France and then to another station in an English town with the charming name of Goonhilly Down.

Seven years later, in 1969, the first moon landing was carried by satellite to an audience of more than a hundred million viewers.

TELEVISION PROGRAMMING

TV programming in the late 1940s was a haphazard attempt at entertainment. One popular wrestling show of the period featured an announcer, Dennis James, delivering loud sound-effect crunches to complement the staged antics of the wrestlers.

The first important TV star was Milton Berle with his hilarious Texaco Star Theatre. Who of the first generation of TV watchers can forget the three Texaco service station men as they belted out the spirited commercial, "We are the men of Texaco, we work from Maine to Mexico, there's nothing like this Texaco of ours . . . "

By 1950, there were 104 TV stations in the United States. Programming became more professional and more varied. Soon the three networks were supporting the production of brilliant comedy shows like Sid Caesar's "Your Show of Shows" and the memorable dramatic series "Playhouse 90." The influence of TV soared. In the words of the eminent social scientist Marshall McLuhan, the medium soon became the message.

Today, television is by far the most powerful force in entertainment. TV production and programming is a major industry. Billions of dollars are spent by advertisers to tap TV's vast audience. Its reach is worldwide, with more than 700 million sets in use. With new technologies in systems and instruments still being developed, TV's influence and scope are limitless.

What's in store for television? Consider this scenario: Before the end of this century, there will be a billion TV sets in worldwide use, most of them equipped with pay-per-view capabilities. A major new movie opens, but instead of releasing it to 1,200 to 1,500 theaters, the studio decides to feature it first on pay-per-view TV. If only one half of 1 percent of the world's TV audience paid an average of $20 per home to see the movie, it would gross $100 million in only one night, more than most movies gross during the whole of their general theatrical release. And this approach still allows for additional distribution of the movie in theaters, TV reruns, and the powerful home video market. Television looks likely to remain the dominant medium in the field of entertainment.

THE IMMEDIACY AND INFLUENCE OF TELEVISION

On January 16, 1991, as Baghdad was hammered by waves of U.S. warplanes, the world heard the Persian Gulf War begin live. Over telephones from a sixth-story room of the Al Rashid Hotel, three CNN correspondents opened their windows to hear the sounds of bombing and antiaircraft fire.

"The sky is lighting up to the south with antiaircraft fire and flashes of red and yellow light," CNN correspondent Peter Arnett reported. "There's another attack coming in. . . . It looks like the Fourth of July." His associate, John Holliman, added, "It's like the center of hell." Later, turning poetic, Holliman reported, "It looks like one hundred fireflies, like sparklers on the Fourth of July, as we look out about four miles. . . . The blast of air was like that you feel at Cape Canaveral when a rocket goes off."

As allied aircraft arrived in four-plane waves, about fifteen minutes apart, and lit up the Baghdad skies, Americans sat immobilized before their TV sets, watching these three intrepid correspondents and their crew bringing viewers the intense drama of a live war. It was the hottest-breaking war story since World War II's Normandy invasion. Not only President George Bush and his adversary, Saddam Hussein, but other world leaders were watching this fantastic coverage as well. On the first night of the war, when CNN called the Palestine Liberation Organization in Tunis to ask if its leader, Yasir Arafat, would appear on camera, Arafat's aide responded: "President Arafat is in the situation room watching CNN and cannot be disturbed."

CNN's prime-time viewership exploded that first evening from its normal 560,000 to an astonishing 11.4 million. Its programming was also carried on more than forty stations in at least twenty-five countries.

The day after the war's outset, newspapers carried dozens of news stories and in-depth commentaries on events in Iraq. Yet none could match the immediacy of the TV medium, and in subsequent days TV continued its leadership with graphic coverage of the Persian Gulf War. It soon became a bizarre routine in American homes; "Let's watch the war on TV" was the byword.

In the years following the Persian Gulf War of 1991, television coverage made us eyewitnesses to momentous world events. We watched military operations in such far-flung places as Somalia, Bosnia-Herzegovina and, in 1993, Iraq again.

TV MARKETS ACROSS THE UNITED STATES

If you are determined to be an anchorperson with the clout and compensation of a Peter Jennings, Tom Brokaw, or Connie Chung, you'll have to be prepared to start at a much lower level and in a small market.

What is a television "market" and how is it measured? Markets are designated for the purposes of audience measurement. The Arbitron Company, a leading broadcast research organization until it ceased TV services in October 1993, ranked the country into areas of dominant influence (ADI) that consist of a major city and its periphery and assigned each a rating that reflects the total number of TV households.

To give you an idea of TV's geographic scope, Table 1 shows some 1993 Arbitron ADI rankings and the number of TV stations in these areas. There are 1,100 commercial stations across the country. You'll note that the market area ranking does not necessarily correspond to the number of stations operating in it. Of course, many stations in the smaller markets do not have large audiences.

TABLE 1. NUMBER OF TV STATIONS IN THE TOP TEN MARKETS

MARKET AREA	ADI RANKING	# OF TV STATIONS	TV HOUSEHOLDS
New York	1	16	6,750,000
Los Angeles	2	19	4,900,000
Chicago	3	14	3,000,000
Philadelphia	4	15	2,600,000
San Francisco	5	18	2,200,000
Boston	6	15	2,100,000
Washington, D.C.	7	10	1,780,000
Dallas/Ft. Worth	8	15	1,760,000
Detroit	9	8	1,700,000
Atlanta	10	10	1,450,000

Source: The Arbitron Company

PRIME-TIME TV IS BIG-TIME DOLLARS

TV broadcasters divide the day into nine "dayparts" or segments (see chapter 10). The most important daypart is prime time, from 8:00 P.M. to 11:00 P.M. During prime time, TV draws its largest audience and the networks and other stations trot out their most expensive programming to compete for the largest number of viewers. Advertisers pay for their commercials based on audience size, found by a rating system.

What are ratings? Briefly, a rating is an estimate of the number of people watching a specific program at a given time. Ratings are expressed as a number and relate to the percentage of all 94.2 million TV homes. For example, if a given show has a 13 rating, that means 13 percent of 94.2 million, or 12.2 million homes, are watching that show. You can learn more about ratings in chapter 9.

Prime-time shows with high ratings mean big bucks. A show such as CBS's "Murphy Brown," with an audience of about eighteen-million TV homes, can charge over $250,000 per thirty-second commercial. The total advertising revenue for the show is more than $3.25 million. On the other hand, stars like Candice Bergen receive salaries of about $200,000 per show. Each network's cost for a full season's prime-time programming is estimated at $1.5 billion. Network TV, and prime time in particular, is a big-league sport. We'll discuss the economics of prime-time TV in chapter 12.

TELEVISION AS AN ADVERTISING MEDIUM

Advertisers make major commitments to network TV as an advertising medium. In 1992, for example, of the top five advertisers in all media, Procter & Gamble spent $535 million on network television alone, General Motors $450 million, Philip Morris $410 million (other than tobacco products), PepsiCo $280 million, and Kellogg $254 million. Procter & Gamble's total commitment to all of broadcast and cable TV advertising was approximately $1 billion.

SOME SALIENT STATISTICS
ABOUT TV AUDIENCES

The A. C. Nielsen Company, the leader in TV research, has developed some interesting statistics that bear on the viewing habits of TV audiences. Here are a few of the highlights:

* Households that view TV most often are those with three or more people, those having pay cable, and those with children.
* In general, women watch TV more than men do, younger children more than older children, and older adults more than younger adults.
* Situation comedies continue to attract the largest prime-time audiences; feature films rank second, and suspense-mystery, third.
* In 1991, TV sets were turned on in American homes for an average of seven hours each day. That's not the nation's highest level. In 1985, the average was seven hours and ten minutes.
* 65.6 percent of all TV households, besides the set in the living or family room, had a set in the bedroom, and 10.7 percent had a set in the kitchen.
* Nine out of ten Americans get their news from TV.
* At this writing, VCRs are found in over 68 percent of TV households.
* In 1991, advertisers spent over $27 billion to reach TV audiences, second only to newspapers, where $30 billion was spent.
* By 1993, cable TV had a total of fifty-five million subscribers, about 60 percent of all TV households. Of these fifty-five million cable subscribers, 52 percent subscribed to one or more pay-cable networks.
* Adults spend more time with TV than with all other major media combined.

WORKING IN TELEVISION

The universe of television employment encompasses programming, production, acting, scriptwriting, news- and sportscasting, advertising sales, engineering, syndication sales, and camera and technical functions. Hundreds of thousands work in local and network TV, in TV production companies, and for newsgathering agencies. Tens of thousands more are employed at ad agencies to evaluate and purchase TV advertising. TV is a glamorous profession that attracts millions of high-school and college graduates and career switchers each year.

This book will make anyone who is interested in a television career familiar with the operation of the networks, stations, and production companies. It discusses the duties and salaries of jobs in TV, and it gives advice on how to break into this popular field.

In the second half of the book we explore the field of radio, a profession that employs upwards of 125,000 people. As in TV, we will discuss jobs, salaries, and the way stations function. In short, this book is an introduction to the whole field of broadcasting.

CHAPTER 2

How TV Is Structured: An Overview

THE RELATIONSHIP OF THE NETWORKS AND THE PRODUCTION COMPANIES

"Murphy Brown," single mother and target of political conservatives, reigns as Queen of the Airwaves on Monday-night, prime-time television. On average, eighteen million homes have their sets firmly focused on CBS to watch this sophisticated hit comedy. A look at the logistics of bringing the show to this vast audience will show the economic factors and relationships of the networks and the production companies.

CBS, the network, owns seven TV stations in New York, Los Angeles, Chicago, Philadelphia, Minneapolis, Green Bay, and Miami. Besides these stations, another 200 stations across the country contract with CBS to carry its programming, including "Murphy Brown." These stations are called "affiliates." In any season, the affiliates will carry most of CBS's prime-time programming (8:00 P.M. to 11:00 P.M.) as well as the network's sizable news and sports output.

CBS neither produces nor owns "Murphy Brown." An independent producer, Shukovsky/English Productions, owns the show in association with a major TV studio, Warner Brothers Television. This means that there is a financial partnership arrangement between Shukovsky/English Productions and Warner Brothers, whose physical facilities will be used in shooting the show. The independent production team produces the show and assumes all its expenses. CBS "licenses" the show from the production company, that is, CBS negotiates a price for some number of half-hour episodes. In the case of "Murphy Brown," CBS is committed to show 26 new episodes during a TV season. The network's license also includes the right to rerun each episode one more time at no additional cost.

The cost of a show such as "Murphy Brown" may run as much as $2.5 million per episode. Often the network does not pay the production company as much per episode as the show costs to produce. How does the production company handle this deficit financing? The answer is "syndication" (discussed below).

But what about the poor network? Besides paying a substantial licensing sum, CBS must also compensate its 200 affiliates for carrying the show. Where does CBS derive its income from broadcasting "Murphy Brown" and its other programming? Where else?—from selling commercials.

CBS sells about thirteen minutes of commercials per prime-time hour. The average thirty-second commercial for a hit show ran about $280,000 in 1992. Simple arithmetic gives us a total revenue to the network of about $3.64 million per "Murphy Brown" broadcast—enough to pay the licensing, the affiliate compensation, and overhead.

Let's not forget the hapless production company, saddled with a deficit of perhaps $300,000 or more per episode. To the rescue comes "Syndication." After a prime-time show has been running for two or three years, qualifying it as a hit, the production company sells "independents," cable stations, and foreign broadcasters the right to air reruns. Independents are local television stations that have no network affiliations. (Some producers use a syndicator as an agent in licensing rerun rights.)

Shows can go to stations for straight "cash," or on a barter basis, with stations accepting programs in return for running some commercials sold by the syndicator. In this case, the station retains some commercial slots and sells time locally. On any basis, a hit show like "Murphy Brown" will yield gold for its producers and syndicators once it reaches this lucrative market. Viacom Enterprises has exclusive syndication rights for the megahit "The Cosby Show." The show began syndication in 1986 and by 1990 it had yielded $600 million, of which Viacom retained one-third. The show's producers, Carsey-Werner, got the rest, with Mr. Cosby himself receiving a good portion of that golden egg.

Traditionally, syndication rights to a show are sold only after the show has been successful for at least three years. We'll get into syndication in more detail in chapter 15.

Understanding television as a business means knowing how the players interact. The accompanying chart shows the relative positioning of all the participants in the TV picture. We offer a brief explanation of their activities and, in subsequent chapters, describe these activities in detail.

THE STRUCTURE OF TELEVISION AND CABLE

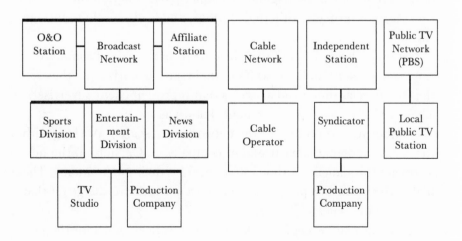

THE FOUR BROADCAST NETWORKS

There are four broadcast networks: NBC, CBS, ABC, and Fox. Each of these networks may own as many as twelve TV stations, the limit established by the Federal Communications Commission (FCC). The networks have also contracted with a combined total of more than 600 privately owned stations—called affiliated stations—that carry the networks' programming under various financial arrangements. Today, networks transmit most programming to the local stations by satellite.

The networks are active in programming and production. The largest portion of their program output—sitcoms and dramas—are licensed from studios and independent production companies similar to the one that produces "Murphy Brown."

The studios that create these TV shows contract with the actors, producers, directors, and technical crew involved in their productions. Various craft unions represent these employees.

The networks themselves produce much of the news and sports programming. Examples of these are NBC's "Today" show, CBS's "60 Minutes," ABC's "Monday Night Football," and NBC's "1992 Summer Olympics." The staffs of these shows are typically network employees. The networks' original news and sports programming is carried on their own and affiliated stations, and is often sold to foreign stations.

Networks derive most of their income from the sale of commercial time. They maintain large staffs in their sales departments that sell the commercial time to ad agencies that represent client advertisers. These TV advertisers are commonly known as sponsors.

Another important arm of the networks is research. Working with the major audience-measurement company, A. C. Nielsen, the networks get the audience estimates (ratings) for their programming. The higher the rating of a program, the more a network can charge for that show's commercials.

Networks employ engineering and technical personnel for the production of their own shows, and for the transmission of their programming to their stations. The stations themselves also have engineering staffs.

CABLE NETWORKS

Cable was originally developed to improve TV reception in areas that were either not served or underserved by standard broadcast stations. The system ran a coaxial cable from an antenna perched on a high point down to homes in low-lying areas. Later, engineers found that they could use microwave relay stations to bring TV signals to cable homes. This method gave birth to community antenna television (CATV)—a system that receives TV broadcasts by antenna and relays them to paying subscribers in areas where direct reception is poor or impossible. Later developments increased the capacity of CATV systems to more than one hundred channels. This growth introduced a new element into cable programming, and what started as an engineering process became a programming source. Today, cable serves about 60 percent of all TV households and is integrally involved in programming.

Cable system operators are the companies that install and maintain local cable hookups. They charge their subscribers a monthly fee for a basic cable service that includes several free cable channels like Ted Turner's Cable News Network (CNN), Entertainment Sports Programming Network (ESPN), Discovery, C-Span (the public affairs channel), and the Arts and Entertainment (A&E) network. In addition, cable system operators offer subscribers certain pay-cable networks such as Home Box Office (HBO) and Cinemax. Both pay-cable and free cable services share in the subscriber fees paid to the cable system.

Today, cable operators are large companies that construct and maintain local systems. The cable networks derive their income from their portion of subscriber fees and from the sale of advertising commercials. These advertising spots are both national and local. For example, a national advertiser may advertise on the entire CNN network, a basic cable service. However, a local restaurant may buy only local advertising. We discuss the entire cable process in chapters 16 , 17, and 18.

OTHER TV PLAYERS

Independent Stations

Independent TV stations are neither owned nor affiliated with the networks. Large companies such as Gannett and Viacom Broadcasting own a number of independent stations. These stations are free to run any programming they choose. It may consist of a locally produced news show or reruns of hit shows that initially appeared on broadcast network stations.

In their arrangements with syndicators, independents retain more commercial slots than do network-affiliated stations. The independents can also select their programming from the best shows available rather than being limited to the network programs—many of which have low ratings—as affiliates are. So, independent stations are often more profitable than network-owned or affiliate stations. Independents carry both national and local commercial advertising spots.

At times, when a network-affiliated station chooses not to run some of the network's programs, the network may offer them to independents.

PBS

The Public Broadcasting Service (PBS) is a network of some 340 noncommercial stations. Despite the name "Public," the stations are independent of political and governmental control or interference. PBS is owned and controlled by its member TV stations, which in turn are accountable to their local communities.

Funding for PBS comes from many sources, including local subscribers, foundations, corporations and the Corporation for Public Broadcasting (CPB). Besides being a funding source, CPB acts as a link with Congress and federal agencies. It is the CPB's job to respond to hundreds of congressional inquiries each year on public broadcasting issues.

PBS, the network, does not produce programs. Its programs come from independent and foreign producers, and from the PBS member stations themselves. For example, Maryland Public Broadcasting produces the popular PBS program "Wall Street Week" and WGBH in

Boston produces the home improvement program "This Old House." Member stations can air the programming of their choice.

The FCC

The principal broadcast regulatory agency is the Federal Communications Commission (FCC), a federal body created with powers of regulation over TV, cable, and radio. It establishes guidelines for station ownership, enforces broadcast regulations, and reviews programming content. It is also concerned with the number of commercials carried by stations. FCC headquarters are in Washington, D.C.

CHAPTER 3

Who Does What: Jobs at Networks and Stations

Most TV jobs fit into two basic categories—those at the networks and the stations and those in TV production where programs are created. This chapter will explore jobs at networks and stations. The next chapter looks at jobs in production.

How many people work in television? Although the numbers are not definitive, the Bureau of Labor Statistics reported in February 1993 that there were 387,000 people employed in some phase of TV and radio. Of course, this figure includes such jobs as secretaries, cable installers, and maintenance people, rather less glamorous jobs than on-air work.

Announcers and newscasters, for example, hold only about 60,000 jobs. For every on-air performer there are hundreds of workers and technicians whose earnings may be a fraction of the salaries of these celebrated performers and behind-the-scenes top executives.

The main TV positions for graduates in journalism and mass communications are in the news department, programming, production, advertising, and promotion. Only a few people come before the cameras as newspersons or in positions requiring on-air talent.

Other jobs at TV networks and stations include directors, writers, reporters, producers, publicists, and engineers.

There is positive news on the horizon. According to the Department of Labor, television employment is expected to grow faster through the 1990s because of an increase in TV stations and the growth of cable TV. Competition will be keen for entry-level positions because this field traditionally attracts large numbers of job seekers.

Most jobs for recent college graduates will be at small stations outside large urban areas. New York City, Los Angeles, and Chicago stations, for example, are primarily interested in hiring highly experienced personnel. The value of work experience, besides a college degree, cannot be overemphasized. Those seeking work at small TV stations would do well to gain experience through internships or part-time work while in college.

This chapter and the next can help you decide whether there is a place for you in the TV industry. By understanding the functions of each department and job, you can better comprehend the entire TV broadcasting universe.

We will first list job descriptions and then discuss salaries at the end of the chapter.[1]

JOB CATEGORIES

Networks are organized differently from stations, and there is also a vast difference among stations, depending on their size. Networks, of course, employ more people and specialists in every area than are found in any station, so the structure is correspondingly more complex. Let's examine the operations of one of the largest networks, CBS, as a representative example.

The CBS/Broadcast Group is composed of six divisions dealing with the company's TV operations:

CBS News Division
CBS Sports Division
CBS Entertainment
CBS Marketing Division

CBS Affiliate Relations Division
CBS Television Stations Division
CBS Enterprises Division

The Broadcast Group is headed by a president, and each division has its own chief executive officer. There are also several vice presidents, many middle management executives, and other employees in each division.

The News Division creates and broadcasts news programming for the network.

The Sports Division produces events and programming aired by the network.

CBS Entertainment creates some programs and licenses programs from production companies.

The Marketing Division sells advertising time on the network's stations and its affiliates.

Affiliate Relations deals with the relationship between the network and its affiliated stations.

The Television Stations Division manages the network's owned and operated (O&O) stations.

The Enterprises Division leads the network's involvement in new technologies, and it licenses programming to cable and video markets at home and abroad.

At other networks, the management structure may vary, so that the sports division also encompasses daytime and children's entertainment. A separate division can be responsible for early morning and late night entertainment and another directing the broadcast operations and engineering area. At an individual TV station, whether O&O, network affiliate, or independent, the job breakdown generally follows this lineup:

MANAGEMENT

General Manager
Assistant General Manager/Station Manager
Business Manager/Controller
Operations Director/Manager

SALES

General Sales Manager
National Sales Manager

Local Sales Manager
Account Executive
Traffic/Continuity Supervisor
Research Director

PROGRAMMING

Program Director
Production Manager
Producer
Director
Assistant Director
Stage Manager
Production Assistant

NEWS

News Director
Assistant News Director
Managing Editor
Executive Producer
Producer
Assignment Editor
News Anchors
Correspondents and News Reporters
News Photographer
Sportscaster
Weather Reporter
News Writer
Video Journalist

ENGINEERING

Chief Engineer/Director of Engineering
Engineering Supervisor
Operator Technician
Technical Director
Floor Director
Film/Tape Editor
Film Director
Production Assistant
Staff Artist
Traffic/Computer Operator
Maintenance Engineer
Transmitter Engineer
Audio Control Engineer
Video Control Engineer

Master Control Engineer
Videotape Engineer
Engineering Assistant or Technician
Electronic News Gathering (ENG) Team

Management

At the top level of a station is its management staff, charged with directing all departments and personnel. These individuals are well paid, but, if a station is not profitable enough, the station's ownership may question their work.

General Manager The general manager is most often a corporate officer who reports directly to the station's owner, the home office, or a board of directors. Seven major departments—programming, production, promotion/publicity, sales and marketing, news, business, and engineering—report to the general manager.

The general manager is ultimately responsible for the station's finances, profitability, and community relations. Most general managers come from the ranks of TV sales and business management.

Station Manager The station manager at a TV station is its chief operating executive. He or she is responsible for the day-to-day operations of the station's departments and personnel. Most get to this coveted spot after careers and training in sales, news, programming, or engineering.

Business Manager The business manager handles all financial transactions, develops business plans and goals, and supervises the activities of a business department that generally includes accountants, bookkeepers, billing clerks, and others. The business manager usually reports directly to the station's general manager. Many business managers are certified public accountants (CPAs) or have extensive accounting experience.

Operations Director/Manager At some stations "operations" is synonymous with "traffic." The operations manager is responsible for the station's "log," a document that lists the timing of all programs, commercials, and public-service or promotional announcements. The operations manager also provides advertisers with verification of their commercials. This department also tells the sales staff how much time can be sold. For a network or affiliate station, the time it can sell depends on how much time the network controls as part of its station agreement. Operations managers often come from sales ranks. Since most stations use automated logging systems, computer training is a prerequisite for operations jobs. At smaller stations the operations manager also writes promotional copy. Larger stations use continuity writers for this purpose.

Sales

Networks and stations make their money selling airtime. Additionally, network affiliates receive affiliate compensation (see chapter 6) from the networks. Station and network sales forces sell three basic kinds of airtime: network TV, spot TV, and local TV.

Network TV sales are aired on stations affiliated with a major broadcast network. An example would be General Foods' buying a thirty-second spot on "Murphy Brown" that would then appear on all 200 CBS affiliates. About 50 percent of network sales are for prime-time programs and 20 percent for sports programs. In 1992, ABC, CBS, and NBC sold about $10 billion in network advertising.

Spot sales are made by an advertiser that, because of product distribution or new product testing, elects not to advertise in every market, but only in selected, "spot," markets. A beer advertiser might wish to run spots in only those cities that are broadcasting NBA basketball games.

Local businesses buy local TV airtime, sometimes called "local availabilities" or simply "local avails," to appear on a local TV station. It is most often sold by the station's own sales staff.

The networks and stations sell spot time on the basis of ratings, such as those developed by Nielsen. These ratings estimate the number of viewers watching a specific program at a particular hour. Usually, the higher the rating on a given program, the more the networks or stations can charge for its commercials.

Separate departments at the networks are in charge of selling spot sales. Stations also rely on "rep" firms to sell their time. A rep firm is an organization with offices in major cities and a headquarters staff in

New York or Chicago. The rep company represents many stations across the country. Thus, a rep salesperson will make sales calls to an ad agency for several stations. This practice is more economical and efficient for an individual station that would otherwise have to employ a very large sales staff. Rep companies generally work with the stations on a commission basis.

General Sales Manager The general sales manager is in charge of producing all advertising revenue for a station or network. He or she analyzes the inventory of airtime available for commercials and then works with the program director and the station's general manager to match programs with specific advertisers. Other major responsibilities include supervising the sales staff, developing sales plans and goals, previewing programs, and helping to set the station's advertising standards and policies.

The position requires long experience in TV sales and a thorough knowledge of the competitive market. An undergraduate degree in marketing, advertising, or business administration is essential. The general sales manager usually comes from a station's sales ranks and is highly compensated.

National Sales Manager The national sales manager sells local TV advertising to national ad agencies and national advertisers. In this effort, he or she contacts client rep firms that place advertising on local stations for national accounts.

Most national sales managers reach their position after experience selling local advertising. Others come from ad agencies or from the networks.

Local Sales Manager Local advertising is the lifeblood of most stations' revenues. The local sales manager supervises the sales staff, makes sales calls, analyzes ratings, and monitors available airtime. He or she must also become involved in community relations. Local sales managers reach this level after training and service as account executives in radio or TV.

Account Executive Account executives are the foot soldiers of TV sales. They work with local ad agencies and call on local advertisers directly to sell airtime. The job requires a persuasive personality since local advertisers often have limited budgets and may be committed to other media such as radio or newspapers. Often, an account executive will help create a local advertiser's commercials.

Traffic/Continuity Supervisor The traffic/continuity supervisor holds an entry-level position with a great deal of responsibility. He or she works with the station's operations manager and general sales manager. This individual informs the sales department of all commercial time available during and between shows, when it is sold, and how it is scheduled.

The traffic/continuity supervisor also writes the station breaks and announcements promoting the station. Generally, a college education

---

CAREER TIP

If you think you have a sales personality, apply for a job as a junior salesperson at a TV station in a city of about 100,000 population. There you will sell to local retailers and establishments. The starting salary probably will not run higher than $15,000 a year plus commission. Commission is usually given after a certain sales level is reached. If such a job is too difficult to obtain, try to gain your experience in a similar position at the local newspaper or radio station; then consider a shift to TV in the same city. Even if you're a college graduate, gain your first TV experience as a traffic/continuity supervisor or sales coordinator. Many opportunities are available for the right person who is alert, bright, detail-oriented, and able to operate a computer and/or word-processing equipment. Then, after working at these entry-level jobs for a while, you will be in a better position to make your move into sales or programming.

Don't overlook the research and promotion aspect of sales. Perhaps less remunerative than sales, it is no less challenging. A computer background helps in research; writing courses are good preparation for promotion jobs.

A good way to get started is selling time for a small radio or TV station.

with a communications major gives an applicant a competitive edge over someone with less training.

Research Director Most large stations have a research director to develop sales ammunition for the sales staff. He or she must have a total understanding of ratings information and other qualitative data that are used to promote sales. Large stations also employ research associates, analysts, and assistants. Many in this job classification have statistical backgrounds.

Programming

A programming division is central to a network's operation. It acquires the programs that fill the prime time, daytime, late night, and sports schedule for its own stations and affiliates. At O&Os and network affiliates, the network supplies most of the programming, although some shows are produced locally. Similarly, independent stations and public TV stations get portions of their programming from outside sources, like syndicators, and they produce shows in-house.

Programming at TV stations encompasses both planning and production of programs. It also includes liaison with the networks and syndicators.

Program Director The program director is the decision maker and overseer of a station's program department. Along with the general manager and sales manager, he or she defines the station's objectives in terms of the kinds of programs it will acquire and produce.

The program director plans the most effective programming schedule for the station. On a daily basis, he or she must consider the competition, the best shows for each time slot and who should produce these shows. The program director is also responsible for budget and allocations of equipment and manpower.

The program director is responsible for the station's compliance with Federal Communications Commission (FCC) programming rules and regulations. (More about the FCC in chapter 8.) Most program directors get their experience from holding jobs described on the following pages. Some are former directors and performers. Program directors must have a thorough understanding of TV and film production. This job requires a college degree. Specialization in communications, Radio-TV, or marketing gives applicants an advantage.

Production Manager The production manager handles the myriad details that go into producing the station's entire range of programs. The number of individually produced programs varies according to the status of the station; however, all O&Os, network affiliates, and independent stations produce news, talk, and interview shows. The independents will produce little other original material, relying instead on reruns of network programs and outside programming. Thus, the production manager's role at an individual station is more limited than it is at an O&O or affiliate station; consequently, it draws a smaller salary. The production manager is responsible for the conception, design, development, and scheduling of programs. He or she often supervises freelance and in-house producers, directors, art directors, camera operators, film editors, floor managers, and so on. Many production managers began their careers as members of studio crews or production companies. A college degree with a major in Radio-TV, communications, theater, or journalism is preferred.

Producer The producer plans and oversees a single show or a series of shows. Job duties include the selection of scripts, story development, booking of guests and performers, and the planning of sets, lights, props, camera angles, and overseeing of editing. A producer for news programs selects tape, scripts, and music to accompany the news, and is also responsible for a show's budget. The producer chooses directors (not, however, newscasters or reporters) and handles contracts with performers, technicians, and musicians. The educational requirements are similar to those of a production manager. There is avid competition for this assignment. Many TV jobs depend on the producer.

Director The director reports to the producer. Besides coordinating the details of a production, the director instructs all of those involved in the show—performers, production staff, and technical crew, including camera operators. Most network stations employ directors on staff. Some specialize in news and special events, others in sports. A college degree is recommended. Courses in radio, TV, and communications help. Many have undergraduate degrees in film and graduate degrees from film school. A director, like nearly all of the professionals described here, needs a combination of creativity, technical knowledge, organizational skills, and the ability to motivate.

Assistant Director The assistant director performs many duties of the director but for 20 to 25 percent less salary. A director depends on an assistant director to help execute all responsibilities. Educational requirements are the same as those for the director.

Stage Manager The stage manager works on the studio floor with the cast. He or she coordinates the director's instructions, reads scripts, cues performers, works with the art director and set designer, and oversees props and costumes.

Production Assistant Many on-air performers, producers, directors, program directors, and general managers got their start as production assistants. At most stations, production assistants serve as apprentices, filling in wherever needed. In some internship programs the budding broadcaster functions as a production assistant. In almost all cases the production assistant is an entry-level job. While boring and menial at times, the job nonetheless offers individuals the opportunity to decide what line of TV work they would like to pursue. From the station's point of view, station management scrutinizes production assistants carefully to spot future talent. In a local station, production assistants are very often promoted directly to news, production, and technical jobs.

News

A network's correspondent in the powder keg of the Middle East, a local news anchor in Los Angeles, a news writer for a network's nightly news show, and a weekend anchor and camera team at a network affiliate station in St. Louis—all are part of television news. The scope of TV news is so wide that, for just one network, it involves more than a thousand people and a budget of $1 million a day. Local news is no less important. Stations carry local news programs for as many as four hours a day. At even the smallest markets, stations employ an average of fifteen people in their news operations. But local news is not merely a service to a station's audience; it is also a major profit center. The battle for ratings is fierce in markets where four or five stations present local news shows. High ratings depend on skilled, talented people and high technology. Herein lies the opportunities for newcomers in TV news. The role of the news department is discussed at greater length in chapter 11.

News Director The news director heads a station's news department and is the final authority for the choice of all news: interviews, documentaries, and special news feature programs. In addition, he or she oversees the news budget and monitors the work of the reporting staff. A news director supervises film and video-camera operators, researchers, assistants, secretaries, and anywhere from five to a hundred or more reporters—anchorpersons, sportscasters, weather reporters, news writers, freelance interviewees, and specialists.

The news director must have news judgment—assessing the importance of a particular news story and the appropriate degree of coverage. This coveted job comes after years of experience as an on-air reporter, news writer, producer, and director. Other stations actively recruit a news director who runs a top-rated news show, but the job has a high turnover rate. News directors bear the blame for the failure of a station's news operation.

Assistant News Director At a large station, an assistant news director reduces the news director's load by assuming responsibility for personnel, budget matters, and the satellite communications system. Assistant news directors often come up from the ranks of reporters and news writers. They usually earn about 15 percent less than their bosses. Both news directors and their assistants need college training in mass communications, journalism, or TV.

Managing Editor At a network, the managing editor is a top executive who maintains general supervision of the newscasts. On "NBC Nightly News with Tom Brokaw," Brokaw also assumes the role of managing editor. At local stations, the managing editor is just under the news director in responsibility for the direction and content of the newscasts.

Executive Producer On a network news show, the executive producer makes the final decisions on the stories covered, who is interviewed and for how long, and the general tenor of the show. At local stations, the job title is often interchangeable with managing editor. Where the job of executive producer exists, it falls below the level of the news director. All of the news positions we have discussed require college training in mass communications, journalism, or TV.

Producer A network news show has many segments, each organized and coordinated by a producer. At the station level, individual newscasts are assigned to producers who coordinate their efforts with the news director, managing editor, and executive producer. The producer must take the raw product—news—and mold it with visuals into provocative, appealing, and informative segments. A producer is constantly under time constraints, as when a planned interview segment is dumped in favor of a late-breaking story. Changes like this are everyday occurrences in the TV-news business. Newscast producers usually gain their experience as reporters or in the production ranks of TV news. College training in journalism or Radio-TV production is desirable, although on-the-job experience may lead to the same objective.

Assignment Editor The assignment editor, with guidance from the news director and managing editor, makes camera, reporting, and writing assignments. He or she checks out stories, directs news bulletin coverage, edits news material, and supervises newsroom activities.

Here is an example of the assignment editor's function: A newsroom that constantly monitors police and fire department scanners learns that a disgruntled former patient has opened fire at the city's largest municipal hospital, critically wounding three doctors and terrifying more than a hundred emergency-room patients. The assignment editor chooses two reporters and a camera crew for this important, late-breaking story. It will preempt all other coverage on that evening's 10:00 P.M. news show. With just a few hours of lead time, the assignment editor tells the reporters to interview the hospital's spokesperson and a police official. The station wants the complete story of the disaster. The reporters will also interview a witness to the shooting and photograph the assailant as he is led away by the police.

Assignment editors move up the ladder after experience as reporters, camera operators, or field technicians. Note: The job of editor does not exist in TV as it does on newspapers. The managing editor and the assignment editor perform the editor's function at a TV station. On a network news show like NBC's "Nightly News with Tom Brokaw," one person assumes the role and title of editor and works with the managing editor and foreign editor. At times the chief anchor also functions as the managing editor.

News Anchors When we think of television news we think of those glamorous people without regional accents who are paid staggering amounts of money to read the evening news. Yes, a handful of superstar anchorpersons are paid million-dollar-plus salaries, but then so are superstar actors, athletes, and rock musicians.

Bear in mind, however, that these people are network stars with vast viewing audiences. Also, the swing of just one rating point (1 percent of 942,000 TV households) from one network's nightly news show to another can mean as much as $100 million in annual revenues.

Top network anchors like Dan Rather, Ted Koppel, Peter Jennings, Tom Brokaw, and Bryant Gumbel are reported to earn more than $3 million a year. Even the top network correspondents earn huge salaries. In 1989, when Diane Sawyer moved from CBS to ABC News, she was reported to receive $1.7 million on the new job. The annual salary of the 200 other network correspondents averages over $100,000.

Of course, none of the highly paid anchors start at the top—nor do they merely read the news. They must be seasoned newspeople who can interview, coordinate live reports from several sources while on camera, and write and develop news stories.

These anchors are the all-stars in the big leagues. If you're an anchorperson in Quincy, Illinois, the country's 153rd market, you'll likely earn closer to $30,000 a year.

For those interested in TV news, a background in local investigative reporting is a good starting point. ABC's Peter Jennings began his career in 1959 as a reporter on a Canadian radio station. David Brinkley got his start as a reporter for United Press. ABC's Barbara Walters was the youngest producer with NBC's New York station. She then became a writer for CBS News. Most anchors started as reporters or writers.

Although it is not written policy, news anchors, both network and local, are physically attractive. Viewers prefer watching good-looking people. In a noted court case, Kansas City anchor Christine Craft sued her former station, claiming discrimination. She said it fired her because she wasn't pretty enough to suit her employers. She lost the case. Craft subsequently became the news director of radio station KFBK-AM in Sacramento, California, where she is not on camera.

Local stations usually have a two-anchor team and, in larger markets, three teams of anchors can split the broadcasting day. Local anchors are more involved in the selection and writing of stories than their network counterparts. Again, as at the networks, ratings are the barometer of success.

Correspondents and News Reporters   The role of correspondent exists primarily at a network. Correspondents provide news coverage from areas all over the world. A correspondent may be based in Frankfurt, Germany, but his or her territory might include central Europe and even the Middle East. During a crisis, a network relies on its correspondent for reports and analysis. Although the airtime allotted may be small, the correspondent is expected to provide a visually exciting and concise presentation.

Correspondents often start out as desk assistants, later becoming news writers at a network's home office, progressing to jobs as video journalists and then correspondents and field producers. Many correspondents began their careers in radio.

On-air TV reporters need all the attributes of news anchors, but they use certain skills more often. Reporters must gather news from many sources, discuss the scope and length of the story with the news director or assignment editor, and write and deliver the story on the air. At larger stations, a reporter may specialize in covering politics, consumer news, crime, health, or business. A skillful TV reporter is a digger. Covering a crisis like the hospital shootings discussed earlier goes beyond filming the on-camera statement of a spokesperson. In this situation, an interview with a doctor at the emergency room or with a frightened patient gives the on-air report meaning and interest. Radio or newspaper training in small markets is good preparation for on-air jobs at a TV station. College journalism and communications courses are also good preparation. Getting an on-camera reporting job is difficult in any market. The lure of fame and large salaries draws many candidates to the medium. It may be best to concentrate instead on the less glamorous but more plentiful jobs in television.

News Photographer The news photographer operates cameras, including ENG equipment (discussed toward the end of this chapter), and may also be responsible for editing the film or tape's visual and audio aspects.

Sportscaster Sportscasters at networks are a part of large sports divisions. At larger stations, sportscasters report to a sports director. At smaller stations, sports may be a one-person department. Many sports-minded people are drawn to this field without realizing how few people can make it.

Sportscasters report the outcome of local games and contests. They review, select, and report on the films and videotapes of sporting events and news of national interest.

Some sportscasters provide play-by-play descriptions of live events, interview sports figures, and create features and documentaries that are aired before and after major events. Some network sportscasters receive salaries well over six figures. "Color coverage" on sportscasts is usually a job for former athletes. Stations and networks favor them, especially if they are articulate and physically appealing, because (it is hoped) they can turn their established following into viewers.

Most sportscasters who are not athletes have undergraduate degrees in journalism or mass communications. Writing sports for a college newspaper is a good way to get started. Covering a sports event for a college or local radio station is even better because it gives the aspirant a tape to use with his or her resume. On-air experience is, of course, the best background.

Weather Reporter You probably don't need a college degree to get a job as a weather reporter at a small station where all you'll do is read the National Weather Service's statistics. At many of these stations the anchor does the weather, or a traffic reporter combines weather with other coverage. At larger stations, however, the weather reporter is usually a trained meteorologist, familiar with the latest weather-measuring technology and equipped with sophisticated visual devices. Because few stations employ more than one or two weather reporters, prospects for employment in this field are limited.

About thirty colleges around the country offer a Bachelor of Science degree in meteorology or, its more formal title, atmospheric sciences. Veteran meteorologists, particularly those at the networks or in larger markets, can earn substantial yearly salaries.

News Writer The news writer edits and processes all continuity (scripts) for news programs, writes continuity for news documentary programs, correlates tape or film news, screens news film, supervises editing, and writes appropriate news continuity. Networks and stations, large and small, need news writers. They do not go on camera, but their function in TV news is no less important. They are the people who write what anchors say and viewers hear. Writers receive tapes and communications from the network's bureaus, from news services like the Associated Press and Reuters, and from reporters and correspondents. They work with producers to prepare video reports or interviews. At some stations, news writers arrange interviews. The ability to write concise, thought-provoking copy is the essence of TV-news writing. College training in journalism is essential. If news writing is your goal, take a job at a small newspaper or radio station to learn the disciplines and techniques of news writing.

Video Journalist At the entry level, video journalists work in-house and are responsible for gathering and editing videotape. At a network, video journalists examine video coming in by satellite for technical flaws. At a TV station, video journalists work in the field, often on assignment with an ENG camera person. It is this team's job to report, shoot, and transmit a story back to the station.

Engineering
Comparing today's television technology to early broadcasting is like comparing space travel to the airplane of the 1920s. Today, engineering personnel deal with electronic, newsgathering equipment that relays information and visuals from the field without requiring film editing at a station. Satellite transmissions assemble news packages and programming from all parts of the world, quickly and efficiently. Video compression allows a single satellite channel to carry up to a dozen TV

programs. High definition TV, with its movie-theater quality pictures, will soon be a reality. A network facility or a large TV station may employ as many as 150 to 350 engineering and technical personnel. Small stations employ chief engineers and assistants, maintenance people and, often, mini-cam operators and electronic newsgathering crews as part of their engineering and technical team. Many TV engineering people have degrees in electrical engineering and computer systems, although a rare few in this field are self-taught. With the spirited competition for any TV job, we advise the formal education route. For further information on the engineering function, see Bruce Sidran's interview in chapter 32.

Chief Engineer The chief engineer, sometimes called the director of engineering, must be experienced in all technical aspects of broadcasting, have a thorough understanding of electronics principles, and be able to design technical systems that meet the station's needs. An understanding of communications law is also essential. An FCC license is desirable as well, along with some form of technical certification.

While some chief engineers began as engineering technicians straight out of high school or technical school, most have degrees in electrical engineering, physics, or science and have technical training from a technical center or college.

Engineering Supervisor At smaller stations, the assistant chief engineer also performs the work of the engineering supervisor. At larger stations, an engineering supervisor directs the work of audio, video, maintenance, master-control, transmitter, and videotape engineers. He or she is responsible for maintaining equipment, keeping alert for malfunctions or failures, and seeing that sound and picture meet FCC regulations.

Most supervisors have had a minimum of two years' experience as an engineer as well as technical school training. Some have degrees in engineering or physics; most have an FCC license and technical certification. The next step is the job of chief engineer.

Operator Technician The operator technician works under the supervision of the chief engineer and must be able to run all the station's technical operational equipment.

Technical Director The technical director oversees the technical quality of a program and operates the production switcher, which controls the choice of camera images and special effects fed into the videotape recorders and over the air. During planning, the technical director analyzes a production's requirements and works with the director to satisfy them. During rehearsal and performance, the technical director sits in the control room with the director and runs the switcher, implementing the director's camera and videotape choices. Most technical directors reach this level after two or more years of experience as engineers. The next step upward is the job of engineering supervisor.

Floor Director When a program is produced in-studio, a floor director supervises the floor people (camera, lighting, and technical staff), making sure that all necessary preparations are made.

Film/Tape Editor The film/tape editor edits film or tape to meet time limitations and provides films on request.

Film Director The job of film director is a general one and includes the responsibility for the supervision and work flow of the film department.

Production Assistant Often an entry-level position, the production assistant has a catchall job that includes checking the physical condition and reproduction quality of all commercials, promotionals, and public service assignments.

Staff Artist The staff artist designs print media advertisements, various graphics for on-air usage, and graphics for use in commercials.

Traffic/Computer Operator The traffic/computer operator prepares the minute-by-minute schedule of a station's on-air programming, commercials, and public service announcements. He or she may be responsible for entering all pertinent data into the computer and generating all the necessary reports.

Maintenance Engineer Maintenance engineers are much in demand. They maintain cameras, switchers, audio consoles, video monitors, microphones, videotape recorders, and other equipment. He or she works in an engineering shop. A high school diploma is required, plus training in electronics at a vocational or technical school, and a minimum of one year of TV-maintenance experience. An FCC license and technical certification are desirable.

Transmitter Engineer The transmitter engineer keeps the TV transmitter and antenna system in compliance with FCC regulations. Daily duties include testing the performance of the transmitter to ensure uninterrupted broadcasting, keeping operations records for the chief engineer, and inspecting the transmitter tower and building. This job requires the same training as that for a maintenance engineer.

Audio Control Engineer The audio control engineer is in charge of the electronic controls that make up the station's audio and video equipment. Duties include placing microphones, producing special sound effects, and monitoring sound levels. During the editing process, the audio control engineer may add music or other sound elements to tape. The position carries final responsibility for the technical quality of the program's sound.

Video Control Engineer The video control engineer sets up and aligns the cameras, controls brightness and color levels, monitors transmission quality, and creates special visual effects. At some stations, an audio-video engineer handles both functions.

Master Control Engineer The master control engineer coordinates the video and audio portions of programming that come from the studio, the networks, prerecorded segments, satellites, ENG crews, and other sources. He or she then delivers the signals via the master control switchers and processing equipment to the transmitter. The master control engineer also cues and rolls the film and videotape to ensure smooth transitions from program to commercial to station breaks, maintains the station log, and ensures that the output meets FCC technical requirements. Training and background requirements are similar to those of audio-video engineers, that is, training in electronics at a vocational or technical school or earning a degree from a college with a broadcast engineering program. This individual must be calm, alert, able to make quick decisions, and must understand the workings of a wide variety of audio and video equipment. There is a good market for this job.

Videotape Engineer The videotape engineer sets up and operates a wide variety of videotape machines that record, play back, and edit programs, although the actual editing of videotape is done by camera or electronic news gathering (ENG) operators. The engineer evaluates videotapes and satellite feeds, duplicates taped material, and assembles tape segments for broadcast. He or she also monitors the audio and visual quality of videotape recordings and works with the master control engineer and other audio-video engineers.

CAREER TIP

Television photography and editing have been dramatically improved with the use of videotape. Film consumed time for developing and processing before it was available for transmission. Today, with videotape technology, film has become obsolete. Videotape's greatest asset is its ability to be played back immediately without processing.

Many college theater departments videotape their productions for analysis and study. Students thus gain valuable experience handling video cameras. Experience with a home video camera can also help in mastering techniques needed in preparation for a video job.

Video engineers generally spend time as engineering assistants or technicians before promotion to this position. An FCC license and other technical certification are desirable.

Engineering Assistant or Technician This is the entry-level job on the engineering ladder. Engineering technicians handle the setup, operation, maintenance, and construction of technical equipment and facilities. The job entails working on every piece of equipment the station owns. The opportunity to advance is limited only by the technician's own capabilities. Requirements are a high school diploma and some vocational training. An interest in electronics and broadcast equipment operations is, of course, an advantage. To enhance chances for employment, a candidate should have an FCC license and be preparing for technical certification.

Electronic News Gathering (ENG) At many stations ENG crews are part of the engineering team. They gather local news with portable video-tape cameras, and then transmit the results from the field to the station. In smaller stations the person who shoots the footage in the field may also edit it.

FCC LICENSES

The FCC no longer conducts examinations for broadcast engineers, and a license is needed only for transmitter operations and maintenance. Technical certification now replaces the license examination and is conducted by groups like the Society of Broadcast Engineers. (For more information, write to the Society of Broadcast Engineers, P.O. Box 50344, Indianapolis, IN 46250.) Tests are tailored for various areas of broadcast engineering. As you gain experience, you can take additional certification tests to prove your expertise in a variety of broadcast-engineering jobs. Certification shows a potential employer that an applicant is willing to work hard for a job and is interested in improving performance.

WHAT PEOPLE EARN

There is no comprehensive information source about salaries in TV because rates vary too much. Network jobs pay more than jobs at individual stations. Usually, you will make more money if you work at a union job, but you must get the job before you are eligible to join the union. NBC and ABC have contracts with the National Association of Broadcast Employees and Technicians (NABET) for many technical and production jobs. This union represents thousands of TV and radio employees at hundreds of stations across the country and at the two networks. The International Bureau of Electrical Workers (IBEW) has the union contract with the CBS network and its O&O (owned and operated) stations.

Seven unions have jurisdiction over television employees. Besides NABET and IBEW, they are: the American Federation of Television and Radio Artists (AFTRA), the Directors Guild, the Writers Guild, the International Alliance of Theatrical Stage Employees (IATSE), and the Screen Actors Guild (SAG). Besides higher salaries at union shops, the fringe benefits are far more liberal than at nonunion shops.

TV salaries depend upon the size of the station and the size of the station's market area. For example, the average annual salary for weathercasters is about $50,000; however, the range goes from a low of $22,000 to a high of $146,000. Sportscasters average about the same salaries. A beginning newsperson at a small TV station can expect to start at about $20,000 per year, as of this writing. Earnings among experienced news people are much higher. TV news anchors averaged about $72,000 in 1993, but, of course, the heavy hitters skew the average. The range goes from about $22,000 in the smallest markets to more than $1 million in the largest.

Washington, D.C., is the seventh leading TV market in the nation, with 1.78 million TV households. In 1993, top anchors at Washington's NBC-owned station and the ABC and CBS affiliates earned between $400,000 and $600,000. A top sportscaster on one of these stations earned between $400,000 and $500,000, and a top weatherperson about $300,000. For the two or three stations in the Washington market ranked below the top three, an anchorperson will earn between $200,000 to $225,000 and a weatherperson $150,000. By contrast, in 1992, the weathercaster in Harrisonburg, Virginia, the 200th largest market, earned only $15,000 a year and doubled in some other capacity.

Most people in television start working at small stations to gain experience. According to Richard Herbst, vice president and general manager of Quincy Broadcasting in Quincy, Illinois, the country's 153rd largest market, "Reporters [at Quincy] begin at about $15,000 a year and can get up to $25,000 as an anchor. We get people with some, but not much, experience. Usually they have worked at a station in the town where they were attending journalism school. But, if they have the personality to become an anchor, in five years they'll be earning $150,000 or more in a larger market."

Job Titles and Salaries

The salaries listed in Table 2 for various TV station jobs are the average yearly rates for employees working at a network affiliate TV station in ADI market numbers 51 to 75. According to the Arbitron population area designation, Albany, New York, is the nation's fifty-first ADI market and Paducah, Kentucky, is the seventy-fifth. Salaries in the top ten ADIs are from 50 percent to 100 percent higher than the figures used in our example. Further, salaries for employees with four years' experience at a network-owned station (O&O), where a union contract is enforced, are substantially higher than in the fifty-first to seventy-fifth ADI. Sometimes, no reliable figures are available for a particular job.

TABLE 2. AVERAGE SALARIES FOR JOBS IN TELEVISION

JOB TITLE	APPROXIMATE YEARLY SALARY
Management	
General Manager	$113,000
Asst. Gen. Mgr./Station Manager	72,000
Business Manager/Controller	43,000
Operations Director/Manager	50,000
Sales	
General Sales Manager	84,000
National Sales Manager	65,000
Local Sales Manager	66,000
Account Executive	41,000
Traffic/Continuity Supervisor	27,000
Research Director	32,000
Programming	
Program Director	42,000
Production Manager	34,000
Producer/Director	25,000
Assistant Director	(not available)
Stage Manager	(not available)
Production Assistant	16,000
News	
News Director	58,000

TABLE 2. AVERAGE SALARIES FOR JOBS IN TELEVISION

JOB TITLE	APPROXIMATE YEARLY SALARY
News	
Assistant News Director	46,000*
Managing Editor	(not available)
Executive Producer	39,000*
Assignment Editor	27,000
News Anchors	53,000
Correspondents and News Reporters	26,000
News Photographer	21,000
Sportscaster	37,000
Weather Reporter	45,000
News Writer	52,000*
Video Journalist	63,000*
Engineering	
Chief Engineer/Director of Engineering	49,000
Engineering Supervisor	(not available)
Operator Technician	22,000
Technical Director	58,000*
(includes field engineer and station engineer)	
Floor Director	20,000
Film/Tape Editor	21,000
Film Director	22,000
Production Assistant	16,000
Staff Artist	22,000
Traffic/Computer Operator	16,000
Maintenance Engineer	58,000*
Transmitter Engineer	33,000*
Audio Control Engineer	37,000*
Video Control Engineer	33,000*
Master Control Engineer	58,000*
Videotape Engineer	63,000*
Engineering Assistant or Technician	(not available)
ENG team	(not available)

National Association of Broadcast Employees and Technicians (NABET) union scale of minimum salaries with one to two years on the job for NBC network and O&O stations.

NOTE

[1] *We are indebted to the National Association of Broadcasters for providing some information in this chapter.*

CHAPTER 4

Who Does What: Jobs in Programming and Production

THE PEOPLE WHO CREATE AND PRODUCE TELEVISION PROGRAMMING

As mentioned in chapter 2, the networks do not produce most prime-time programming. They rely on more than 300 independent production companies to conceive and produce the shows.

The network entertainment divisions do maintain sizable staffs to develop prime-time programming and oversee the output of the production companies. At the ABC Entertainment Division, for example, almost forty executives are responsible for prime-time TV. More than two thirds of these executives are based on the West Coast. Some of ABC Entertainment's executive assignments and job responsibilities are as follows:

* Two executive vice presidents have general responsibility for ABC's prime-time schedule. They report directly to the president of ABC Entertainment.
* A senior vice president in charge of motion pictures and miniseries spends most of his or her time in meetings with studios and pro-

duction companies working on ideas for production. The job carries considerable responsibility since a network programs as many as twenty or thirty movies of the week (MOWs) each year and several miniseries.

* A vice president in charge of on-air promotion oversees the promotion and publicity for the current season's programming and for future shows.
* The Entertainment Division employs a vice president and two departmental directors to develop comedy programming. They listen to ideas for new shows and assign pilots for shows in more advanced stages of development.
* A vice president and two departmental directors are in charge of dramatic series development.
* Two vice presidents for program planning and scheduling develop programming for future seasons and select replacements for programs that have been canceled during a season. They report to the three top executives of ABC Entertainment. There is also a parallel assignment on the East Coast.
* Three executives hold the title Director, Current Series Programs. They are responsible for liaison with the production companies and studios that produce current programming. For example, when a show's ratings sag, these executives meet with the producers to discuss ways to improve results.
* ABC Entertainment employs four casting directors on the West Coast and one on the East Coast. They work with production companies and studios to line up top talent for the network's programming.
* Headed by an executive vice president, ABC Entertainment has four vice presidents on the West Coast and four on the East Coast who make the deals and complete the contracts for the network's programming. Most of these executives are lawyers who work with lawyers from the production companies and studios. Other executives are involved in public relations and affiliate marketing services, and broadcast standards and practices.

The Production Team

In their arrangements with the networks, the independent production companies are responsible for all phases of production. Often, these companies form partnerships for financing and physical facilities with television studios like Warner Brothers Television, Lorimar Television, Paramount, and Buena Vista Television (Disney). These studios also produce their own series. There are over 300 small TV production companies and about 35 major production companies. Most are located near Los Angeles or New York City. Some produce as many as ten prime-time series at once.

A typical prime-time series, miniseries, or movie-of-the-week (MOW), fills the following job classifications: We list them here and then give a brief description of each job:

Actors	Music Director
Executive Producer	Sound Editor
Creator	Film Editor
Supervising Producer	Floor Manager
Producer	Unit Manager
Executive Story Editor	Costume Designer
Writer	Publicity Director/Manager
Production Designer	Camera Operator
Director	Wardrobe Supervisor
Director of Photography	Graphic Designer
Production Manager	Carpenter
Lighting Director/Designer	Property Master
Casting Director	Makeup/Hair Specialist
Special Effects Director	

Other, less important, technical credits are not listed.

Actors This category includes stars like Bill Cosby, Candice Bergen, and Ted Danson, and, at the lower end of the scale, actors who barely get to read a line. Incidental roles are filled show-by-show. A miniseries typically has more stars and featured players than a prime-time series.

The rule about unions prevails in this specialty as it does in others: you cannot join the union until you have a job, so you need to be hired first.

Competition is spirited for each acting assignment. Auditions are called for new productions. Hundreds of actors often read for key roles. An agent helps one's chances, but agents are reluctant to take on new, inexperienced talent. Gaining experience in college, amateur, and regional productions is a sound way to get started, as is dramatic training at any of many fine schools.

Executive Producer This title is often reserved for the originator and owner of a show. On CBS's "Northern Exposure," Joshua Brand and John Falsey are the executive producers. They are the show's creators and

have a proprietary interest in it with Universal Studios. Many executive producers also serve as writers.

Creator This title is sometimes synonymous with executive producer.
"Murphy Brown" was created by Diane English. English and Joel
Shukovsky are its executive producers. Their production company,
Shukovsky/English Productions, owns the show in association with
Warner Brothers Television.

Supervising Producer A TV series may have an individual producer for a
given show. The supervising producer, however, is in charge of the production of the entire series and is involved in casting, writing, and technical production. Supervising producers sometimes double as writers.

Producer The producer plans and oversees a TV show. Duties include
the selection of material and performers and the planning of sets, lights,
props, and camera angles. The producer hires the director and actors
either directly or with the supervising and executive producers.

Executive Story Editor/Story Editor Hundreds of manuscripts are submitted to a running TV series. The story editor arranges the screening procedures. He or she works with the show's regular writers on plot
lines and enlists the services of additional freelance writers when required.

Writer Writers often conceive of a TV show or write segments of a series. A running TV series may have one writer or a team of writers,
some on staff, others freelance, and it usually has a head writer. Many
writers work at home or at an office, but they must attend story conferences, and often are present at the taping to make last-minute
changes.

The number of writers on a show varies. PBS's "Sesame Street" has
eighteen writers on staff, "Saturday Night Live" has fifteen writers,
and "Late Night with David Letterman" had fourteen writers.

Most TV writers belong to the Writers Guild of America (WGA),
which has branches in New York and Los Angeles. (More about writers' work appears in chapter 12.)

Director The director reports to the producer. Besides coordinating a
production's details, the director instructs everyone involved in the

show—actors, production staff, and the technical crew, including camera operators. An assistant director performs many duties of the director, who depends on him or her to help execute all responsibilities.

Training to become a TV director is as rigid as it is for feature films. Many directors work in both fields. Directors are represented by the Directors Guild of America (DGA). Of its 4,400 director members, most are employed in TV commercials, sports and entertainment programs. The DGA also conducts workshops and seminars on various aspects of the craft. A college degree with courses in TV and communications is recommended for those pursuing careers as directors. Many TV directors have graduate degrees from film schools. In terms of qualifications, a director, like nearly all the professionals described here, needs a combination of creative talent, technical knowledge, organizational skills, and the ability to motivate people.

Production Designer/Set Designer/Art Director Not every TV show employs all three of these classifications, and their roles are similar. The designer or art director "dresses" a production. If the production is a period piece, for example, it is his or her job to make the show look like its period. The production designer is responsible for building a show's sets, scouting locations for a shoot, and budgeting the costs of sets, locations, materials, and personnel. Many work in feature films as well as in TV.

Director of Photography This job is sometimes called cinematographer, or even camera operator. The director of photography directs the operators who run the cameras. Typically, the director of photography supervises the camera and lighting crews.

The steppingstone to the job of director of photography and camera operator is assistant camera operator. Camera operators need a high-school diploma and some training in photography (still or motion) and/or audiovisual equipment. College training in TV, film, or communications, however, will place the job seeker in a preferred spot.

Production Manager The production manager reports to the producer and is responsible for assembling and maintaining the budget and for expediting all the aspects of a show's production. He or she often supervises art directors and floor managers. Most production managers have substantial experience in lesser positions and have majored in TV or communications at college.

Lighting Director/Designer The lighting director is in charge of designing and preparing lighting for a TV production. The job requires technical know-how; the lighting director must overcome TV's technical and budgetary limitations by using spots, floods, and filters. He or she oversees a small crew of technicians who install and position lights. The lighting director usually reports to the production manager.

Casting Director Casting is a very creative activity, as integral to TV as it is to feature films. For a new TV or dramatic show, the casting director prepares a cast breakdown that contains a brief précis of each role. These breakdowns go to talent agents and personal managers. The casting director calls in prospects, interviews them, and ultimately holds auditions, readings, and screen tests for the director and producers.

Casting directors work for TV commercials as well as TV productions. Most are based in Los Angeles; some work in New York or in both cities.

Special Effects Director Feature films, TV productions, and even TV commercials use special effects. Today, special-effects wizardry can be visual or optical, mechanical or computer-generated. Although special effects do not often fit into the budgets of a series, TV movies often use them. Special-effects directors and technicians are well paid, about as much as cinematographers. Most film schools, undergraduate or graduate, offer courses in special effects. With new advances, especially in the area of computer-generated special effects, this field offers increased opportunities in film and TV for those trained in this creative specialty.

Music Director The music director works with composers, arrangers, and orchestrators to create the proper background and incidental music for a production. This highly creative task involves music scoring, timing, and music editing. A variety show obviously uses more music than a comedy or dramatic series.

Sound Editor The sound editor integrates the production's dialogue, sound effects, and music into a final mix. The sound editor must have both technical competence and experience. For a made-for-TV movie, the sound editor will often use the facilities of a mixing studio.

Film Editor TV uses videotape predominantly. It is easier to edit than film, though the editor of video is no less important to the final product than the editor of film. Editing is part of feature films, documentaries, industrial films, music videos, TV commercials, and TV productions.

Although the process is a technical one, it demands highly creative skills. The talented film editor has a sense of timing, pace, and creativity. Experience begins as an editorial room assistant and branches out after an apprentice period.

Floor Manager The director's extension to the cast is the floor manager, who ensures that everything meets the director's instructions. He or she reads scripts and cues performers during rehearsal and shooting, works with the art director and set designer, and oversees props and costumes.

Unit Manager The unit manager is responsible for all preproduction scheduling and for the setup, maintenance, and operation of equipment. He or she also organizes the stage and light crews and camera operators—all the production staff—during preproduction and rehearsal.

Besides scouting locations and scheduling transportation, food, and lodging for location shoots, the unit manager is in charge of the shooting facilities, sets, and technical crew. The title of unit manager sometimes describes the person in charge of the daily operation, organization, and budgeting of a TV series.

Costume Designer Costume designers work on miniseries, made-for-TV movies, and TV series. Working from firm budgets, they must purchase or rent, design and supervise the making of all costumes for a production. One trains for this demanding specialty by working at the assistant level. Formal training in fashion design may help to get the first job.

Publicity Director/Manager On a running TV series, miniseries, or made-for-TV movie, the publicity director must develop and distribute publicity about the production and its stars. He or she arranges interviews in a variety of media. Sometimes the publicity director of a show is on staff, but more often this assignment is freelance. On network shows, the network maintains a large publicity staff that works closely with the show's publicists.

Camera Operator On feature films, camera assignments involve a director of photography or cinematographer, a camera operator, two or three assistants, and electricians, known as gaffers. Made-for-TV movies use this same arrangement. On a TV series, the camera operator and crew operate the camera under the instructions of the director. Making it to the top in this field may mean going to film school, but, in a more practical sense, it means starting as a gofer and working your way up the ladder.

Wardrobe Supervisor The wardrobe supervisor works with the costume designer and floor manager to maintain a production's costumes.

Graphic Designer The graphic designer works with the art director and production designer, decorating sets and props. On location-shoots, this role becomes more creative and demanding.

Carpenter The carpenter works with the production designer and the set construction foreperson in building, setting up, and maintaining sets for a production.

Property Master A property master keeps the inventory and maintains all the props for a production.

Makeup/Hair Specialist Makeup artists organize and supervise the makeup and hair design of all the actors in a production. The skills are considerable on any production, but on a period piece they are even more demanding.

PRODUCTION FACILITIES COMPANIES

If you drive for a mile or so down Hollywood's Vine Street, you'll see the signs of hundreds of production facilities companies. These specialists perform services for the studios and production companies.

They are involved in editing, sound mixing, dubbing, music scoring, special effects, sound studio rental, and all the phases of postproduction. Although many of these companies employ small permanent staffs, they do rely on freelancers to complement their personnel. There is no reliable figure on the total number of employees working in TV production at these facilities, since many serve both motion picture production and television. However, the total number of people who work primarily in TV production is substantial.

WHAT PEOPLE EARN IN TV PRODUCTION

As in jobs at TV stations and the networks, there is no comprehensive information source about salaries in the production phase of TV. Seven different unions represent these employees. If a network or production company has a contract with any of these unions, the salaries and fringe benefits are higher than at nonunion shops. But remember, you will have to get the job first and then join the union.

Another factor in TV production salaries is the nature of this employment. Many production people are neither employed by the week nor by the project, but instead are hired daily. The network executives responsible for programming are well paid. Executives with vice-presidential rank earn $100,000 a year or more. Although not many people are in this category, yet even their staffers are highly paid.

Job Titles and Salaries
The salaries listed in Table 3 specify the source when available. Sometimes there is no reliable figure, or the salary varies too much for an accurate estimate. Similarly, at the producer level, although salaries are high, there is no accurate information available.

TABLE 3. SALARIES IN TELEVISION PRODUCTION

JOB TITLE	YEARLY, WEEKLY, OR DAILY SALARY OR RANGE
Actor for made-for-TV movie	$1,620/week*
Actor for 30-minute series	$1,925/episode*
Actor for 60-minute series	$2,023/episode*
Executive Producer	not available
Creator	not available
Supervising Producer	not available
Producer	not available
Executive Story Editor	not available
Writer for 30-minute network prime-time	$14,519/show**
Writer for 60-minute network prime-time	$21,354/show**
Writer for 60-minute soap	$20,684/five shows**
Director for network prime-time show/one half hour	approx. $14,500/show
Assistant Director for MOWs	$2,400/week min.
Director Photography	$360/day minimum***
Production Manager	approx. $2,000/week in studio, $2,800 on location
Lighting Director/Designer	$230/day minimum***
Casting Director	not available
Special Effects Director	$220/day minimum***
Music Director	$220/day minimum***
Sound Editor/Mixer	$1,100/week
Film Editor	not available
Floor Manager	not available
Unit Manager	not available
Costume Designer	$240/day***
Publicity Director/Manager	approx. $1,000/week
Camera Operator	$200/day***
Wardrobe Supervisor	not available
Graphic Designer/Set Designer	$1,000/week
Carpenter	$160/day***
Property Master	$180/day***
Makeup/Hair Specialist	approx. $1,350/week

*Screen Actors Guild (SAG) minimum 1993
**Writers Guild of America (WGA) minimum 1993
***NABET minimum 1993

PART II

The Networks, the Stations, and the Public Broadcasting System

Courtesy National Broadcasting Company

CHAPTER 5

Those Mighty Networks

Today, there are three major television networks—CBS, NBC, and ABC—and one mini-major, Fox. Three of the four—CBS, NBC, and ABC—originated as radio networks and emerged as TV pioneers in the post–World War II period. Rupert Murdoch's Fox network got started in 1986.

CBS broadcast its first black-and-white television programs to a single New York station in 1941 and developed a system for color television in 1948. NBC followed in color broadcasting in 1949, but neither network made the important move into coast-to-coast live transmission until 1951.

Early-TV network programming was a mixed bag of comedy and drama with wrestling and boxing providing live-action mayhem. Before the introduction of sophisticated TelePrompTers and videotaping, talk shows were often precarious adventures. In 1950 I watched Lady Iris Mountbatten nervously snap her fingers on camera for what seemed like a minute and a half while she waited for the next cue on her interview show.

By the early 1950s, with improved technology, the networks moved aggressively into the promising new medium. They established their own stations and produced a variety of programs to fill the broadcasting day. The growth of networks in the next twenty years was exponential, their influence global.

THE STRUCTURE AND FUNCTION OF THE TV NETWORKS TODAY

In this chapter we present an overview of network functions, the economics of their operations, and their current problems. We also take a close look at each individual network.

A network is typically divided into two main divisions, the broadcast group and the television network group.

A network's broadcast group, typically, attends to the operation and profitability of its owned and operated (O&O) stations. FCC regula-

---

VHF and UHF

VHF (very high frequency) is a term that describes stations that broadcast over the electronic-spectrum band from 30 to 300 megahertz. VHF encompasses channels one through thirteen in the United States and Canada. UHF (ultrahigh frequency), the TV band in the electronic spectrum from 470 to 890 megahertz, encompasses channels fourteen through eighty-three.

Most early TV sets were not equipped to receive UHF, but by the mid-1980s close to 90 percent of all TV sets had this capability. In theory, the UHF band can handle the broadcasts of up to 3,000 stations in the United States, far beyond the number that VHF can use. Because of VHF's head start and lower channel numbers, however, it has always dominated, although in recent years many independents have chosen UHF because of availability. By the late 1970s there were only 350 UHF stations, of which 195 were commercial. By 1993, there were about 550 commercial and 125 public VHF stations on air, and about 560 commercial and 230 public UHF stations.

tions, until the mid 1980s, let a network own and operate up to seven VHF stations (see box), provided their total reach did not exceed 25 percent of the nation's TV households. In 1984, the number of VHF stations a network could own was increased to twelve stations.

In addition, the broadcast group oversees television advertising sales and, at some networks, video and cable enterprises and radio stations.

The TV network group distributes programming to the network's affiliated stations. It also produces or licenses news, sports, and entertainment programming. While news and sports are usually produced in-house, entertainment is both produced in-house and licensed from production companies. A network's news and sports arms account for a large amount of programming, and they maintain large staffs in their in-house production units.

The TV network group is also responsible for broadcast operations and engineering. In this function they provide technical and logistical support for their various components.

A network also employs an information and publicity staff to handle public relations for its programming and network operations.

Individual networks, which we discuss later in this chapter, break down these divisions into further subcategories.

The FCC permits a network to be involved in cable and video operations. Often this takes the form of venturing a financial interest in a cable TV network besides supplying programming to domestic and foreign cable and to video networks.

THE PROBLEMS FACING TV NETWORKS TODAY

Until about 1976, the networks had the game all to themselves on their own playing field. Their share of the prime-time audience was 92 percent. Advertisers were generally willing to pay high prices for their commercials because they knew they were buying the maximum number of viewers in this peak period. But starting in the mid-1970s, a new threat, cable, began chipping away at the networks' cache. To make matters far worse, in the mid-1980s VCR use further eroded network TV audiences, especially during prime time. Odd viewing habits developed. A working couple, for example, could tape a soap or an afternoon talk show on their VCR and then view it at their leisure during prime time.

Long is the litany of network woes in recent years:

* From 92 percent of the prime-time audience in 1976, the networks' share for the 1992–93 season plummeted to under 40 percent.
* Cable, the pesky newcomer, is clearly here to stay. In the mid-1970s, the average cable-home had seven cable channels. By 1990, that figure had increased to thirty-three channels. Viewers with a satellite dish and the new technology will soon have 500 channels.
* Network news was once a major profit center for the networks. Today, however, the cost of covering the world's news has escalated enormously. By 1993, the three largest networks were spending more than three quarters of a billion dollars a year on news and employing about 3,000 people in their news division. With this huge expense, it is virtually impossible for the networks to make a profit on their news operations. To make matters worse, the networks' share of viewers for their nightly newscasts has been plunging rapidly. Cable TV's CNN network has certainly been responsible for much of the networks' audience loss. In another important development, independent stations (not affiliated with the networks) have shown that they can produce inexpensive morning news shows that can beat out the networks' top shows, "The Today Show" and "Good Morning America," in the ratings.
* Many advertisers find network TV too expensive and are switching their budgets to cable and local independent TV stations and to other media such as magazines, newspapers, direct mail, and contests.
* By 1993, the three biggest networks were paying their affiliates about $300 million a year to carry their programming. Efforts to lower these fees substantially have not been successful.
* The cost of prime-time programming has increased exponentially. For the networks the best way to offset these costs is by owning the shows. Then, when the shows go into syndication, the networks themselves can reap the rewards; however, before 1991 the networks could produce and own only 25 percent of their programming. The FCC amended this rule so that after 1991, they could produce 40 percent of their programming. Yet, by 1993, the networks had come nowhere near this level. They continue to rely on the studios and production companies for most programming.
* Programming a prime-time lineup remains a guessing game. Each season the networks trot out their shining new favorites in hopes of achieving ratings domination, but they seldom succeed. It contin-

ues to be difficult to predict the shows the public wants to see.

* The high cost of broadcast rights have made network sports programming increasingly expensive. CBS, for example, lost over $320 million in 1991 on their major league baseball and NFL football coverage and $50 million on the 1992 Winter Olympics. NBC paid an unprecedented $400 million for the rights to the 1992 Summer Olympics in Barcelona.

To make a profit, the networks must charge inordinately high prices for commercials on these events. When advertising time remains unsold or the price for commercials declines, network sports coverage loses money.

* Pay-per-view video movies could prove to be hazardous to the networks' health by the mid-1990s. Under this system, viewers will select from a menu of hundreds of recent movies merely by pressing a button. If successful, the development looks certain to harm the video and movie theater business, and it may mean a sharply reduced audience for the networks.

Many observers have predicted that the networks as we know them are a dying breed and will not survive to the next century. But don't write them off just yet. While we may see some consolidation and changes in the way the networks operate, they remain a powerful force. The three largest networks attract an average weekly prime-time audience of thirty-four million TV households and yearly advertising revenues of almost $9 billion.

Now let's take a closer look at the individual networks.

NBC

In 1986, the giant RCA company merged with the supergiant General Electric. At the time of the merger, RCA had sales of $8.97 billion and earnings of $369 million (1985 fiscal year). NBC was the number one network and first in prime-time programming. For the next five years it stayed on top of the ratings race, only to lose out to CBS in the 1991–92 season. It was the first network in TV history to rank first in every week of a 52-week broadcast season.

The NBC network is a television pioneer. In 1939, RCA chairman David Sarnoff stood before the cameras at RCA's pavilion at the New

York World's Fair. It was the first time that television covered a news event. The TV set of that era had a nine-inch screen.

These days, NBC continues to innovate by making important advances in the field of high-definition TV. In a joint venture with Cablevision Systems, NBC provided uninterrupted coverage of the 1992 Summer Olympics through an unprecedented pay-per-view package that supplemented NBC's own Olympics coverage. Unfortunately, the experiment did not attract a large audience.

NBC breaks its operations into three major divisions: NBC Television Network, NBC Entertainment, and NBC Sports.

The NBC Television Network is responsible for the network's six O&O stations in Chicago, Denver, Los Angeles, Miami, New York, and Washington, D.C. In addition, the network serves more than 200 affiliated stations and employs about 4,000 people.

NBC Entertainment is responsible for the programming and scheduling of prime-time, daytime, and children's programs. This division developed the groundbreaking "Saturday Night Live" and "Late Night with David Letterman." Letterman moved to CBS for the 1993–94 season.

NBC Sports is an active participant on the sports scene, covering the NFL's American Football Conference, the National Basketball Association, the National Hockey League's All-Star Game, and many golf tournaments.

This division also includes NBC News, which provides NBC's O&O stations and affiliates with news coverage, primarily on the national level. It produces "NBC Nightly News," "The Today Show," "NBC News at Sunrise," and the venerable "Meet the Press," which has aired since 1947.

NBC Today

In the 1991–92 season, NBC relinquished its long hold on the top spot in the ratings to CBS. By 1993, General Electric, NBC's owner, publicly expressed dissatisfaction with the network's profit margins and rumors circulated that they wanted to sell the network. Whether or not NBC finds a new home, it will certainly continue to be an important player in the broadcast business.

CBS

William S. Paley died on October 26, 1990, at the age of eighty-nine. While still in his twenties, Paley took over a struggling network of 160 radio stations and amplified it into a billion-dollar news and entertainment media empire called CBS. Under Paley's stewardship, CBS became known as "the Tiffany network." From 1955 until 1976 it remained number one in the ratings—an incredible record. Although he sold control of the network to the Tisch family in the 1980s, to broadcast veterans, CBS will always be identified with Bill Paley.

Today, the company employs about 4,000 people in two major divisions, CBS Broadcast Group and CBS Television Network.

The CBS Broadcast Group has TV stations in New York, Los Angeles, Chicago, Philadelphia, Minneapolis, Green Bay, and Miami, more than 200 affiliate TV stations, and 20 radio stations.

The CBS Television Network comprises three divisions: CBS Entertainment is responsible for the development, acquisition or production, and scheduling of all entertainment programs on the network; CBS Sports produces high-profile sports events including Major League Baseball, 1992 Winter Olympics, NFL Football, and the NCAA Basketball Championship; CBS News maintains news bureaus around the world and provides news coverage for its O&O (owned and operated) TV and radio stations and affiliates. It also produces a half-dozen news programs, including the "CBS Evening News with Dan Rather and Connie Chung" and the top-rated "60 Minutes."

CBS Today

CBS had financial reversals in the late 1980s due, in part, to its huge investments in sports programming and rights, and reduced advertising revenues; however, by 1992, the company had halted this downward trend. It reported a net profit of $160 million that year.

In the prime-time ratings war, CBS is making sweeping progress with such programs as "Murphy Brown," "Murder, She Wrote," "Love and War," and "Northern Exposure." By the spring of 1993, CBS had five programs in the top ten, and was number one in the ratings over ABC and NBC, respectively.

ABC

In 1985, in a friendly consolidation, ABC merged with Capital Cities to form Capital Cities/ABC, Inc. Although ABC was already an established broadcasting network, it gained stations and other media investments that made the combined company a giant. Capital Cities/ABC today is diversified into newspaper and magazine publishing, cable TV and video, as well as broadcasting, with annual revenues of over $5.4 billion. Besides its broadcasting activities, the company has become a major factor in the cable business. It owns 80 percent of ESPN (Entertainment Sports Programming Network) and a third of both Arts and Entertainment and Lifetime.

Capital Cities/ABC's broadcasting operations fall into two groups, the ABC Television Network Group and the ABC Broadcast Group. The ABC Television Network Group distributes programs produced by ABC News, ABC Sports, and ABC Entertainment to 230 affiliated stations. In addition, ABC has about thirty secondary affiliates, the network's second choice within a given market to carry programming. The ABC News, Sports, and Entertainment Divisions are responsible for the development, acquisition, production, and scheduling of programs.

The ABC Broadcast Group owns and operates eight VHF-TV stations in New York, Chicago, Philadelphia, Raleigh-Durham, Los Angeles, San Francisco, Fresno, and Houston. Six of these stations are located in the nation's top ten markets.

ABC Today

In terms of ratings, by early 1993 ABC was in second place among the networks, behind CBS but ahead of the longtime leader, NBC. ABC's biggest hit, "Roseanne," and its newer prime-time successes, "Home Improvement" and "Coach," were comfortably ensconced in the top-ten of the ratings charts.

Although faced with the same problems as the other networks—diminished audiences and cyclical losses in advertising revenues—ABC is still a profitable network and one whose video and cable investments will continue to make it a leader into the 21st century.

THE FOX BROADCASTING COMPANY

In the 1970s and 1980s, several attempts were made to form a fourth network. None succeeded until Rupert Murdoch came along in 1985. With a huge bankroll and much determination, he prepared to outdo the Big Three at their own game.

Murdoch, let us understand, was no Aussie tenderfoot when he stalked this big game. He owned one third of Britain's newspapers and had already made his mark in American magazine and book publishing. Before he moved into television, he purchased a major movie studio, 20th Century-Fox. The movie company, Murdoch reasoned, would be a profit center and provide programming for the TV network.

In 1985 Murdoch plunked down $2 billion for Metromedia's TV stations in Los Angeles, Chicago, Washington, D.C., Dallas/Ft. Worth, Houston, Salt Lake City, and the profitable WNEW in New York, now renamed WNYW. In 1993, Fox added an eighth station, in Philadelphia. The next step was to line up stations unaffiliated with the other three networks. The hook: a generous package that offered cash and extra advertising time beyond the usual amount allotted affiliate stations by the networks. By 1993, 140 stations were affiliated with the Fox Broadcasting Company.

The new Fox network inaugurated its broadcasting schedule in April 1987 with several new half-hour sitcoms and other entries. Fox aimed its signal at young audiences, but much experimentation was needed (and many bombs were endured) before Fox found the right formula for appealing to young tastes. In a bold move, they positioned their wacky hit "The Simpsons" on Thursday night at 8:00 P.M., opposite the seemingly invincible "The Cosby Show." "Cosby" had a larger audience, but not in the twelve through thirty-four age group. "The Simpsons" won that easily.

Of course, word travels with the speed of light in the TV business. Once the three major networks realized the impact Fox was making on the youth market, they scrambled to meet this youth revolution. One industry commentator asked, "Are we approaching youth-quake overkill?"

Fox Today

The verdict is not in yet on Fox. By the 1992–93 season's end, only five shows, led by "The Simpsons," were in the top 50 in the ratings and none were in the top 20. The Fox network, called by an industry correspondent "the little network that could," expanded to a seven-day, prime-time schedule in June 1993. Clearly, at this point, Fox Broadcasting has yet not earned the designation of the fourth major TV network.

CHAPTER 6

The Network Affiliates and Those Independent Independents

The Los Angeles market area, number two in the nation, has nineteen broadcast channels and twenty-four cable channels. Broadcast channels are those whose signals are transmitted "over the air" whereas cable channels transmit their signals to subscribers through coaxial or fiber optic cable. Four of the nineteen broadcast channels in Los Angeles are O&Os (owned by the four major networks), fourteen are independents, and one is a public broadcasting channel.

The Walt Disney Company, which makes few mistakes, paid $320 million a few years ago for KCAL-TV, an independent station in this lush Los Angeles market. When this major gamble proved unprofitable, Disney swapped a share ownership in KCAL for a stake in a major New York independent, WWOR. Independent stations may be very profitable, but perhaps not so much as to warrant a purchase price of $320 million.

The much smaller market area of Boise, Idaho, the 136th market nationally, with about 158,000 TV households, has six TV stations—three are network affiliates, one is a public TV station, and the other two are small independents.

As we saw, the three largest networks—CBS, NBC, and ABC—own a total of twenty-one stations (O&Os) and have about 200 affiliated stations each. Fox owns eight stations and has 140 affiliates. The remaining 300 commercial TV stations are independents, or "indies" as they are referred to in the business. These figures do not include public television stations. Some independents are small, locally owned stations while others are powerful stations owned by major media companies.

How does each category of station fare in viewership? During one representative week in March 1992, the breakdown was:

Network-affiliated stations	63 percent
Basic cable channels	24 percent
Independent stations	11 percent
Pay TV channels	5 percent
Public TV stations	3 percent

(Note: The total is over 100 percent because of multiple-set households.)
(Source: A.C. Nielsen Company)

By far, network-affiliated stations attract most viewers. This group includes the twenty-nine stations owned by the four networks and the 700-odd stations affiliated with the networks.

The next largest share of viewership watches the basic (free) cable channels like CNN, ESPN, TNT, and A&E.

The nation's 300-odd independent stations make up the third largest viewership group, followed by the pay TV channels (HBO, Showtime, Bravo) and the smallest group, public TV stations.

These figures show the loss in viewership of traditional over-the-air (broadcast) stations to both basic and pay-cable channels. Cable offers viewers a menu of more than thirty channels and people are very selective.

The independents are hardest hit among all these groups. The loss of viewership has forced them to choose increasingly innovative programming. Of course, all groups have lost out to the increasing use of VCRs.

Here is a closer look at the categories of broadcast stations. We cover public broadcasting and cable in chapters 7, 16, and 17.

O&Os

The O&Os, or stations owned and operated by the networks themselves, are usually located in large TV market areas. For example, all four networks own stations in New York, Los Angeles, and Chicago, the nation's three largest market areas. Among the largest networks, ABC, CBS, and NBC, there is little shuffling in the ownership of their O&O stations. Fox, the newcomer in this elite group, purchased seven of its eight stations, formerly independents, from Metromedia. As an industry practice, O&Os are rarely bought and sold.

In terms of programming, the O&Os, naturally, carry all of a network's prime-time programs, sports, and national news shows; however, most O&Os air locally produced evening news shows. They are somewhat flexible on what they program for the late-night period.

O&Os, affiliates, and independents compete heavily over ratings for their locally produced news shows. Stations are constantly experimenting with format and personnel to attract more viewers. It is not unusual for a station in a leading market to pay a news anchor a high six-figure salary, especially if it wooed a popular newscaster away from another station.

Affiliates

As we have stated, the three major networks each have about 200 affiliated stations and Fox has about 140 stations. These stations are not owned by the networks but enjoy a very close relationship, particularly in terms of programming. Typically, you'll find a network affiliate in each of the 300 largest market areas except in those markets where the network owns a station. Many affiliates are themselves owned by large broadcasting or media companies. For example, Westinghouse Broadcasting, the Gannett Company, Cox Communications, and Gillett Holdings own many network affiliates.

How the Network-Affiliate Relationship Functions

Typically, a network maintains an exclusive relationship with its affiliated station in a particular market. There will not be two CBS affiliates, say, in the same market area. In a representative contract, a network agrees to supply at no charge about half an affiliate's daily programming, including all the prime-time shows, much of their sports programming, and the morning and evening network news.

How does this arrangement benefit both sides? When the affiliate airs the network's programs it also runs the network's commercials. The network is then able to tell advertisers that their advertising messages will be beamed to a large "network" of more than 200 stations. Of course, this is a basic guarantee, since the network cannot know how well its programming will fare within each market and what ratings each show will get.

These commercials are the network's primary revenue source. During each hour of prime-time programming, the network lets an affiliate sell two minutes, about 17 percent of the total commercial time. This commercial time provides the affiliate with as much as 40 percent of its total revenues.

In addition to the free programming and adjacent-commercials time (commercial spots between programs), the network compensates the affiliate station for an average $500,000 a year for this exclusive relationship; however, if the affiliate preempts some network programming, it loses part of the compensation. Each of the major networks spends more than $100 million a year on affiliate compensation.

For the transmission of the network's programming, the network provides a station with a schedule of satellite signals. An affiliate's engineering staff aims its satellite dish to capture the signal, which it either tapes or transmits live.

So far this relationship seems ideal. Both sides benefit: the network gets a large audience for its programming and can charge advertisers the maximum amount the ratings allow for its commercial time; the affiliate gets free prime-time programming, receives substantial affiliate compensation from the network, and can sell the valuable adjacency time. Until a few years ago affiliates had pretax profits of as much as 40 percent of their total revenues.

But there is trouble in affiliateland. For one thing, the affiliates face stiff competition for viewership from cable, independent stations, and VCR use. Affiliates are often dissatisfied with the networks' programming, particularly new, untested series. Alternatives may be very attractive, such as running low-cost, syndicated shows. In an average market, an affiliate can buy a group of old half-hour sitcoms for about $7,000 a week and then sell local commercials that bring in about $35,000 a week.

These preemptions are anathema to the networks. They base commercial sales on the total viewing audience of their own stations and those of the affiliates. Preemptions reduce that audience, thereby reducing the price they can charge advertisers.

Both affiliates and independent stations are offered programming like religious specials that air without commercial breaks. Billy Graham's one-hour specials on Sundays are examples of this kind of programming. In this case, the sponsor buys the time outright, paying, say, $25,000 per station for the hour. The special may bring contributions far beyond this cost and it has image-building benefits too. This formula is more profitable for an affiliate than network programming. Here, the affiliate wins, the network loses.

A network may offer a preempted hour to another station in the same market or, when preemptions occur frequently, the network may seek another affiliate in the same market. Of course, that opportunity may not exist in a small market.

Networks are moving aggressively to reduce the amount of yearly compensation they pay affiliates. Some networks have even threatened to charge affiliates for certain prime-time hit shows. This is a very controversial move. Industry watchers doubt that it will work. Anyhow, the whole network-affiliate relationship is changing and, clearly, change is in the interests of both sides.

THOSE INDEPENDENT INDEPENDENTS

In 1980 there were only ninety-five independent TV stations. By 1990, the number of "indies" had quadrupled and threatened the domination of the network affiliates in many cities. The independents are not affiliated with any of the networks and are usually smaller than the local network stations; however, some independents are major stations in their market areas and are often owned by large media organizations.

KTLA in Los Angeles, for example, is a powerful independent station that competes aggressively with the four O&Os and the other independents in its market. The station's locally produced morning-news show has enjoyed higher ratings than the three national news shows run on NBC, CBS, and ABC. It also has broadcast rights for three major sports teams: the Kings, Angels, and Dodgers. In prime time, KTLA has endured against the networks' programming by running recent movies that that they acquire at a relatively low cost.

Independents share about 11 percent of the nation's TV audience. Their ad billings are about $2.5 billion—almost 25 percent of total TV national and local sales and, most important of all, their net profits are about 25 percent of their total revenues.

Independents are found in both large cities and small ones. New York, the nation's largest market area, has sixteen broadcast channels. Two of the six largest stations are independents and one station, WNYW, was formerly an independent but is now part of the Fox network. It is one of the most profitable stations in the country. Rupert Murdoch purchased it for Fox for about half a billion dollars in 1986.

Howard Stringer, president of CBS Broadcast Group, says that "the network's fiercest challenger is not cable but the independent broadcast stations. They have siphoned away viewers and torrents of ad revenues that the networks once took for granted."

The battle between the networks, the affiliates, the independent stations, and the cable channels will go on for a long time, or until someone devises a more workable system.

CAREER TIP

Affiliates and independents do not offer much production or on-air work, except on their local news shows. There are, however, opportunities in sales. In very small markets, an independent may be your only option, but it is a good place to get started.

CHAPTER 7

The Public Broadcasting System

Dozier, Alabama, Bethel, Alaska, Pago Pago, American Samoa, Cotati, California, and Broomfield, Colorado have one thing in common—they all have member stations of PBS, the Public Broadcasting Service. As of 1993, there were 341 noncommercial stations in this network. During an average week, viewers in more than fifty million homes watched public television at some point.

PBS, alone among the world's public TV systems, is entirely independent of political and governmental control or interference. It is owned and controlled by its member TV stations, which, in turn, are accountable to their local communities. This freedom does not mean that PBS operates without controversy, particularly in terms of its programming. In recent years conservative and religious groups have lobbied to withhold government funding (the federal share is about 15 percent) because of a purported liberal bias of PBS programming.

At the other end of the spectrum stand liberal advocacy groups that decry the probusiness slant of the network's political programs. These complaints have often been expressed in public TV's twenty-four-year history. Yet somehow this vital broadcasting voice has survived.

A SHORT HISTORY OF PUBLIC BROADCASTING

The nation's first public TV station predates the creation of PBS. KUHT in Houston, Texas, got its start in 1953. One of its productions, "Children's Corner," had a weekly budget of $150, which included salaries and props. We can just guess at the producer's fee.

By 1962 there were seventy-five such stations, most operated by educational institutions. The distribution system used in those days was indeed primitive. When offered for nationwide use, a program had to be "bicycled"—a few copies would go to key stations that would air the program and send them on to other stations.

The Public Broadcasting Act, signed by President Lyndon Johnson in November 1967, initiated governmental support for public broadcasting. At the same time, the Corporation for Public Broadcasting (CPB) was founded as a buffer between stations and federal agencies. It was to protect programming from governmental influence, develop television and radio systems with alternative programming, and help support these stations. After consultation, representatives of the CPB, the Ford Foundation (a longtime supporter of public television), and public stations recommended formation of "Public Broadcasting Service." PBS signed its charter on November 3, 1969.

PBS started with 128 member stations and a budget of $7 million. In the first year, its audience was treated to a diet of such productions as "The French Chef," "Washington Week in Review," and "The Nader Report."

Through the 1970s, PBS introduced provocative programming like "The MacNeil/Lehrer News Hour," "Bill Moyers' Journal," "Nova," "Masterpiece Theatre," and "Live from the Met." It also continued the successful children's program "Sesame Street." By the 1990s, about ninety million people were watching public television each week.

By 1993, the total budget for public TV was about $1.4 billion, of which more than 80 percent came from nonfederal sources. Of this nonfederal portion, approximately equal amounts came from subscribers, state governments, and corporate contributions.

The Corporation for Public Broadcasting funnels federal funds to qualified noncommercial TV and radio stations. It helps insure production of high-quality programs from diverse sources. It also provides training, instruction, recruiting, research, and fund-raising services.

HOW DOES PUBLIC TELEVISION OPERATE?

PBS is a nonprofit corporation with a staff of about 300 headquartered in Alexandria, Virginia. It neither produces programs nor controls its member stations. It acquires programs from member stations, independent producers, and foreign sources.

The primary focus of PBS is on program acquisition and scheduling. It is also concerned with education services, press relations, video promotion, audience research, station development, revenue-producing activities, broadcast and technical operations, and engineering development.

PBS's share of the $1.4 billion budget for all of public TV is about $156 million a year. Almost 73 percent of this figure comes from its member stations.

PBS's member stations produce many of the shows aired on the network. Such long-running shows as "American Playhouse," "Nova," "Live from Lincoln Center," "Washington Week in Review," and "Wall Street Week" are produced by member stations. Funding for these productions comes from subscribers, grants, corporations, foundations, and the government.

Besides producing programming for national distribution, member stations produce programs for local viewing.

The PBS member stations with the largest budgets serve the largest market areas. New York's WNET/Thirteen, one of the network's largest stations, has an annual budget over $100 million. About $6 million of that came from the CPB. This station has produced such critically acclaimed series as "Heritage: Civilizations and the Jews," "The Brain," and "A Walk Through the 20th Century with Bill Moyers."

Smaller member stations also produce programming for the PBS network. WGBH in Boston, for example, produces "Nova," the often controversial "Frontline," and "This Old House."

PBS PROGRAMMING: A CASE STUDY

Public TV differs from commercial TV by both its lack of commercials and the innovative excellence of its programming. "The Civil War," a series by award-winning filmmaker Ken Burns, is an example of public TV at its best. Premiered on PBS in 1990 and rebroadcast in 1991, 1992, and 1993, this epic, eleven-hour documentary combines scholarship and riveting entertainment. It was the highest-rated series in PBS history; its first showing attracted an audience of fourteen million people for each of its five evenings.

A series like "The Civil War" is extremely expensive, though not by commercial TV standards. General Motors was the sole corporate sponsor of the series and contributed to its promotion. Beyond providing an unforgettable experience for millions of viewers at home, the value of "The Civil War" was extended in several ways:

* Eighty thousand study and teacher guides were distributed free to high schools nationwide.
* An educational resource package was sold that included a complete set of videocassettes, a teacher's guide, a timeline poster, a Civil War map, and an index of people, places, and events.
* The series became available as a college-credit course in January 1991, licensed to colleges by the PBS Adult Learning Service.

Rarely, if ever, does a commercial TV series have the educational impact of "The Civil War."

Raising the Money for a PBS Series

Financing any documentary, and particularly an extended series, is a heroic task, often filled with frustrations. Producers know the money sources, but getting them to write a check is another issue.[1]

Ken Burns, the producer of "The Civil War," was an established filmmaker who had already produced two Academy-Award documentary nominees, when he conceived of the series in 1984 and initially budgeted the project for $2.7 million.

A PBS member station, WETA, in Washington, D.C., made a token contribution of $20,000 to get him started. Later, PBS added a second $20,000 to his ante as an informal grant. This seed money enabled

Burns to hire grant-proposal writers and support himself for a year, but he still needed the serious capital.

He got $1,050,000 from the National Endowment for the Humanities, and a commitment from General Motors to contribute production money and additional funds for promotion. The Corporation for Public Broadcasting was the next stop on Burns's financing trail. When he approached CPB in 1988, they were considering 750 projects seeking financing, but, after a couple of tries, Burns received a commitment of $200,000.

He still needed almost one million dollars to complete the production, now budgeted at $3.2 million. Burns made the rounds of the charitable foundations and raised $650,000 from the Arthur Vining Davis and MacArthur foundations and another $300,000 from the National Endowment for the Humanities. The laborious quest for financing had taken Burns six years. Consider how much more difficult financing the project would have been, if possible, for a producer without Ken Burns's track record.

A QUANTUM JUMP IN TECHNOLOGY

In 1978, PBS took a giant leap when it became the first TV system to distribute its programs via satellite. In 1984, PBS purchased four transponders from Western Union, giving the system the capacity to provide public TV stations four streams of programming simultaneously. (A transponder is a device on a satellite that receives, amplifies, and retransmits broadcast signals.) In 1993, PBS switched to a new satellite that provides a high-definition system to deliver a sharper picture and allows interactive school programming.

For hearing-impaired Americans, PBS spearheaded the development of the closed captioning system that puts subtitles on sets connected to special decoding devices.

Since its inception, public TV has been active in broadcasting college education. About 250,000 students a year enroll in courses using PBS's Adult Learning Service. These programs use satellite and microwave technology. In addition, PBS feeds telecourse programming from a studio classroom to its satellite and delivers the programming directly to schools with satellite dishes. For schools without dishes, local public TV stations send the signal over the air or through cable.

THE PBS STATION: A CASE EXAMPLE

KCET is an innovative, public TV station in Los Angeles. It has won many awards for excellence in broadcast journalism and is active in the production of programming for all the PBS stations. In 1990, for example, KCET produced Arthur Miller's adaptation of Ibsen's "An Enemy of the People" for American Playhouse. In 1991, the station produced "The Astronomers," a series narrated by Richard Chamberlain. In 1992, KCET produced "Millennium: Tribal Wisdom and the Modern World" and a daily preschool series, "The Puzzle Factory."

TABLE 4. KCET'S REVENUE SOURCES

REVENUE	AMOUNT	PERCENTAGE
Individual subscription, unrestricted grants from major donors, corporations, foundations, donated goods and services	$23,189,000	61%
Program production and broadcasting grants	$8,463,000	22%
Corporation for Public Broadcasting community service grant	$2,180,000	6%
Product Sales	$1,533,000	4%
Contract production	$1,498,000	4%
Interest and miscellaneous	$1,082,000	3%
TOTAL	$37,945,000	100%

KCET operates on a budget of about $38 million. Tables 4 and 5 list its sources of revenue and expenses for the fiscal year ending June 1992. These figures reveal the significance of individual subscriptions and corporate and foundation donations, which together make up four-fifths of the station's revenues. Also notable is the expense of producing their own shows and acquiring programming from other sources. This expense also includes the physical costs of the station's own broadcasting operations.

THE WOES OF PUBLIC TELEVISION

We have mentioned the problems public TV faces from pressure groups over its programming. Perhaps even more important is the ever-prevalent matter of money. The poor economy of the early 1990s yielded fewer dollars during the stations' fund-raising efforts. The stations use these moneys for their own operations and to help PBS pay for

TABLE 5. KCET'S EXPENSES

EXPENSES	AMOUNT	PERCENTAGE
Administration and general support, including interest, legal, accounting, insurance, etc.	$4,600,000	12%
Public information: KCET magazine, publicity, advertising	$2,341,000	6%
Fundraising: Subscriber services, marketing and development, donated goods and services	$7,619,000	20%
Production, programming, and broadcasting	$21,799,000	58%
Production marketing	$1,097,000	3%
Campaign activity	$480,000	1%
TOTAL	$37,936,000	100%

program development and acquisition. As income dwindled, PBS has had to reduce its commitment to programming. Some series feature fewer episodes; others have been cut altogether.

One remedy for this shortfall is the acceptance of "commercials," much to the disapproval of many public TV viewers. The content of these commercials varies from the soft sell of a sponsor/supporter's name to a fifteen-second spot that looks and sounds like an ad appearing on commercial television. Of course, public TV stations see these commercials as good business. They encourage companies to make larger contributions than they would if this privilege were not available. Meanwhile, the debate over the propriety of commercial advertising on public TV continues, perhaps not to be reconciled until an acceptable formula is achieved.

At the time of this writing, public TV faces a dilemma. It must continue to produce high-quality programming while reducing its costs. It is a problem without a simple solution.

PUBLIC TELEVISION AS A CAREER

Readers interested in a rewarding career should consider public television. Few other fields offer this combination of education and entertainment.

As pointed out earlier, there are public TV stations everywhere. Many of these stations, as well as PBS headquarters in Alexandria, Virginia, have informal internship programs. There are also opportunities to become a volunteer fund-raiser at a local TV station. Success in this role has often led to paying jobs in development (fund-raising).

Except for sales, the table of organization of a public TV station is similar to that of a commercial station. In smaller cities, public TV jobs pay less than their commercial counterparts. In larger cities like New York and Los Angeles, salaries are about equal.

Breaking into public TV is no less difficult than breaking into commercial television, unless you have exceptional skills and training. The job spectrum is about the same, the major difference being that fund-raising replaces ad sales. While there is even more financial pressure

to meet budgets in public TV, there is also an esprit that may be miss-
ing in commercial TV. Perhaps it is based on the lack of constraints
from advertisers. A good route to follow is to get experience on a PBS
production, even if it means being a "gofer." From there, your experience may lead to a more responsible assignment on another PBS production or to prime-time, commercial TV production.

NOTE

[1] Larry Leventhal, "How Ken Burns Managed to Pay for the Civil War," Variety, September 21, 1992,
p. 73.

CHAPTER 8

The Federal Communications Commission

The Federal Communications Commission (FCC), the American public's protector of the airwaves, is an independent federal agency. It was created in 1934 and has considerable regulatory powers over television, cable, and radio. Its chairperson and four other commissioners are appointed by the President and serve for five years. Their appointments must be confirmed by the Senate.

Through the years, the activities of the FCC have varied, depending upon the dynamism of its chairperson and commissioners. From the 1980s until the early 1990s, the agency was an instrument of change in the television industry, principally concerning competitiveness between the networks and the suppliers of programming.

Although there are outcries to reduce TV violence and improve the quality of programming, the FCC mandate does not include the regulation of programming (although a new scheme for networks to self-police violence has just been announced).

FCC ACTIVITIES

One can better understand the function of the FCC by examining some of its activities.

Broadcast Regulation

The FCC allocates broadcast frequencies, rules on applications for new stations, and regulates existing stations, including the licensing of transmitter operators and the transfer of a station's license from one party to another. It is the FCC, for example, that decides how many stations one person or corporation may own and sets the term of a station's license (five years).

In recent years, the FCC's interpretation of the financial interest rule, commonly known as "fin/syn," has stirred serious concern among the networks. Originally, the networks could produce news and sports programming as well as made-for-TV movies and miniseries; however, the networks were allowed to produce only three of the twenty-two hours of weekly, prime-time programming. Later, that number rose to five hours. The bulk of prime-time programming was to be produced by independent production companies and studios. Of course, if the networks don't own these shows, they cannot participate in the lucrative syndication market.

In April 1991, after much protesting and lobbying by the networks, the FCC changed the fin/syn rule to let the networks produce up to 40 percent of prime-time programs. Since they could now produce more shows, they would also own them and benefit from their syndication; they could also co-produce with studios and production companies and engage in domestic and foreign syndication. In April 1993, the FCC lifted most limits on financial ownership and syndication of programs. The networks can now own a stake in the programs they broadcast and then market the reruns worldwide.

Programming Oversight

The commission periodically reviews station performance in terms of equal-opportunity employment and public-service programming. These reviews are part of a license-renewal application and determine whether a station has met its obligation to serve the public interest.

During political campaigns, the FCC prescribes that all legally qualified candidates for any public office be afforded equal opportunities to state their views. This practice is commonly known as the "equal time provision."

Advertising Oversight

The FCC does not regulate individual commercials, but it does have jurisdiction over the number of commercials a station may broadcast in a given period. In the early 1970s, the commission was instrumental in banning cigarette and alcoholic beverage advertising, not including beer, from TV and radio.

New Technologies

The FCC has been active in fostering the growth of new technologies like high-definition television. It also regulates the use of home satellite-dishes and the distribution of signals to these units.

CAREER TIP

Considerably less glamorous than working for the networks or in TV production, a job with the FCC can nonetheless be fulfilling. It may be especially attractive to those who would like to work in Washington, D.C. The FCC employs some 1,800 people, of whom about 250 are lawyers. Other than the five commissioners, who are appointed by the President, employment in the FCC is nonpartisan.

PART III

Programming and Production

CHAPTER 9

All You Need to Know about Ratings

Ratings and programming are related. The objective of all programming is to achieve high ratings. For commercial TV, high ratings translate into high advertising rates, but ratings are important for public TV too since a highly rated series like "The Civil War" brings in new subscribers.

WHAT THE RATINGS ARE ALL ABOUT

Audience ratings determine how much broadcasters can charge advertisers for commercials. If you're an advertiser like General Mills or General Foods, and spend millions of dollars on TV commercials, ratings tell you who each program reaches; that is, ratings tell you the number of households that saw the ad and what types of people live in them. Such information helps advertisers predict sales performance and later tells them what they received for their money. Ratings guide advertising agencies in the buying of TV time, and then help them evaluate the efficiency of their buys. Ratings also serve as both programming and sales tools for the networks, stations, and program suppliers.

For the first-run prime-time TV season of 1992–93, which ended in April 1993, CBS led the pack with an A. C. Nielsen rating of 13.4. ABC followed with 12.5 and NBC trailed with 11.0. Nielsen tabulates ratings for the thirty-week period from mid-September to mid-April. The numbers reflect the average percentage of U.S. homes with TV sets watching each network.

Each rating point represents 942,000 TV homes. CBS's rating of 13.4 means that 12.62 million TV homes are watching that network in prime time (8:00 P.M. to 11:00 P.M.).

Besides points, ratings report "shares." A share refers to the percentage of homes with TV sets on and tuned to a specific program or network. One week, for example, the show "Roseanne" might have a 22.5 rating and a share of 35, meaning that the show reached a total of 21.2 million households and 35 percent (share) of homes with TV sets on in that period.

Prime-time ratings set the stage for network profitability in the years to come. The difference of one rating point can be worth $100 million in advertising revenues.

Shows that do not achieve high enough ratings early in a TV season are vulnerable and may be canceled after the season's first half; however, some low-rated shows may be continued if they appeal to a special target audience that advertisers want to reach. The network makes the final decision.

Ratings "sweeps" take place four times a year. Sweeps are the periods the networks use to calculate commercial-time charges. The A. C. Nielsen Company's audience measurements during a "sweeps" serve as the basis for network rates during the following season. During the sweeps periods, the networks pull out all the stops on programming to get the highest ratings. By the November sweeps, the networks will have already replaced their weakest shows of the new season, which begins in September. They may also have juggled time slots to position shows around an emerging hit show.

By the time the February sweeps roll around, the networks will have learned which of their new shows are popular and which of their previous season's programs have staying power. The network's O&O stations and their affiliates base their rates for the forthcoming season on the sweeps numbers.

Network ratings and shares have generally gone down in recent years, victims of competition from cable and home video viewing. In 1987, "The Cosby Show" had a season average rating of 34.3 and an average share of 52. In 1992, the year's top-rated show, ABC's "Roseanne," had a rating of 22.5 and a share of 35.

THE MAJOR TELEVISION AUDIENCE RESEARCH COMPANY

The A. C. Nielson Company is preeminent in the field of TV audience sampling and ratings. It has been at this numbers game since 1936, starting with radio broadcast research. Back then, it used a device called an "audimeter" that linked the tuning dial on a radio receiver with a moving roll of paper that kept a permanent record of dial position (i.e., station tuned to).

Nielsen started the Nielsen Television Index in 1950 when the medium was in its infancy. A "Golden Age" of television eclipsed radio in just a few years. Technology advanced and, in 1950, the Nielsen TV Index began providing network-audience activities. Nielsen's first index was based on a sample of 300, which grew to 450 households in 1951, and 700 in 1953. The system used a "mailable audimeter," which included a replaceable film cartridge that was mailed from the sample home to Nielsen every week. In those days, 3.8 million households, or 9 percent of U.S. homes, had TV sets. Today, more than ninety-four million households, 98 percent of all U.S. homes, have one or more.

The Nielsen Company grew along with the medium, with ever more sophisticated techniques to meet the demands of the industry. In 1980, Nielsen issued its first cable report. It could measure cable, pay cable, subscription-TV, and super stations with a monitoring device placed in 4,000 homes. These homes represent a scientifically-selected sample of all TV viewers. Nielsen can also tell whether a VCR is on playback or recording a program.

Although A. C. Nielsen dwarfs all other research companies, with total revenues of $1.305 billion in 1992, there are many other organizations in this field. The Artbitron Company was active in TV audience research until October 1993, when they discontinued their efforts in TV audience measurement. They continue to be America's largest local-market, syndicated radio audience measurement service.

In 1966, Arbitron conceived of the Area of Dominant Influence (ADI) as an exclusive marketing area for TV. A geographic designation, ADI provides advertisers with the relative standing of each market area's number of measurable viewers.

For example, New York (the greater New York City metropolitan area) is the nation's leading ADI. It has roughly seven million TV households (homes with at least one set) out of the nation's total of ninety-four million. We therefore refer to New York as the "number-one market." In contrast, San Diego is the 25th market, with about 900,000 TV households; Las Vegas is the 79th, with about 310,000; and Panama City, Florida, the 162nd market, has about 96,000 TV households.

These market rankings are important to advertisers, who will pay more to reach larger markets, or to reach specific markets for product testing. At the time of this writing, the ADI geographic designation continues to be used even though Arbitron is no longer in the TV measurement game.

THE IMPORTANCE OF RATINGS

Movie producers reading critics' unfavorable reviews of their pictures often dismiss the criticism by saying, "What does he know about movies?" TV producers and networks that receive low ratings will often say, "You know that those ratings are inaccurate."

Since advertisers spend billions of dollars to reach TV households, which average more than fifty TV-viewing hours per week, research on this vast audience is vital. Several advertising agencies spend almost a billion dollars per year in TV for their clients.

Consider, too, the cost of this advertising. In 1965, the average cost per thirty-second commercial on prime-time TV was $19,700. By 1990, it had reached $100,000. Total TV advertising for 1992 was more than $30 billion.

For the networks, audience measurement is essential. Many new shows are introduced each year, requiring audience measurement to find their popularity. Of course, ratings are also necessary for evaluating existing shows.

THE TECHNIQUES OF AUDIENCE SAMPLING

TV-audience research like that provided by Nielsen measures the size of a show's audience, as well as finding the viewers' age, education, and so on. These are quantitative, not qualitative, measurements.

The national Nielsen Television Index samples only 4,000 homes, but this sample is adequate to provide a reliable estimate of national TV-viewing habits and trends.

Nielsen puts a small electronic device called a "people meter" into each scientifically-selected, sample household. The meter can connect with up to four TV sets and VCRs. Of course, the test households must approve the placement of meters in their homes. The device stores information at one-minute intervals, showing whether each set is on or off and, if on, to which channel it is tuned. The meter transmits its information to Nielsen, giving the central-office computer a full day's viewing information in five seconds. In effect, the channel selection knob on each set in each sample household is "wired in" to Nielsen's computers. They can learn exactly how those knobs are switched around, minute-by-minute, over a twenty-four-hour period.

The meter device checks whether the set is on, but how does it tell who is watching? The answer lies in using scientific sampling procedures in the 4,000 households randomly selected. The findings within the sample are then "projected" to national totals, and therefore carry a small margin for error. Each permanent member of the selected household is given his or her own number, which is punched into the "people meter" each time a viewer stops or starts watching the set. In this way, Nielsen can report what programs are watched and the demographic information on age, sex, and so on of the family members doing the viewing. Nielsen is developing a "passive" meter that will automatically register the presence of people in front of the TV set without requiring any manual input. You cannot volunteer to be in the sample; you must be selected by scientific-sampling procedures. A household stays in the sample an average of two years.

Nielsen collects and tabulates all this information for distribution to networks, TV stations, ad agencies, production companies, and the like. Nielsen has two systems to measure programs. The national Nielsen Television Index measures programs seen on networks, on cable channels, and in syndication. The local service, Nielsen Station Index, measures viewing of local TV programs.

CAREER OPPORTUNITIES IN TV RATINGS AND RESEARCH

A. C. Nielsen employs thousands of computer and research specialists to implement its various programs. Its activities today are global, with foreign revenues exceeding those in the United States. There are many other organizations involved in research; the October 18, 1993 issue of *Advertising Age* lists 100 companies, their locations, and phone numbers. Geographically, research companies are spread across the nation. Of the top twenty in the *Advertising Age* list, only three are in the New York metropolitan area. A. C. Nielsen is headquartered in Northbrook, Illinois; Information Resources, Inc., the second-largest research company, is in Chicago; and others are in fifteen other cities.

The networks and ad agencies employ research personnel on both coasts to evaluate audience measurement data. These evaluations are then passed along to the programming and sales departments.

CAREER TIP

Audience research companies like Nielsen employ people in engineering, field operations, program records, meter and diary checking, data processing, writing report publications, and conducting telephone interviews. College students and graduates with talent in mathematics, statistics, and computer science might consider employment in this demanding field. Salaries for the entry-level job of research analyst with an audience-research company start at about $18,000 a year. After three or four years, with normal promotions, pay progresses to about $25,000. In contrast to such areas as TV production, this field affords good job stability.

CHAPTER 10

The Fine Art of Programming

THE HOWS AND WHYS OF TV PROGRAMMING

Essentially, TV programming is the selection and scheduling of programs for a particular period at a station or network. How is programming done at the various types of stations? At the network-owned stations (the O&Os), the networks provide both the programming, except for local news and sports shows, and the schedule. At the network affiliates, stations have greater flexibility in their scheduling. Although the networks want affiliates to follow their schedule, at least in prime time, the stations often preempt network choices in favor of shows they think will bring larger audiences.

The program director at an affiliate will make extensive use of research to define the local audience. He or she may, for example, determine that a larger audience can be pulled on Monday nights by running syndicated shows than by carrying the network's made-for-TV movie.

Of course, the affiliate that preempts the network's programming choice is also reducing its affiliate compensation. Thus, the revenue it realizes from its preemptive choice must exceed the amount it would have received from the network for airing the program. Further, the affiliate's programming decision must also consider the programming of its competitors in the same market.

Independent stations have more choice in programming. Independents carry an ever-increasing number of locally produced news and sports shows, but they also may choose from the vast menu of the syndicators' fare. Again, the programmer decides what will work best in each time slot. That decision rests on research and much trial and error.

When an affiliate rejects the network's programming, the network may offer independent stations the option of purchasing these programs.

Jobs in programming vary. At a network, programmers help develop series. They evaluate and assign scripts, produce pilots, and test new programs with focus-group audiences. Working in network programming is the big time. Successful programmers go right to the top of the networks' pecking orders—with salaries to match.

Stations have less program development but do more research into what will work in a particular market.

THE DAYPARTS OF PROGRAMMING

Any discussion of programming must begin with a definition of "dayparts." A daypart is a particular segment of the broadcasting day. The day is broken down into these dayparts:

Early Morning: 6:00 A.M. to 9:00 A.M.
Morning: 9:00 A.M. to Noon
Afternoon: Noon to 4:00 P.M.
Early Fringe: 4:00 P.M. to 6:00 P.M.
Early Evening: 6:00 P.M. to 7:30 P.M.
Access Time: 7:00 or 7:30 P.M. to 8:00 P.M.
Prime Time: 8:00 P.M. to 11:00 P.M.
Late Fringe: 11:00 P.M. to 11:30 P.M.
Late Night: 11:30 P.M. to 6:00 A.M.

Television viewing increases throughout the day, reaching a peak between 8:00 and 10:00 P.M., then declines as people retire for the night.

The following is a brief analysis of the programming strategy for each daypart.

Early Morning

The early morning daypart is traditionally dominated by news and talk shows like NBC's "Today" and ABC's "Good Morning America." The independents generally counterprogram the networks' shows with children's programming. On Saturdays the networks run children's shows in this daypart, while on Sundays it's news and interviews.

Morning

During the morning, the networks run a mixed bag of programs, including syndicated sitcoms, exercise, talk, and game shows. In this daypart, audiences include twice as many women as men and twice as many children as teens.

Afternoon

From noon to 4:00 P.M. is the time for soap operas, those spicy sagas never to be missed (more about soaps in chapter 14). Women make up 70 to 75 percent of this afternoon audience. The three networks produce ten soaps during this period. Although it takes considerable time to win audience involvement with a soap, once a viewer is hooked, he or she is trapped forever.

Stations not carrying soaps on this daypart usually go with movies, talk and interview shows, syndicated series (usually old network reruns), and game shows. On weekends, sports prevail in this daypart.

Early Fringe

The early fringe period is a tough daypart to schedule. The teens are home from school, often pressuring one-set households for MTV. From 5:00 P.M. to 6:00 P.M., the network affiliates usually run local news or news-feature shows. Stations without news experiment with this time slot, often running popular old sitcoms to increase the ratings.

Early Evening

From 6:00 P.M. to 7:30 P.M., the networks trot out their big news guns—the Rather-Brokaw-Jennings bunch along with their highly paid correspondents—for thirty minutes of national and international coverage.

As noted, the affiliates either precede or follow network news with locally produced news or they sandwich the network news between two local-news programs. The independents generally do not carry news in this daypart; instead, they carry syndicated series and game shows.

Access Time

During the interval between the evening news and prime time, the networks and affiliates usually program game shows. One often sees the highly successful "Entertainment Tonight" in this time slot. The independents run game shows or syndicated sitcoms like "M*A*S*H" or "Happy Days."

Prime Time

The stations hope to get the highest ratings during prime time, and commercials sell at the highest rate then. This is a high-stakes game. The networks support this programming with extensive promotion, both on air and in print.

Table 6 shows the Nielsen ratings for the week of February 22–28, 1993. The figures opposite the day of the week represent the average ratings for each network for that particular night's prime-time programs. The number preceding the name of the show is that show's ranking among all prime-time programs. The figures after a show's listing are first its rating and then its share. At the bottom of the table is each network's weekly average ratings and share and its season's figures through February 28, 1993.

What can we learn from this listing?

Note the importance of positioning. On Monday nights, CBS's "Murphy Brown" enjoys a very high rating and the two shows following benefit from this popularity.

Made-for-TV movies are a staple of prime time. ABC and NBC run them on Monday, CBS on Tuesday. Besides these movies, the networks also feature classic and recent theatrical films (produced for distribution in theaters). During this week, ABC ran two of these films, CBS ran three, including "The Wizard of Oz," and Fox ran one on Wednesday night. On Sunday, CBS's "Rio Diablo" led the pack with a high 17.3 rating.

TABLE 6. NIELSEN RATINGS FOR PRIME-TIME SHOWS, FEB. 22-28, 1993

	ABC	CBS	NBC	FOX
Monday	**13.4/20**	**14.8/22**	**14.1/21**	**No Programming**
8:00	42. FBI: Untold Story 11.7/18	32. Hearts Afire 13.2/20	11. Fresh Prince 16.5/25*	
8:30	42. American Det. 11.7/17		19. Blossom 14.9/22*	
9:00	22. ABC Monday Night Movie:	10. Murphy Brown 17.0/24*	30. NBC Monday Night Movies:	
9:30	Between Love and Hate 14.2/21	22. Love and War 14.2/21*	Miracle on Interstate	
10:00		16. Northern Exposure 15.6/25*	880 13.3/20	
10:30				
Tuesday	**14.1/22**	**15.9/25**	**9.1/14**	**4.3/6**
8:00	8. Full House 17.3/26*	12. Rescue: 911 16.2/24*	74. Quantum Leap 7.5/11	86. Class of '96 4.5/7
8:30	14. Hangin w/Mr. C 16.0/24			
9:00	2. Roseanne 21.1/31*	15. CBS Tuesday Movie: Judgment		87. Key West 4.1/6
9:30	24. Jackie Thomas 13.9/21	Day: The John List Story 15.8/25*		
10:00	70. Civil Wars 8.2/14		40. Dateline NBC 12.3/21	
10:30				
Wednesday	**12.5/19**	**20.0/31**	**11.3/17**	**5.7/9**
8:00	60. Wonder Years 9.9/15	3. Grammy Awards 20.0/31*	21. Unsolved Mysteries 14.5/22	85. Fox Night at the Movies:
8:30	59. Doogie Howser 10.0/15			License to Kill 5.7/9
9:00	5. Home Improvmt 18.9/27		65. Homicide 8.9/13	
9:30	18. Coach 15.0/22			
10:00	51. ABC News Special: For Men		53. Law and Order 10.4/17	
10:30	Only 10.7/18			

TABLE 6. NIELSEN RATINGS FOR PRIME-TIME SHOWS, FEB. 22-28, 1993

	ABC	CBS	NBC	FOX
Thursday	**14.2/22**	**11.1/17**	**14.7/23**	**11.2/17**
8:00	30. Matlock 13.3/20	44. Top Cops 11.6/18	38. Cheers 12.5/19	27. Simpsons 13.7/21*
8:30			25. Wings 13.8/21*	37. Martin 12.6/19
9:00		53. Street Stories 10.4/15	7. Cheers 18.6/27*	55. ILC Great Bits 10.3/15
9:30			5. Seinfeld 18.9/28*	68. ILC: First Season 8.3/12
10:00	13. Prime Time Live 16.1/26*	45. Knots Landing 11.3/19	41. L.A. Law 12.1/20	
10:30				
Friday	**11.6/19**	**12.3/21**	**11.2/19**	**7.8/13**
8:00	25. Family Matters 13.8/23*	32. CBS Movie Special: The Wizard of Oz 13.2/22*	72. Days of Our Lives: Night Sins 7.9/13	68. Amer's Most Wanted 8.3/14
8:30	28. Step By Step 13.4/22*			
9:00	63. Dinosaurs 9.5/15		35. 9th Annual Soap Opera Awards 12.9/22*	74. Sightings 7.5/12
9:30	74. Camp Wilder 7.5/12			80. Sightings 2 7.0/11
10:00	36. 20/20 12.7/22*	57. Rescue: 911 10.2/18		
10:30				
Saturday	**8.7/15**	**11.3/20**	**9.0/16**	**8.8/15**
8:00	78. ABC Saturday Night Movie: City Heat 7.4/13	20. Dr. Quinn, Medicine Woman 14.6/25*	74. Almost Home 7.5/13	66. Cops 8.8/15
8:30			73. Nurses 7.7/13	57. Cops 2 10.2/17
9:00		62. CBS Saturday Movie: Mother of the Bride 9.6/17	45. Empty Nest 11.3/19*	71. America's Most Wanted: Mobsters 8.1/14
9:30			55. Mad About You 10.3/18*	
10:00	45. The Commish 11.3/20*		67. Sisters 8.6/16	
10:30				

TABLE 6. NIELSEN RATINGS FOR PRIME-TIME SHOWS, FEB. 22-28, 1993

	ABC	CBS	NBC	FOX
Sunday	**12.8/20**	**19.2/29**	**10.9/17**	**8.6/13**
7:00	64. Life Goes On 9.2/15	1. 60 Minutes 22.8/36*	81. NBC News Special Report 6.5/10	83. Batman 5.8/10
7:30				83. Shaky Ground 5.8/9
8:00	28. Am Fun Home Vid 13.4/20	4. Murder, She Wrote	49. I Witness Video 11.0/16	48. In Living Color 11.2/17
8:30	52. Am Fun People 10.5/15	19.5/29*		50. Roc 10.8/16
9:00	17. ABC Sunday Night	8. CBS Sunday Movie:	34. NBC Sunday Night	39. Married w. Chil 12.4/18
9:30	Movie: Not in My Family	Rio Diablo 17.3/26*	Movie: Journey to Center of	61. Herman's Head 9.7/14
10:00	15.1/23		the Earth 13.1/20	79. Edna Time 7.1/11
10:30				82. Married w. Chil 6.2/10
Week's Avgs.	**12.5/20**	**15.1/24***	**11.4/18**	**7.8/12**
SSN. to date	**12.5/20**	**13.5/22***	**11.1/18**	**7.18/12**

*Ranking/Show [Program Rating/Share]   * Winner of time slot*

Source: Nielsen Media Research. Reprinted with permission from Broadcasting & Cable, *March 8, 1993.*

Saturday night has become the loneliest night of the week for TV programmers. The audience has receded to a point where the highest rated show had only a 14.6 rating, and the others fell below 11.3.

Special events often bring big ratings. CBS's "Grammy Awards" show had a whopping 20.0 rating for its three-hour broadcast on Wednesday evening, but NBC's "9th Annual Soap Opera Awards" had much less appeal.

Reality-based programming has become a mainstay of prime time. The networks have been actively pursuing this format because these shows cost less than sitcoms and drama programs, and enjoy relatively high ratings. In the week shown in the table, ABC had five in this category, including the highly rated "Prime Time Live" with a 16.1 rating; CBS had four, including a repeat of a "Rescue: 911"; NBC had three and Fox had six, including reruns of "Sightings" and "Cops."

Fox had no programming on Monday of the week shown; however, the network went to seven-night programming in Summer 1993.

CBS's hardy perennial, "60 Minutes," was the highest rated show of the week we are examining, with a 22.8 rating, translating to an audience of 21.5 million TV homes on Sunday evening. The other networks cannot even come close to unseating this champion.

Two weeks prior to the one on our chart, ABC had a blockbuster prime-time ratings winner when it broadcast Oprah Winfrey's ninety-minute, live interview with Michael Jackson. The show registered a 39.3 rating and a 56 share, meaning that it had an audience of 37 million households and reached 56 percent of all the homes watching TV at that time.

Late Fringe

Traditionally, the late fringe time slot is reserved for late news, sports, and weather, usually carried at 11:00 P.M. by the networks' O&Os and affiliates. Independents that carry their news at 10:00 or 10:30 P.M. usually run syndicated series during this late-fringe period.

Successful syndicated programs of such old shows as "Cheers," "Taxi," and "I Love Lucy" predominate in this daypart. They earn huge sums for the series' original owners, but seldom make much for the actors and writers.

Late Night

Until the minirevolution of 1993, NBC owned the late-night daypart. Johnny Carson had long been the king of this realm with his "Tonight" show. Carson was succeeded by Jay Leno without the show's suffering much audience loss. "Late Night with David Letterman" followed "Tonight," and NBC's "Later with Bob Costas" filled the latest late-night slot. In 1993, Letterman jumped to CBS, attracted by a $14 million-a-year salary and a head-on shot against Leno.

If you wonder how the networks can afford these astronomical outlays, bear in mind that the late-night daypart is responsible for advertising revenues of about $600 million a year. When NBC had all three shows, its share of this megapie was about $270 million.

ABC and the independents tried to compete with these blockbusters with news shows and a patchwork of other formats. In the 11:30 P.M.

slot, ABC's "Nightline" with Ted Koppel has made a major impact. Arsenio Hall has attracted a substantial following on independent television.

By 1:00 A.M., when most of us are asleep, the insomniacs are watching old movies. The ratings are low, so national advertisers stay away. At this hour the pitchmen for a potpourri of products come out of the woodwork to ply their wares on a not-too-alert audience.

THE HIGH ANXIETY OF THE PROGRAMMING PROCESS

We now know how the ratings work and that an increase of one rating point for the season in prime time may mean $100 million a year to the network. In planning a forthcoming TV season, the top network executives responsible for news, sports, and entertainment, and their programming staffs, are charged with developing a lineup that will generate high ratings and destroy the competition. Of course, most of the planning is done a year or more in advance because programming production takes time.

News
A network's news division bases its decisions on the number of hours it must fill and its annual budget—from $250 million to $300 million a year. Provisions must be made for unforeseen situations like the Persian Gulf War. Covering a national political convention runs about $10 million and requires a staff of about 300 people.

Placing news shows in the proper slots is a rather straightforward matter. The morning and evening network news for the three largest networks have fixed schedules. News specials are scheduled at random.

Sports
The commitments for sports events are made far in advance. The networks must conclude their arrangements with the various sports leagues and associations years in advance. A once-every-four-years event like the Summer Olympics requires the purchase of the rights, advance

planning, and staffing years before the Games take place.

Network sports are predominantly scheduled on weekends, although occasionally a special is held on a weekday night. ABC's "Monday Night Football" has been standard Monday evening fare for more than twenty years.

Entertainment

The Herculean task of developing and programming the twenty-two hours of weekly, prime-time TV is the responsibility of a network's president of entertainment and his or her large staff of talented nail-biters.

The late Bill Paley of CBS justifiably called programming an art, not a science. Some of the considerations and questions affecting these decisions:

* Cost. The three major networks spend between 75 and 85 percent of their total budget on programming. It costs about $1.5 billion per network to buy a season's worth of prime-time shows.
* Although comedy and drama series occupy most of the prime-time schedule, the network has to guess whether a less costly movie-of-the-week will produce higher ratings on a given night.
* How extensive is the market for cost-effective "reality-based" programming like "Rescue: 911," "America's Funniest Home Videos," "Unsolved Mysteries," and "Street Stories"? These shows cost between $400,000 and $600,000 an hour to produce, about half the cost of a drama or action-adventure show.
* Is it productive to slash the number of weeks in which the networks provide original series from thirty-five weeks to twenty-two or twenty-five weeks?
* Is there still a market for expensive miniseries? Many have bombed out.
* How can the networks attract younger viewers? Then again, how can they attract women eighteen- to forty-nine-years-old, a group much desired by advertisers? And, finally, how can they stem the flow of viewers from the networks to cable and home video?

PROGRAMMING FOR PRIME TIME

The network-TV, prime-time season ends in April. In May, the network's president of entertainment and the programming staff engage in the stress-filled ritual known as "Decision Week," when the lineup of shows for the start of the September fall season is announced. It is the culmination of a year of high anxiety for many individuals at the network and at the studios and production companies. In the weeks after Decision Week, the network programming executives listen to pitches from writers, producers, and studios for new shows for the following season. With so many pitches, their presentations must be short. Often the idea is merely a rehash of an old successful formula with perhaps a minor new twist.

Thousands of new ideas are pitched to the networks; few are chosen. As we explain in greater detail in chapter 12, the odds on an idea moving ahead to a script, a pilot, and then a series are slim indeed. Each network orders only about thirty new pilots a year.

While the final programming decisions are made at the very top, the network's programming executives move the production process along. Besides listening to endless pitches, they suggest ideas for shows

---

CAREER TIP

Consider TV programming as a career. Program selection is a sophisticated craft. Research is widely used. Network programming's largest expenditure goes to series development—evaluating and assigning scripts, producing pilots, and testing. Network programming is the big league. Successful programmers go right to the top of the networks' pecking order—with salaries to match. Try to get any job, even secretarial, at a network's east or west coast entertainment division. Then, learn all you can about the programming process so that you'll be ready to make your move. Several colleges in New York City and Los Angeles conduct extension courses or Saturday seminars on the subjects of prime time and programming. UCLA, for example, has an excellent six-session extension course called "Developing and Selling Television Shows: The Reality and the Art." Programming is the essence of this course. Even at the local station, there is a need for programming talent. Jobs are not readily available, but persistence is the key.

to writer-producer teams and to studios. About 75 percent of new program ideas come from the networks. The studio executives and the producers work with writers who have been assigned scripts. They are also involved in casting and work with agents to attract new acting and directing talent.

After announcing the fall lineup of shows, the programmers fill in the blanks of the actual weekly schedule. There is a great deal of experimenting here, but programmers also rely on accepted formulas of what works.

Finally, an important consideration for network programmers is cost. With $500,000 as the average per-episode licensing fee for a half-hour show, and $900,000 for a one-hour show, the networks can ill afford many mistakes.

CHAPTER 11

The Who, What, Where, When, and Why of TV News

As head honcho at ABC News, Roone Arledge runs a division with more than 1,200 employees including million-dollar news superstars Peter Jennings, Barbara Walters, Ted Koppel, Diane Sawyer, David Brinkley, and Hugh Downs. Arledge is responsible for an annual budget of over $250 million. He has been with ABC, a division of the media conglomerate, Capital Cities/ABC, for over twenty years. His employers obviously appreciate Arledge, paying him a huge salary plus perks, including a chauffeur-driven Bentley. But, such are the vagaries of network news, should pesky newcomers like CNN take big bites out of ABC News's audiences and should its ratings fall, Arledge too could be a casualty of the media wars.

Let's examine the broad area of TV news, both national and local, and network, independent, and cable news programming.

THE NETWORKS

The three largest networks—ABC, CBS, and NBC—maintain large news divisions responsible for daily evening news programs, like ABC's "World News Tonight," CBS's "Evening News with Dan Rather and Connie Chung," and NBC's "Nightly News with Tom Brokaw." The networks supply these shows to their own stations (O&Os) and to their affiliates.

Most of the networks' O&Os and affiliates produce local, early evening news shows that run for one or two hours.

In Los Angeles, for example, the NBC O&O station produces a 4:00 to 5:00 P.M. news show, another show with a different set of anchors from 5:00 to 6:00 P.M., and still another from 6:00 to 6:30 P.M. After that, the station picks up the network-produced "NBC Nightly News with Tom Brokaw."

In addition, the networks' news divisions produce two-hour week-day morning news shows. As of March 1993, ABC's "Good Morning America" and NBC's "Today" shared the lead for morning shows, followed by CBS's "CBS This Morning." These morning shows are fed to the O&Os and affiliates, who intersperse the programming with local news and weather.

The major networks also produce prime-time newsmagazine programs led by the venerable ratings leader, CBS's "60 Minutes." CBS also produces "48 Hours," anchored by Dan Rather. ABC is in the prime-time newsmagazine competition with "20/20," hosted by Hugh Downs and Barbara Walters, and "Prime Time Live" with Diane Sawyer and Sam Donaldson. NBC is a player in these sweepstakes with "Dateline NBC." ABC has created a valuable niche in the late-night daypart with "Nightline," hosted by Ted Koppel. Its formula of news and hard-hitting interviews has made it a ratings winner since its launch in 1980.

Not to be overlooked is the substantial audience that the networks have built and retained for Sunday morning news programming. NBC's "Meet the Press" is the longest-running program on network TV, having debuted on November 6, 1947. It originated as a radio program in 1945. CBS produces "CBS Sunday Morning" and "Face the Nation," and ABC produces "This Week with David Brinkley."

Producing this vast amount of programming for the networks takes two teams—the first, reporters and correspondents, covers the news worldwide, and the second team, editors and producers, selects, edits, and presents the news in an interesting and informative framework.

Each of the three largest networks employs from 1,000 to 1,200 people in their news divisions and has an annual budget of between $250 million and $300 million.

"NBC Nightly News with Tom Brokaw"

"NBC Nightly News with Tom Brokaw" airs Mondays through Fridays from 6:30 to 7:00 P.M. Eastern time. Brokaw has been the program's chief anchor since 1983, although many eminent broadcast journalists preceded him in this role: John Cameron Swayze was the anchor from 1949 to 1956; Chet Huntley and David Brinkley shared the job from 1956 to 1970; and John Chancellor and others had it for several years before Brokaw took over. Today, Brokaw is the anchor as well as managing editor.

"Nightly News" broadcasts daily to NBC's O&O stations and 200-odd affiliates for a half hour each evening. Its basic formula provides "reports and analysis of the day's most newsworthy national and international events." This comprehensive news package is compiled by NBC's large team of correspondents and reporters all over the world.

In New York, where "Nightly News" is produced, a team of thirty-four NBC News personnel and a technical staff is responsible for this half-hour show. The news team includes a managing editor at the top (Brokaw), an executive producer, a director, seven segment producers, two news writers, five researchers, and eleven production assistants and staff. The total makes for a very expensive group behind a half-hour show.

As of this writing, women hold fifteen of the thirty-four positions on the "Nightly News" roster.

NBC's "Today" Show

NBC's "Today" show runs for two hours, five days a week, and is beamed to the entire network. Its formula consists of "the latest international and domestic news, interviews with newsmakers from the worlds of

politics, business, media, entertainment, sports, and weather reports."
The show, which is broadcast live in New York, is hosted by Bryant
Gumbel and Katie Couric, and has a team of seventeen producers plus
a technical staff.

From 1979 through 1991, NBC's news division suffered financial
losses and in 1987 lost about $150 million. In 1992, the page was finally
turned when the division earned about $18 million. What were the rea-
sons for this lackluster performance? One answer is poor ratings, but
another, clearly, is excessively high salaries.

It is estimated that more than 70 percent of the NBC News staff
earns more than $70,000 a year and the average NBC correspondent

---

KATIE COURIC'S CAREER PATH

Katie Couric hurtled to the top. She has been the co-host of the
"Today" show since April 1991, an assignment she assumed while
only in her early 30s. Couric's first job after graduating from the
University of Virginia in 1979 was as a desk assistant in the ABC
news bureau in Washington, D.C. After a year she moved to CNN as
an assignment editor. She later transferred to Atlanta as an associate producer and then producer of a two-hour news and information program. Her first on-air stint came in 1984, when she became
a full-time correspondent, then political correspondent, covering
the 1984 presidential campaign.

From 1984 to 1986 Couric was a general-assignment reporter at a
TV station in Miami. From 1986 to 1989 she filled a similar slot at
NBC's station in Washington, where she won an Emmy. Her work at
this station brought her to the attention of NBC News's network management. In 1989 she became the deputy Pentagon correspondent,
and in 1990–91, a national correspondent for the "Today" show.

In April 1991, Couric was named co-anchor of "Today," a job whose
daily routine includes interviewing presidents, world figures, and
newsmakers. It is a testimonial to the perky Ms. Couric that since she
became co-anchor, the show has improved its ratings to run almost
even with the leader, ABC's "Good Morning, America."

earns about $180,000 a year. Their four-star correspondents are reported to earn an average of $600,000 a year.

Even lesser folk share in this largesse. The average NBC camera crew member earns about $100,000 a year and field producers about $80,000.

Why are NBC and the other networks willing to suffer losses or small profits on their news operations? The answer is the prestige factor, to some extent, but also the fact that news is a valuable service to a network's O&O stations and affiliates. Along with prime-time programming, news is the essence of the networks' structure.

Other NBC News Shows

"Dateline NBC" is a one-hour, prime-time weekly news show. It follows a newsmagazine format and includes investigative reporting on a wide range of topics.

"Meet the Press" was forty years old in 1993. It broadcasts on Sundays for thirty minutes and features interviews with world-renowned figures.

"NBC News at Sunrise" appeals to the early risers. It broadcasts from Monday through Friday from 5:30 to 6:00 A.M. Its menu includes news, weather, sports, and feature stories.

ABC's "World News Tonight"

Peter Jennings is the host of ABC News's top-rated "World News Tonight." This show evolved from a three-anchor team, with the late Max Robinson in Chicago, the late Frank Reynolds in Washington, and Jennings in London in 1978. Jennings spent several years as an ABC national correspondent and twelve years as an ABC foreign correspondent, six of them in Beirut. From 1978 to 1983, while part of the three-anchor team, Jennings also was ABC's chief of foreign correspondents.

So that we can better understand the TV news process, and because the evening news is the most prominent news format on TV, we will chronicle a typical day in the newsroom of ABC News's "World News Tonight." This will provide an understanding of how a news team functions and will delineate various job responsibilities.

As we saw, the television news team divides into two groups: one, reporters and correspondents, and the second, editors and producers.

The day's activities start early in the morning as correspondents, producers, and camera crew receive their daily assignments. Assignment decisions are based on information received from ABC domestic and international news bureaus, ABC-affiliated stations all over the country, stories from the "futures" file (which anticipates stories that may break months later), and information received from the wire services—Associated Press, United Press International, and Reuters.

The senior producers made a final check on the assignments the previous night to prepare the "troop movement," or positioning of staff members.

9:00 A.M.: The senior news staff, including the executive and senior producers, arrive. All have carefully read the morning newspapers and are familiar with the overnight news. They hold a "reading in," a review of overnight dispatches and cables, and receive the daily "situationer" that tells them where the events are happening and how they are being covered. The situationer is a billboard that keeps track of assignments, breaking stories, and important news events. This situationer is updated all day.

10:00 A.M.: A conference call is held between the executive producer and senior producers in New York and all ABC News representatives in the United States and overseas. They discuss and evaluate the relative weight and importance of particular stories, relying on information from the field.

10:30 A.M.: The senior producers and editors hold a meeting to line up stories and choose a "lead" story. The lead may be a group of related events involving a particularly hot area of the world, like the Middle East. The stories are then "blocked" into segments divided by commercials. At all times, the editors try to make the stories flow from one to another by grouping similar stories.

10:30 A.M. to noon: By noon, the field producers have evaluated their stories and all bureaus have reported in. Also, new information from the wire services and newly arrived videotapes are reviewed.

Noon to 2:00 P.M.: The anchor, managing editor, and senior producers discuss the organization of the first draft and the selection and length of stories. The group also chooses the show's visuals and graphics, reviews the editing of the videotapes with the tape producer, and deals with technical problems regarding satellite time, late-arriving material, and the like.

2:00 P.M. to 3:00 P.M.: The lineup must be adjusted for late-breaking news. If new "news" is light, it may serve as a "show ender." Typically, two or three complete changes in the lineup are needed.

3:00 P.M. to 6:00 P.M.: More tapes arrive and are reviewed. All have been edited, but they need cutting because every second counts. The hardest part of editing is balancing the visuals with the narrative to ensure continuity.

The anchor, especially if he serves as managing editor, is integrally involved in the selection and rotation of stories, as well as their presentation. Now the anchor's copy is prepared, his hair is styled, and makeup is applied. The anchors and writers prepare the introductions and narrations for the shorter pieces. These narrations are called "voice-overs" or "tells."

6:30 P.M.: "World News Tonight" goes on the air. The first feed is broadcast direct from the control room in New York City. The "feed" refers to the transmission of a broadcast to stations via satellite or other network systems. For ABC's "World News Tonight," the network signal is "uplinked" or transmitted from ABC's roof in New York to a satellite, and is received by the affiliates at their earth stations. An earth station is a terminal equipped to communicate with satellites.

A second feed, carrying stories updated since the first feed, goes from ABC in New York to stations in later time zones.

So there it is: twenty-two minutes of news that represents more than twenty-four hours of planning, writing, filming, and editing, just so that you can sit back comfortably in your living room and effortlessly absorb a summary of the most important events of the day.

In the highly charged world of TV news, ratings leadership in early evening network news is a coveted honor, and substantial financial rewards go to the winning network. Since 1989, ABC's "World News Tonight" has led its competition at the other two networks.

ABC's Other News Shows

"Nightline" with Ted Koppel has been an ABC late-night success since it was launched in 1980. It has been estimated that the show yields an annual profit of more than $20 million.

"Good Morning America" is ABC's early morning news, talk, and interview show. Until 1992, it was the number one early morning show for many years. In 1992 and 1993, NBC's "Today" closed the gap and ran even with "Good Morning America."

"20/20" and "Prime Time Live" are ABC's prime-time, once-a-week newsmagazine shows. "20/20" is hosted by Hugh Downs and Barbara Walters and has continually held high ratings. "Prime Time Live" features veteran Sam Donaldson and Diane Sawyer. Its ratings have run a good bit behind its sister show, "20/20." On Sunday mornings, ABC broadcasts the profound news commentary of veteran David Brinkley in "This Week with David Brinkley."

The news operations of all three networks have faced profit squeezes in recent years. High-priced talent is clearly a factor, as is the huge cost of providing comprehensive coverage of wars, disasters, and special events. ABC has effected some downsizing of personnel and instituted other cost-cutting procedures. These measures seem to have worked. At this writing, ABC News is a profitable operation.

CBS and the News

Until 1987, "The CBS Evening News with Dan Rather" was the ratings leader, but in recent years it has given up this standing to ABC's "World News Tonight." Rather is one of newsdom's highest-paid anchors, earning a reported $13,409 a day.[1] Rather also anchors CBS's highly rated "48 Hours," which airs on prime time once a week.

In the newsmagazine field, CBS's venerable and respected "60 Minutes" is the most-watched news broadcast. It is also considered the most profitable single show in television. For sixteen consecutive seasons, through 1992/93, it has been in the top-ten rankings. Its average audience is about twenty million TV households.

There have long been attempts to emulate the formula of "60 Minutes," usually with little success; however, network news departments continue to try, chiefly for the financial advantage. It costs less to pro-

duce a newsmagazine in prime time than it does to produce an entertainment show, about $500,000 per hour versus $1 million or more.

In 1991/92, CBS introduced another prime-time newsmagazine,
"Street Stories," anchored by "60 Minutes" reporter Ed Bradley. "CBS
This Morning," the network's competition with "Today" and "Good
Morning America," has continued to languish in third place in the rat-
ings race.

CBS News also produces "Eye to Eye with Connie Chung," "CBS
Morning News," with the witty and urbane Charles Osgood as co-an-
chor, "Sunday Morning," and the forty-year-old public affairs program,
"Face the Nation."

CBS News broadcasts more than forty hours of regularly scheduled
news programming each week. Its full-time complement numbers about
1,000, and it also employs about 250 part-time personnel.

THE NEWSMAGAZINE AND PRIME TIME

By the 1993/94 season, there were six newsmagazine shows on prime-
time television, led by "60 Minutes." All but one, NBC's "Dateline,"
finished first or second in the ratings in their period. The group also
included CBS's "48 Hours" and ABC's "20/20" and "Prime Time Live."

The networks value newsmagazines for several reasons. We have already pointed out that they can be produced economically. Newsmagazines can also sustain their popularity for a long time. Witness
the success of "60 Minutes" and "20/20." Newsmagazines have also
proven popular with younger audiences, a group coveted by advertisers because of their flexibility on brand preferences. Since the networks own newsmagazine shows, they are not required to negotiate license fees, as they do with the prime-time fare produced by studios
and production companies.

HOW THE INDEPENDENTS MANAGE
THEIR NEWS COVERAGE

A few years ago, an independent TV station in Massachusetts laid off ten of its sixteen-person news staff. Instead of a locally produced 5:30 P.M. newscast, the station opted for a CNN package of national and world news. Local news was now supplemented with five-minute updates every hour, 3:00 P.M. to 10:00 P.M. It also had a fifteen-minute nightly newscast at 10:00 P.M. to cover local and national news. The remaining six-person news staff at the station consisted of two reporter-anchors, an executive producer–anchor, two news photographers, and a meteorologist.

The message here is economy. News is seldom a profit center at an independent station and, by cutting its staff and buying the CNN package, the station served its audience and sharply reduced its overhead. According to Dr. Vernon A. Stone of the University of Missouri, about three-quarters of broadcast news operations at network affiliates make money, but only 43 percent are profitable at independent stations.

For most local TV stations, news is its largest, most expensive department. Yet all these stations, affiliates and independents alike, are responsible for local news coverage, often a costly operation.

Some independent stations in major markets produce morning news programs that combine local and national news. In Los Angeles, for example, a local independent station, KTLA, owned by Tribune Broadcasting, produces a two-hour morning news show that competes favorably in the ratings with the network shows. The station also produces a one-hour news show at 10:00 P.M. in prime time.

Few independents carry news in the early evening daypart, but many have been successful with news programs in late prime time. Independents often supplement their coverage by running news segments purchased from CNN or other news services like the Associated Press and Group W News Services.

Today's news director, particularly those at independent stations, must think budget as much as news coverage and ratings.

PUBLIC TELEVISION AND THE NEWS

Just as public broadcasting is often an antidote for commercial TV, so is the "MacNeil/Lehrer News Hour" a formidable alternative to network news. In 1993, it reached more than 3 percent of all households watching TV in that time slot.

The program is a success primarily because it is targeted to those people who are "entertained" by a serious approach to the news. The philosophy of Robert MacNeil and Jim Lehrer is simple: "We believe the American people are smart enough to figure it out for themselves, and what we want to do is to help them figure it out for themselves rather than tell them what to do."[2]

"MacNeil/Lehrer" is co-produced by public TV stations WNET in New York and WETA in Washington. The program's annual budget is about $25 million, about 10 percent of the budget of each of the three largest network news operations. It is financed by the Corporation for Public Broadcasting, corporate and foundation sponsors, and by the viewers of public TV.

Jim Lehrer explained how the "MacNeil/Lehrer News Hour" is put together. "It's divided into a beat system. We have senior producers who function, in newspaper terms, as desk editors, and we have staff who work for them on economics, foreign affairs, domestic politics, etc. Each Friday, they prepare status reports and we talk about the next two-week planning cycle, penciling them in. Then on a given day, we have a 10:15 A.M. meeting and those very same producers come forward with their recommendations based on what's already been planned and what's happened in the news in the last twenty-four hours."[3]

Jim Lehrer started out as a newspaperman. He has also been a novelist and a playwright. Robert MacNeil's early career included acting and radio drama before he joined NBC and went on to spend seven years there and eight with the BBC. The pair launched the "MacNeil/Lehrer Report" in 1975. It became an hour-long show in 1983.

NEWS SOURCES AND SERVICES

Associated Press Broadcast Services

The Associated Press started with newspapers that needed coverage outside their geographical boundaries. If a major story was breaking in Chicago or Los Angeles, a paper in New York had to have the details fast; however, it wasn't economically feasible to employ full-time correspondents in these areas. Therefore, news organizations—cooperative and private—sprang up to fill this gap by providing reporters and correspondents to bring the national and international news to local papers.

In May 1848, a cooperative of six New York City newspapers formed the Associated Press. The purpose: to work together to increase news coverage of the United States and the world. The first year's budget was less than $20,000.

By the 1980s, that six-paper, nonprofit cooperative had grown into an organization serving more than 1,299 newspaper members and 3,890 broadcasters in the United States. Its services are printed and broadcast in 115 countries. Its present budget is in excess of $280 million.

From the outset, Washington and foreign news were staples of AP coverage. Its first Washington correspondent, Lawrence Golright, reported on such momentous events as the start of the Civil War and President Lincoln's assassination. By the early 1980s, the Washington staff numbered 128 newspeople, and the global network was staffed by 93 Americans and 589 foreign nationals.

In 1875, AP established the first leased wires dedicated exclusively to the transmission of news. The wires ran from New York to Washington and carried 20,000 words a day. Today, AP's telephone, cable, and satellite circuits circle the globe and carry millions of words daily at speeds up to 12,000 words a minute. It maintains 141 domestic bureaus and more than 80 foreign bureaus.

AP news wasn't available to broadcasters until 1942. Today, although the networks maintain large domestic and foreign staffs, they still need services like AP to complete their own operations.

Twenty-four hours a day, seven days a week, Associated Press TV feeds coverage of all the news. APTV member stations have a direct connection to AP's broadcast news computers via an AP-provided satellite receiver or local telephone line. Two high-speed circuits link dedicated printers (printers that connect exclusively with a station) or a computer running on an AP News Desk program. This program is designed to run on any IBM-compatible personal computer.

One circuit delivers state and regional news, sports, and weather. A second circuit carries national and international news, sports, weather, features, and the AP Washington Daybook—the authoritative planning calendar for the nation's capital.

In late 1990 the AP launched its on-line TV news graphics service, called the AP GraphicsBank. It is a comprehensive electronic library of high-resolution graphic elements and finished images formatted for TV. Images like maps, head shots of national and international leaders, and other newsmakers can be retrieved on demand.

CAREER TIP: JOB OPPORTUNITIES WITH AP

* Apply for AP writing, on-air, and technical employment at your nearest Associated Press bureau. There you will fill out an application, take a vocabulary and newswriting test, and be interviewed.
* Generally, applicants should be college graduates with a minimum of two years of newspaper or broadcast experience. A few temporary openings are available for those who lack the two years of professional experience.
* You may also apply directly to Associated Press Broadcast services, 1825 K Street, N.W., Washington, DC 20006-1253. Contact the general broadcast editor.
* For TV and radio jobs, experience with tape-editing equipment and other standard tools of the broadcast industry is necessary.
* AP has a thirteen-week summer minority internship program for African-Americans and Hispanics who have completed their junior year of college.
* To work for AP overseas, you should be fluent in at least one foreign language. Once employed, you may have a choice of assignment location.

CNN's Headline News

The Turner Broadcasting network offers stations a national feed, enabling them to carry some or all of CNN's Headline News. At this writing, more than 220 broadcast affiliates use this service to enhance their own news. By subscribing, stations avail themselves of CNN's 250 journalists in the field, as well as their own newsgathering resources.

Other News Sources

A TV news director has a broad choice of syndicated news sources. In this chapter we have written about the Associated Press, perhaps the most important source of world and national news for newspapers, radio, and TV stations; however, in a news director's search for specialized coverage, dozens of syndicated services are available. Here is a sample of some of these services or "newsfeeds" as they are termed in the broadcasting business:

Accu-Weather is the world's leading commercial weather-service. It provides exclusive local forecasts for radio and TV.

Consumer Reports Television is a syndicated consumer news service.

The New York Stock Exchange offers full broadcast capabilities on its activities.

The News Travel Network give consumer travel reports and a weekend travel update.

Radio Television News Directors Association (RTNDA)

RTNDA is dedicated solely to electronic journalism. Its members are radio and TV news executives and the communications professionals who work with them.

Although RTNDA's primary purpose is to improve relations between news departments and station, group, and network management, it performs other important services as well, including hosting the annual Edward R. Murrow awards for excellence in broadcast journalism.

One important program is its RTNDA Foundation, which works with broadcast journalism schools. The Foundation offers scholarships for both undergraduate and graduate students of electronic journalism, and it gives fellowships for working electronic journalists, new to the field, who wish to enhance their professional background with academic studies.

RTNDA also publishes the excellent monthly publication, the *RTNDA Communicator*. It features advice on technologies and tips on writing, editing, and reporting.

A booklet, Careers in Broadcast News, is available free (send a self-addressed 6x9 envelope). Write to:

RTNDA
1735 DeSales Street, N.W.
Washington, DC 20036.

A Few Statistics on TV News Jobs

In the May 1992 issue of *Communicator*, Vernon Stone reports there are 21,000 full-time employees in TV news and about 2,800 who work part-time. Stone estimates that there are 740 fully staffed news operations at stations across the country. These are encouraging numbers.

In an article in the March 1993 issue of *Communicator*, Stone indicates a wide disparity in salaries paid to newspeople in large and small markets. A typical reporter job in the top 25 markets has a median salary of $47,250. A news director's median salary is $92,500.

In the markets between 51 and 100, the reporters' median salary is $20,500, and the news director $51,470.

There is also a substantial difference in salaries, according to the size of the station's news staff and its geographical location. An assignment editor in a staff of 36 to 180 will earn a median salary of $35,130 compared to $18,250 in a staff of 0 to 10. An assistant news director in the East will earn a median salary of $66,250 against a salary of $42,500 in the West, and $35,150 in the South.

NOTES

[1] *Ken Auletta*, Three Blind Mice *(New York: Random House, 1991).*

[2] *The Paul White Award interview, "The Courage to Be Serious,"* Communicator, *September 1990, p. 13.*

[3] *Speech at Columbia University's DuPont Media Forum, January 1992.*

CHAPTER 12

All about Sitcoms, Cop Shows, and Prime Time

On May 18, 1992, a vast audience of twenty million households watched with rapt attention when Murphy Brown, the most illustrious single mother in the land, announced the birth of her baby on TV. Never mind the political and social implications of the birth. For that half hour Murphy's baby was America's baby.

On an average evening, prime-time TV delivers a cumulative audience of more than forty million American homes. Prime-time TV links more people in a common activity than any other event in human history. Its influence and reach are unprecedented, but for the networks, prime-time TV has serious problems. The audience is eroding. The competition from cable, the independents, and home video is building rapidly. In an economic downturn advertisers race away. Critics are often merciless in their barbs at the programming.

Yet for broadcasters, prime time is very important. In prime time, broadcasters can charge advertisers the highest rate for commercials because prime time has a larger audience than other dayparts.

Who watches prime time? According to the A. C. Nielsen Company, 48 percent of prime-time viewers are adult women, 34 percent adult men, and 18 percent teens and children.

Prime time's arcane world rests on the relationships between the players. Let's first discuss the most powerful force in prime time.

THE NETWORKS

Until June 1993, the fourth network, Fox Broadcasting, was on a five-day schedule. When Fox assumed a seven-day, prime-time schedule, it raised the weekly prime-time programming for the four networks to eighty-eight hours (8:00 P.M. to 11:00 P.M. weekdays and Saturday, 7:00 P.M. to 11:00 P.M. Sunday). Sitcoms and dramas make up about half this mix. The other half is composed of newsmagazines, sports, movies, and the newcomer, reality-based programming.

The FCC's 1993 rulings let the networks produce prime-time programs. They may also co-produce programs with studios and production companies. As of the start of the 1993–94 season, however, the networks still had not taken on the work of producer for most of prime-time programming, particularly in the area of sitcoms and dramatic entertainment. Instead, the networks continued their role of commissioning or licensing programs from studios and producers. This license allows the networks to show each episode twice. A program first runs during the TV season and a rerun typically airs in the summer.

The network feeds the series to its O&O stations and affiliates. It earns revenues from the sale of commercials which run during the broadcast of the series. On a hit show like "Home Improvement," a thirty-second commercial sold for about $325,000 in 1993.

THE PROCESS OF PROGRAM DEVELOPMENT

At the networks, the program development staff is responsible for the scripts and proposals submitted by agents, producer-writer teams, and studios. If an idea is acceptable, it goes through many preliminary steps before it makes the big time—a place on the networks' prime-time schedule. A final step in the development procedure is usually the making of a pilot film. If a project gets that far, the network's program-development people set a firm price that they will pay for the production of the pilot.

Other network staffers deal with ad-agency executives who evaluate new shows before making their commitment. This consultation is an elaborate process, typically done from May to September. The ad agencies consider about one hundred hours of shows before making their sponsorship decisions. They must bear in mind the high failure rate for new programs and the high cost of a pilot. Agencies realize that the pilot has higher production values than the series itself because the networks spend more time and money on it. Usually a premier director who may not work on any series episode directs the pilot.

Network legal and financial people negotiate agreements with the studios for those shows that will be on their program schedule.

The network's ad-sales team works with ad agencies and their clients to secure commercial-time commitments for prime-time programming.

THE STUDIOS AND PRODUCTION COMPANIES

A dozen major TV studios produce the bulk of prime-time programming. These companies do the physical production of a series. Many of them are also in the feature film business. Time Warner, the media conglomerate, owns Warner Bros. Television and Lorimar Television, two major players in TV production. Although they have the same parent, the companies operate independently. They produce comedy, drama, animation, miniseries, and made-for-TV movies. They also provide first-run syndication programs for independent stations.

During the 1992–93 season, for example, Lorimar produced fifteen prime-time, network series and Warner Brothers produced three. These two production companies are responsible for the hit shows "Murphy Brown" on CBS, "Northern Exposure" on CBS, and "Full House" on ABC. Studios develop many of their own series in-house, but they also work with teams of independent writer-producers to create programming. "Murphy Brown" was created by the team of Joel Shukovsky and Diane English. The writer-producers Joshua Brand and John Falsey created "Northern Exposure." Although these two writer-producer teams created these shows, the financial responsibility and ownership resides with the studio. Of course, when a show is successful, the writer-producer team shares in the profits.

Beyond the immediate benefits that a writer-producer reaps from creating a hit show, his or her success leads to additional opportunities. Steven Bochco is famous for conceiving and developing "Hill Street Blues" and "L.A. Law." That work brought a ten-series deal with ABC that calls for $50 million over a period of nine years. Interestingly, the deal with Bochco, signed in July 1988, has since provided the network with one hit, "Doogie Howser, M.D.," one cult favorite, "Civil Wars," that lasted through the 1992–93 season, and two flops.

Many writer-producer teams are involved in multiple projects. The process requires a maximum degree of planning and cooperation and, of course, time and energy. For each prime-time series the writer-producer team supervises a group of writers, directors, and creative and technical staff that may number more than a hundred people. Shooting a series on location makes the work even more complex.

HOW NEW SHOWS MAKE IT TO PRIME TIME

You have probably watched a new comedy or dramatic show on television and thought to yourself, "Gee, I can come up with a better concept than that." Possibly you can, but don't count on getting into next fall's hot new season and becoming rich and famous. Here's why.

First, let's rule out the 99 percent of individuals who send the networks unsolicited manuscripts. Chances are that these will be returned promptly with a polite form letter. The networks cannot afford to risk lawsuits claiming they stole a writer's idea. Returning unsolicited manuscripts unread is the networks' protection against these claims.

Sending outlines and manuscripts to TV production companies like Warner, Paramount, and Lorimar will result in the same response.

Paramount, for example, tells me that they receive about 300 scripts every day for existing shows and dozens of ideas for new shows.

The May 1993 issue of the monthly journal of The Writers Guild of America (WGA) reported that, of the eighty prime-time shows scheduled for the 1993–94 season, thirty-five accepted submissions from agents, forty-four shows had all their scripts committed for the forthcoming season, and only one show, "Star Trek: The Next Generation," was open for unsolicited submissions. Clearly, staff writers or agents provided most of the committed scripts.[1]

For every idea that comes into a major network or production company, hundreds of similar, if not identical, ones have preceded it. A skilled reader can look at an idea, outline, or script and know, almost within seconds of opening the envelope, if it has possibilities and into what category it fits.

At ABC, all submitted material goes to the broadcast standards and practices department. There, a staff of three or four people read the submissions, writes brief synopses of the properties' thrust, and indexes them under subheadings like women, mystery, blood and gore, terror, and sitcom. From there each goes to the appropriate programming department for disposition.

Readers at NBC and CBS merely open submission envelopes to see if they're unsolicited. If so, they send them right back. Again, the networks avoid future lawsuits by following this procedure.

Readers at the networks and production companies are a harried lot. There is always a big backlog of material and when the backlog is reduced more is about to arrive. Junior readers are glorified clerks who spend most of their time going through books and files to check titles. Senior readers do the same thing but also spend more time reading and writing synopses.

At a network the highest level reader-researcher is paid about $35,000 a year; those at lower levels earn a good bit less. English majors who read and write fast are favored for these jobs. If one has the right contacts at a network, there is freelance reading work. The pay—about $40 to $50 for a thirty-five-page script. For a full novel the fee is around $100. The soundest approach for a writer with an outline for a series or a script for an existing series is to get a reliable agent, one who is known to the networks and production companies. The agent can then target a particular executive at a network, studio, or production company. Of course, getting an agent is not easy since they are reluctant to take on nonprofessional writers without credits.

Let's look at a hypothetical situation. Suppose you are an unproduced writer and you have a brilliant idea for a new series, but you don't have an agent. However, your cousin's friend is a receptionist at the powerful William Morris Agency in Los Angeles. You buy her a drink one night after work and tell her about this great idea you have for a sitcom about two New York cops. One is a bigoted Irish male and is 6'2". His partner in the radio car is a 5'2" black woman. They fall in love and she brings him home to meet her parents, both high school principals.

After two drinks, the receptionist agrees to show the outline to her friend, an assistant agent who is moving ahead rapidly. After much cajoling, the assistant agent agrees to send the outline to the three networks. Within a few weeks, the outline comes back to the agent with two polite rejection notes and another one saying that they have received the same idea six times with only the woman's height changed.

When the agent sends the outline to various studios—Warner Bros. Television, Lorimar, Paramount Television, and 20th Century Fox Television—the results are all the same—rejection. You've been turned down, but at least you have an agent.

Long-Shot Odds

There are three to five executives at each network who listen to pitches for new and existing shows. Each network will average 2,000 pitches a year from writers, production companies, and agents, or a four-network total of 8,000 pitches a year.

Each network will order only about 150 scripts a year. A writer's minimum pay is $14,000 to script an existing half-hour show, $21,000 for a half-hour pilot, $20,500 for an existing one-hour show and $30,000 for a one-hour pilot. On average, a network will make a pilot of only one of five scripts it commissions.

The networks budget about $500,000 for a thirty-minute pilot and $1.5 million for a one-hour pilot. These figures vary and a network may invest more in a pilot if the writer-producer has a promising track record.

The chance of an idea being made into a series and then entering a second season is almost infinitesimal. The mathematics is brutal: 2,000 pitches yield 1,850 rejections and 150 scripts; only 1 script in 5 becomes a pilot, so that leaves 120 more rejections and 30 pilots; 1 in 3 pilots becomes a series, so the pilots lead to 20 more rejections and 10 shows. Most shows flop, of course, so of those 10 only 2 can expect to be around for a second season. That is 2 successes per 2,000 pitches and heaven alone knows how many ideas it takes before one is pitched.

The story of "Tattinger's" is all too typical. In 1988, Bruce Paltrow, the creator of the successful "St. Elsewhere," conceived of a new show, "Tattinger's." Paltrow did a pilot at a cost of $2.8 million. NBC contributed $2 million, and his studio, MTM Productions, provided the balance. Nearly a million dollars in the hole already, MTM's luck grew worse. NBC accepted the pilot and the series ran for one unhappy season. The difference between what NBC paid MTM as a license fee and the show's actual cost was $3.5 million. Even the mighty make mistakes.

According to an article in *Broadcasting & Cable*, producers and studios lost an estimated $470 million during the 1991–92 season, a 31 percent increase over the previous season.[2] For example, a producer of twenty-two one-hour episodes would have had a deficit of $6.7 million based on the costs of producing the show versus the license fees paid by the network. Of course, if the show is lucky enough to go into syndication its producers will recoup these losses.

Why are studios and production companies willing to engage in deficit financing? They hope to recoup when a show goes into syndication. However, a show must run on prime time for three years or more to become an attractive prospect for syndication. More about syndication in chapter 15.

The "Cheers" Success Story

In late 1992, the producers of "Cheers" decided to call it quits after eleven highly successful seasons, thus ending TV's longest-running

INTERVIEW:
MEL TOLKIN ON WRITING A PILOT

Comedy-writing giant Mel Tolkin entered television in the early 1950s as a senior writer for the classic "Your Show of Shows" and "Caesar's Hour." His co-writers then were Mel Brooks, Neil Simon, Woody Allen, and Larry Gelbart. More recently, he has written for Bob Hope and he was story editor on "All in the Family" for five years. Mel has been awarded one Emmy and received seven Emmy nominations for his work on various shows.

Asked for his advice on writing a pilot, Mel Tolkin listed the difficulties of selling a pilot and then offered the following suggestions.

Suppose, in spite of the odds stacked against you, you still want to write a pilot. And suppose you have written this pilot. Suppose it is in the proper form, the correct number of pages, all of it neatly typed. And suppose, further, you consider your brain child marvelous, that it will bring a fresh note to tired old TV and may start a rash of imitations.

Don't put in an order for a Rolls Royce or convertible, of course, or call your lover to start packing for a weekend in Paris. Not yet. First, reread your masterpiece and ask yourself these very crucial questions:

Is your cast of characters a family unit? By family unit I mean some cohesive, closed group, like the gang on "Murphy Brown" or the staff in some hospital (plenty of examples there). Or even inmates of a prisoners' camp ("Hogan's Heroes," which ran for ages).

Note that in the above examples of "family," all the members are locked in, either because of love, or because they're too young to go out in the world, or because they risk losing a weekly paycheck if they cut out. Or they're locked in because they're locked in—with locks and guards. Unable to leave, they must solve their problems, fight their battle, then and there.

Do your characters have the potential to grow? A teenage girl is an excellent example of growth. Little Jenny can marry, have a baby—two events that add millions of viewers. The potential of growth in the characters adds to the show's longevity.

Has the show some originality—but not too much? Examine the current crop of "family" family shows. (Mom, Dad, kids, dog, etc.) They all look alike, but on examination you will see there is always some element that makes each show different.

Is there some built-in conflict within the cast of characters? Some basic difference of opinion is absolutely necessary. Examples: Sam the stud versus Diane the romantic in "Cheers." Archie the reactionary versus Mike Stivic the liberal in "All in the Family." Any two people in a family who always agree aren't worth a scene. Conflict—the life blood of comedy and drama.

Does each member in the family (as defined above) have story possibilities? The need for such possibilities is obvious.

Have you considered the budget? Can the permanent cast keep stories going without having to hire expensive guest stars? Or going on location?

Do not suggest for the pilot, "Michael Jackson's limousine breaks down in front of the Gordons' home, and he comes to love them—they're so decent, so simple, especially the dog."

Do not open with location shots of a festival in Kyoto, where Jim and Mary meet romantically. If that is your first line, the producers won't bother reading the second.

Are your characters funny? Consider the cast of the longtime hit, "The Golden Girls." One is dumb, one is a Southern belle type with rather loose morals, one is a cynic, one is old enough not to care what the others think of her cutting remarks. The jokes fly!

Now, if your answer to all the above has been yes, you must still refrain from buying a Maserati or calling your wife or lover with the good news because you have some things to do first.

Get an agent who thinks you have something salable. Getting a reputable agent to represent you, who will work hard for you is very difficult unless you've already sold a pilot, which is impossible without an agent. [Suggestion: Collaborate with a writer who has a track record. Plenty of fame and glory and money for two.]

Suppose you get an agent. Have him set up a meeting with some established producer or a network. Pitch your story. Suppose they like your idea. After sweating through many a rewrite, wait for the network to give the project a go-ahead.

> Your pilot is made. The network then looks at dozens of other pi-
> lots and makes its choice. Yours is one of the lucky ones, say. It is on
> the air, scheduled between "Full House" and "Roseanne," two big-
> gies.
>
> Now buy the car, with cash, and call your travel agent. By then you
> may be too old to get an automobile license. And your lover has gone
> to Paris with a writer with two pilots.
>
> But when you get to that point, you will know that all that sweat
> and the waiting has been worthwhile.
>
> So—good luck, and many renewals! You now have a track record.
> By the way, I have this idea for a pilot. . . .

comedy series. For NBC the show was profitable, yet costly. The network paid $74 million for twenty-six episodes in its final 1992–93 sea-
son, making it the most expensive series on TV. "Cheers" star Ted Danson is reported to have earned $450,000 per show, yet he was in on the
decision to end the show's run before it began to falter in the ratings.
The show had been in syndication for years at the time of its demise.
Its producers, Glen Charles, Les Charles, and James Burrows, and its
star, Mr. Danson, became very wealthy.

MADE-FOR-TV MOVIES

Some in the biz call them "made-for-TV movies," others say MOWs
(not pronounced as an acronym; use the letters). MOW stands for
movie-of-the-week. There is, of course, a distinction between MOWs
that run on prime time and feature films made for theatrical distribution and then shown on television.

MOWs increased in recent years. Although their budgets generally
run to only $3 or $4 million, their production values are quite good. Networks often prefer these original productions because they can be rerun or syndicated in the future and sometimes serve as pilots for series.

The plot for a made-for-TV movie often treats current psychologi-
cal or sociological issues. Stories told in 1992's MOWs included: a

woman's triumph over mental illness after years in an institution; a young widow involved in two relationships—one heterosexual, one lesbian; and a real-life, three-year probe into the police shooting death of a black man.

FORECASTING THE SUCCESS OF A NEW TV SEASON

All the computerized research available will not guarantee a network's successful prime-time season. There is still an element of guessing what shows audiences will watch. For the fall 1992–93 schedule, the four TV networks trotted out a mixed bag of programming that em-

---

CAREER TIP:
BREAKING INTO TV AS A WRITER

My intention is not to dissuade readers from turning their skills to writing for television. Instead, I urge people to be realistic about their chances for success. If you want to write, keep writing as much as you can but don't quit your job. Write as many scripts or outlines of ideas as you have time for. This will give you ammunition to sell your talent. As previously noted, you may have difficulty getting an agent.

Use targeted networking to get people to read your work. Take advantage of any contact you can make at a network or production company. Give them a rationale for reading your material. Get the names of TV writers whose style you think is similar to your own. Then find out the names of their agents and badger them until they agree to read your work. It takes great determination and lots of nerve to get to this stage in your development as a writer.

Pay heed to the message of successful TV writer-producers Billy Van Zandt and Jane Milmore: "Don't write a line you wouldn't want to say. . . . Do shows on what you want to watch."

Remember, too, that TV sitcoms and dramatic series are a major industry, one that employs directors, camera operators, actors, producers, lighting and sound specialists, and editors, as well as writers.

phasized shows targeted at the eighteen-to-forty-nine-year-old market. This age group is particularly attractive to advertisers since they are still forming brand loyalties and are raising children.

Note that there were four reality-based programs in the list below of new shows for 1992–93. Reality-based programming has been popular on prime time since 1990. This category includes nonfiction shows about police and crime. Others involve humorous true-life videos sent to the studios and packaged as programming. These reality-based shows cost about half as much to produce as the traditional dramas, action-adventure, and comedy shows. For 1992–93, there were about a dozen of these, out of the total of eighty-odd prime-time shows.

Here is a list of thirty-four of the networks' highly regarded new shows that were launched in the 1992–93, prime-time season:

Hearts Afire	S
Love and War	S
Going to Extremes	D
Hangin' with Mr. Cooper	S
Class of '96	D
Key West	S
Laurie Hill	S
The Hat Squad	S
Mad about You	S
Delta	D
Rhythm and Blues	S
Martin	S
The Heights	D
Camp Wilder	S
Golden Palace	S
Bob	S
Picket Fences	D
Final Appeal	R
What Happened	R
The Round Table	D
Covington Cross	D
Likely Suspects	D
Frannie's Turn	S
Crossroads	D
Here and Now	S
Angel Street	D
The Edge	S

Up All Night   S
I Witness Video   R
Secret Service   R
Ben Stiller   S
Great Scott   S
Woops!   D
Flying Blind   S

(Key: S=Sitcom, D=Drama, R=Reality-based)

By season's end, the list was small indeed. Only these stalwarts made the cut:

Heart's Afire
I Witness Video
Love and War
Mad about You
Hangin' with Mr. Cooper

Another subject for speculation is who will win the prime-time ratings wars. CBS, in last place in 1991–92, jumped into first place in 1992–93. It based its success primarily on "Murphy Brown," "Murder, She Wrote," "Northern Exposure," and the stalwart "60 Minutes." Yet, as we know, success is indeed fleeting in prime time.

For the networks, studios, production companies, and advertisers, the guessing game is a rite of spring. They must pick the shows that will succeed and the category that will dominate. For the 1993–94 season, the four networks were betting on comedies over drama series by two to one. NBC, the loser in the previous season's ratings, was the most innovative. It planned twelve miniseries and a heavy slate of thirty-one made-for-television movies.

As we already know, the higher a show's rating, the more a network can charge for its commercials. For the 1992–93 season, the season's highest-rated show, "Roseanne," commanded the hefty price of $237,000 per thirty-second commercial, followed by "Murphy Brown" at $236,000 and "Cheers" at $225,000. ABC's "NFL Monday Night Football" sold for $265,000 and the highly rated "60 Minutes" cost $193,000 per thirty-second commercial. The new shows and the previous season's low-rated shows sell at bargain rates. "Quantum Leap," number 22 in the 1991–92 ratings, sold for $115,000 per thirty-second, but an advertiser could gamble with three new shows, "Delta," "What Happened," and "Covington Cross," and buy them for $70,000 per spot or less. Of course, none of these shows made it beyond midseason.

THE FUTURE OF PRIME TIME

The economics of network prime-time programming look bleak. ABC, CBS, and NBC each spend between 57 and 85 percent of their total budget for this programming. Fox will soon operate with similar figures. It costs about $1.5 billion per network to buy a season's worth of prime-time shows. This becomes a particular problem when we consider that the audience for this programming is eroding, with the networks losing ground to cable and video.

In 1980, the networks had an 85 percent share of the TV audience during prime time. By 1990 that figure was down to 63 percent and down to 40 percent by 1993. But don't write the networks off just yet. There will be a prime-time season in the year 2000, even if no one can tell what it will look like or who the audience will be. After all, by then the baby boomers will be in their mid-fifties.

NOTES

[1] Sue Karlin, "The New Producers," Mediaweek, October 14, 1991, p. 20.
[2] Steve Coe, "Production Deficits Top $464 Million," Broadcasting & Cable, June 8, 1992, p. 4

CHAPTER 13

The Wide World of TV Sports

THE SCOPE OF SPORTS BROADCASTING TODAY

In the early days of TV, sports coverage was confined to wrestling, boxing, and the roller derby. Today, we've seen an explosion in TV sports, involving cable stations and broadcast stations at both the network and local levels. Consider this growth: In 1970, the three networks broadcast less than 800 hours of original live sports programming. By 1980, as cable joined the marketplace, that figure more than doubled, jumping to almost 1,700 hours. By 1992, there were more than 4,900 hours of live sports broadcasts per year, not even counting programming on regional sports networks and local stations.

To sustain this huge amount of programming, the networks need increasingly larger audiences. Simply stated, there is now just too much sports programming for the number of available viewers.

How does TV sports work financially? The broadcast and cable networks pay the various sports leagues and associations for the rights to show some of their events. For example, a network will pay the National Collegiate Athletic Association (NCAA) about $140 million for the right to broadcast its college basketball championship tournament in the spring. NBC paid $43 million to the National Football League for the TV rights to Superbowl XXVIII, held in January 1994. To support these huge payments, the networks must sell commercials during these programs. If the programming does not score high enough ratings, the network may have to give rebates to advertisers. With the cost of some thirty-second commercials running more than $250,000 per spot, sports broadcasting has become very risky for all concerned.

SPORTS AT THE NETWORKS

Each of the three largest networks maintains a separate division for its sports operations. At the head of each division is a president whose responsibility includes the acquisition of rights for various individual events and a whole season's coverage of a sport.

In a network sports division, there are about twenty-five announcers; some are generalists and cover several different sports, while others specialize. On NBC Sports' roster, for example, Bud Collins and Chris Evert are the two tennis commentators who cover the Wimbledon and French Open tennis tournaments.

Besides play-by-play announcers, there are color commentators, often former coaches and players, who supplement the coverage with informed analysis. The network sports division may include technical and production personnel to handle the physical aspects of sports broadcasting.

NBC links the sports and news divisions; ABC links sports with daytime and children's entertainment. Sports divisions are not subdivided by a particular sport, although there are specialists in certain areas.

The sports division of a network is typically a profit center; however, in recent years the networks overpaid for the rights to events and series and suffered losses. Rights fees are the largest single cost factor in sports broadcasting, accounting for about eighty-three cents of every dollar spent on sports.

Network sports employ only a limited number of full-time personnel. It has been reported that NBC has only about one hundred full-time employees in sports. To save money, freelancers are often used, particularly in the area of production. For example, a network may produce as many as seven different professional football games on a Sunday. Many camera and technical people for these games are freelancers.

Network sports generate more than $2.6 billion annually in ad revenue, or about 20 percent of all network advertising. One of network sports' major problems today is the competition from cable and regional sports networks which tap the ad-revenue pool. These delivery systems, as they are known in the trade, include ESPN, TBS/TNT (owned by Turner Broadcasting), USA Network, Prime Network, Sports-Channel America, and regional or syndicated sports operations.

In the early 1990s, advertising commitments declined while the costs of rights escalated. The sports divisions of the major networks had to cut their costs dramatically and cover events more efficiently. They reduced their full-time staff and used more freelance production personnel.

Now for a close-up of the individual network sports divisions.

NBC SPORTS

At this writing, Dick Ebersol is the president of NBC Sports. His career is a paradigm of broadcasting success. Ebersol's career path took him from a job as a researcher for ABC Sports in 1967, at the age of twenty, to NBC as a vice president when he was only twenty-eight. He became president of NBC Sports in 1989.

Today, the staff at NBC Sports includes twenty-four broadcasters, many with names familiar to TV sports viewers. This group includes ex-NFL football players O. J. Simpson, Ahmad Rashad, and Bob Trumpy. Clearly, ex-athletes have an advantage in breaking into sports broadcasting. NBC Sports broadcasts a full slate of sports, including Super Bowl XXVII in 1993, NFL football, the 1992 Summer Olympics in Barcelona, selected games of the National Basketball Association (NBA), and golf tournaments sponsored by the Professional Golfers of America (PGA).

CBS SPORTS

Neal Pilson became the president of CBS Sports in 1986. Pilson leads a division that has had many creative triumphs but, along with the other networks, has suffered through the worst sports advertising market in decades. When this factor is coupled with the heat CBS took for paying too much for the rights to broadcast Major League Baseball and other rights, it spells trouble.

How does CBS Sports plan to turn things around? In 1993, Pilson said that the network would spend less for rights, and CBS passed on the rights to Major League Baseball after the 1993 season. It also moved toward using more freelance personnel and independent production units.

CBS Sports' lineup includes Major League Baseball's World Series, NFL regular season football and playoffs, the Olympic Winter Games, the U.S. Open Tennis Championships, the Daytona 500, and golf's Masters tournament.

ABC SPORTS

Dennis Swanson became president of ABC Sports in 1986, having previously served five years as head of ABC daytime and ABC children's programming. ABC's 1991 annual report offered a concise analysis of the state of TV network sports and its own operation in particular. The report maintained that television network sports was unprofitable for all three networks, and ABC Sports' loss for 1991 was in excess of $50 million. ABC blamed this loss on escalating rights fees and declining advertising revenue. It said future success would depend on its ability to reduce the cost of these rights. ABC Sports has broadcast "Monday Night Football" since 1970. The show continues to draw high ratings in prime time, with an audience of more than fifteen million TV households. ABC Sports also covers college football, New Year's Day football bowl games, the Triple Crown of horse racing, and several NFL playoff games.

ESPN

ABC is both a competitor and an owner of ESPN. The parent company, Capital Cities/ABC, owns 80 percent of ESPN, the nation's largest cable TV network. Although ESPN includes some lifestyle shows and early morning business news, its primary focus is on sports.

As a round-the-clock network launched in 1979, ESPN telecasts a broad range of sporting events. Their lineup includes cable coverage of NFL football, college football, professional tennis, the professional golf tour, the America's Cup (sailing), and special events for serious sports aficionados, like the NFL Draft and the Baseball Hall of Fame induction.

ESPN has sixty million cable subscriber households and annual advertising revenues of about $300 million. Anheuser-Busch, the Budweiser people, has a $100 million, five-year deal with ESPN that runs until 1996. ESPN has a distinct advantage over the three largest networks. Besides revenues from the sale of advertising, it receives more than $120 million a year from the cable companies that carry its programming.

OTHER TV SPORTS NETWORKS

Ted Turner owns baseball's Atlanta Braves and basketball's Atlanta Hawks. His Turner Broadcasting Company is active in the TV sports business with the TNT and TBS cable networks. In 1992, TNT was the first cable network to provide live telecasts of the Winter Olympics from Albertville, France. His network telecasts selected sports events from NBA Basketball and NFL Football. The TBS superstation broadcasts major league baseball, professional basketball, professional golf, and NASCAR auto races. Turner's Sportsouth, a regional sports network, offers Atlanta Braves baseball and professional basketball games of the Atlanta Hawks and Charlotte Hornets.

There are other regional sports networks, including Prime SportsChannel, Home Sports Entertainment, Prime Ticket Network, and New England Sports Network. These networks offer live and taped sports events and sports news.

THE ESCALATING COST OF TV SPORTS RIGHTS

An all-star, major-league-baseball lineup of the highest-paid players at each position for 1993 would have had a payroll of $47 million. Now, you may ask, how can baseball's owners afford these huge salaries when their parks are not filled for every game? The answer, of course, is the huge amount the networks pay to major league baseball for the right to broadcast their games. CBS paid $1.06 billion to televise baseball in the 1990–93 seasons. In 1992, NBC paid $401 million to broadcast the Summer Olympics in Barcelona. NBC sold almost $500 million worth of commercials at $335,000 per thirty-second spot, yet it is reported that the network lost approximately $100 million on the event. What went wrong? NBC arranged a three-channel, pay-per-view program with Cablevision. For prices ranging from $25 to $125, Olympics buffs could see nearly all the action live. NBC expected 3,000,000 viewers; unfortunately, only about 165,000 showed up. NBC and Cablevision could have made as much as $225 million if the pay-per-view plan had succeeded. Further, because of NBC's pay-per-view arrangement, viewers of the NBC regular broadcast were shortchanged, seeing fewer events than they might have if there had been no cable telecast.

When CBS paid $275 million for the rights to televise baseball for one season it overvalued the deal, misjudging the amount of advertising time it could sell for the events. The result—a whopping $282 million dollar pretax write-off. ABC pays the NFL $150 million a season for the rights to "Monday Night Football," or about $7 million per game. When ad revenues are in decline, as they were in the early 1990s, the show loses money. In 1991, ABC's telecast of Super Bowl XXV and four NFL playoff games took in $80 million; however, the rights and production costs exceeded these revenues and the network lost money on its telecasts. In 1990, ESPN paid $112 million to telecast twelve NFL football games. It lost about $85 million on the deal. TNT made the same deal, but lost about $95 million because it did not sell its commercials for as much as ESPN. Besides the fees paid for the rights to these events, we must add the enormous cost of production and technical crews and, for the networks, the transmission of the broadcasts to their affiliated stations. Undeterred, the sports networks continue to bid high sums for the rights to sports events.

SPECIAL EVENTS

Any sports event that is broadcast on TV requires planning, whether it's a college basketball game or the Super Bowl. Arrangements must be made a year or more in advance for the rights, the technical coverage, and the use of local facilities. Assignments to broadcasters are made long before the event's coverage. The network must promote the event to its O&O stations and affiliates. The publicity staff must prepare press announcements months prior to the event. The network's sales staff must sell its inventory of event commercials. These arrangements are routine for broadcasting a local college basketball game, but imagine what they are when a network covers an event like the Summer Olympics games.

How NBC Sports Covered Super Bowl XXVII

On Sunday, January 31, 1993, in Pasadena's venerable Rose Bowl, a capacity crowd of 98,374 paid an average $175 per ticket (up to $1,400 when purchased through scalpers) to see the NFC's Dallas Cowboys pummel the AFC's hapless Buffalo Bills by a score of 52–17 in America's biggest sports spectacular, the Super Bowl. But the fans at the stadium were like specks in the cosmos compared to the TV audience for the game. NBC Sports carried Super Bowl XXVII to a TV universe of more than 110 million people in the United States and an estimated 250 million people worldwide. The show was aired on NBC's six O&O stations, more than 200 affiliates, and the Armed Services Network. It had a blockbuster rating of 43.9 and a 65 share, meaning that forty million homes and 65 percent of TV sets turned on watched Super Bowl XXVII.

The Deal: NBC Sports bought the rights to broadcast Super Bowl XXVII from the National Football League (NFL) for a sum of about $25 million (exact figures are not available). Production costs brought NBC's total expenses for the event to $40 million. The network's advertising revenue for the telecast of the game totaled $39 million. NBC Sports just broke even on the game itself; however, revenues from the pregame and postgame broadcasts enabled them to earn a handsome profit.

The Coverage: The telecast schedule began at 3:30 P.M. Eastern Time with a pregame show that included Magic Johnson interviewing three of the Dallas Cowboys and country singer Garth Brooks singing the national anthem. The telecast of the game itself began at 6:20 P.M. Eastern Time and ran for about three hours. At halftime Michael Jackson starred in a fifteen-minute extravaganza live at the Rose Bowl that was beamed to TV viewers worldwide.

The Personnel: More than 200 people took part in NBC's telecast, including production, technical, and administrative and support crews. An executive producer was NBC's top staffer for the show, with another producer and director handling the pregame, halftime, and postgame shows. NBC's veteran sportscaster, Dick Enberg, handled the play-by-play for the game and the network's top commentator, Bob Trumpy, was responsible for the analysis. Former football star O. J. Simpson and Will McDonough served as contributing analysts on the Super Bowl pregame show. Bob Costas acted as host of the pregame show and did postgame locker-room interviews. Gayle Gardner, Jim Lampley, and former player Todd Christensen were reporters on the pregame show. There was also a producer and a director for the pregame show, and another pair for the game itself. Besides these lead people, two other producers worked on the pregame show and two on the game.

Technical Factors in the Super Bowl Telecast: To telecast so big and important a game, NBC Sports needed sixteen cameras plus carloads of additional equipment. Their heavy baggage included:

16 game-coverage cameras, including one blimp camera and one point-of-view camera
14 videotape replay machines
1 paintbox (animation generator)
1 picturebox (image-storing device)
1 Chyron Infinit (graphics device)
1 telestrator (on-screen drawing device)
25 miles of cable (for cameras, electronic devices, etc.)

A crew of approximately 200 technical, engineering, and support personnel handled this equipment.

Behind the Broadcast Scene: Months before Super Bowl XXVII, NBC's sales staff was beating the ad agency bushes to sell its total of twenty-eight in-game commercials. They went for $850,000 per thirty-second spot, or $28,333 per second.

NBC's sales staff was assisted by sales development people who prepared the ammunition—ratings of previous games and expected ratings for this one. They also provided data about the demography of the viewer audience. (Demography relates to the statistical characteristics and buying habits of an audience.) Selling this time was no simple effort since demand among advertisers for commercial time on sports telecasts had slackened. Nonetheless, the sales staff was successful in selling about $39 million for the game.

About a dozen advertisers, including Reebok, Pepsi, Gillette, Budweiser, McDonald's, Seven-Up, Nike, and Lincoln Mercury, spent more than $2 million each on commercials for Super Bowl XXVII. Frito Lay was sole sponsor of the halftime show. Pregame commercials went for $225,000 to $325,000 per thirty-second spot, and the network's sales staff sold seven "prekickoff" thirty-second units at $500,000 each. The unheralded heroes for this achievement was NBC's sales staff.

Other network management personnel, including lawyers and negotiators, were busy on other fronts. They made deals with the NFL and Rose Bowl management for the right to use the stadium's production facilities, and with affiliate stations and the foreign stations receiving the feed.

No less important was the responsibility of NBC Sports' promotion and publicity departments. Their job was to attract viewers. Certainly they had a hand in generating the thousands of words of pregame hype in the media. Despite so much planning, they could not start their feverish push until three weeks before the game, when the participating teams were identified.

For all of us viewing the Super Bowl, comfortably relaxed at home with our beer and pretzels, it was just a game. For the people at NBC Sports, it was how they made their living—glamorous, exciting, demanding, and remunerative.

Focus on "Monday Night Football"
ABC has broadcast "Monday Night Football" since 1970. Its invasion of the regular prime-time schedule was considered a radical move at the time, but the show has always scored high in the ratings. In December 1985, a Chicago Bears–Miami Dolphins game achieved a 29.6

rating and a 46 share, which translates to a viewer audience of twenty-seven million TV homes, 46 percent of the homes watching TV that evening.

ABC pays the National Football League $7 million per game for the rights to broadcast "Monday Night Football" and $150 million more per season for seventeen regular season games and a postseason football doubleheader. Commercials for the show run about $260,000 per thirty-second spot. ABC's commercial revenues for "Monday Night Football" are more than $10 million per show. Of course, we must consider ABC's expenses in broadcasting these games. Al Michaels earns an estimated $2.1 million a year for announcing the play-by-play on ABC's NFL "Monday Night Football" and ABC's coverage of major league baseball. His salary almost matches that of the stars he covers on his TV broadcast. Michaels's co-announcers on "Monday Night Football," Frank Gifford and Dan Dierdorf, are also in a select group of about ten sports commentators who earn over $1 million a year. To the $7 million per game that ABC pays to the NFL, we must add the salaries of Michaels, Gifford, and Dierdorf, the technical costs for the broadcast, and finally the compensation to the 225 affiliated ABC stations.

CAREERS IN TV SPORTS

According to the sports pages, Tim McCarver, the ex–baseball player, earns $1.5 million a year broadcasting baseball. Bob Costas, who served as NBC's anchor on their broadcast of the 1992 Summer Olympics, is said to earn $1.4 million a year, not including his "Later" show. Veterans Brent Musberger and Dick Enberg earn about $1.4 million a year broadcasting various sports. These huge fees do not include the perks— giant expense accounts and free golf rounds at exclusive country clubs. Do these jobs seem attractive? They certainly do, but seven-figure salaries are for the chosen few.

There are many options in this field besides being a broadcaster. Although the network phase of TV sports employs only a few thousand people, there is a diversity of talent involved. As we have seen, people in sports work in promotion and publicity, ad sales, engineering, technical, and legal affairs as well as in on-air jobs.

How They Got Started

NBC Sports published an information booklet for the benefit of the press covering Super Bowl XXVII. In it are bios of some of NBC's key personnel. Here are some highlights of these staffers' career tracks.

Gayle Gardner. Gardner graduated from Brooklyn College and then earned a graduate degree in film and broadcasting from Boston University. She began her career in sportscasting as the executive producer of a pregame show for the New England Patriots, at an NBC affiliate in Boston. Later, she became a full-time sports reporter and a weekend sports anchor for the station. Gardner held these same duties at stations in Detroit and Baltimore for five years.

She then moved to ESPN where she covered baseball, boxing, and the America's Cup races. Gardner made her debut with NBC Sports on New Year's Day, 1988, serving as a studio host for the network's nine-hour coverage of the college football bowl games. More recently, she has covered the Summer Olympics, NFL Football, and major league baseball. Gardner, along with Lesley Visser of CBS and Robin Roberts of ABC, is a top woman in sports broadcasting.

John Faratzis. In 1978, Faratzis graduated from Syracuse University with a degree in broadcast journalism. He started his career as a production assistant at ABC Sports. After working there for one year, he moved to CBS Sports where he spent six years as a staff producer working NFL and NBA games. He returned to ABC Sports for two years and then joined NBC Sports in 1989 as coordinating producer of NBC's NFL football coverage. For the 1992 Summer Olympics in Barcelona, Faratzis was responsible for track and field, diving, and the men's marathon. In 1993, he was the lead producer for Super Bowl XXVII.

John Gonzalez. Gonzalez graduated from Memphis State University with a degree in TV and radio. He began his career as a camera operator for a TV station in Memphis and later became the director of the evening news. After only two years, he joined NBC and, after a few years of miscellaneous assignments, he was appointed director of a sports show at NBC Sports. During the next fifteen years he worked as a director of Super Bowl games. He also worked on the 1992 Summer Olympics and various college bowl games.

These three people made it to the top at the network sports level. Most other sports jobs pay lesser salaries and involve considerably less glamour. How to get started? Follow the same direction as you would in TV news. Get a job at a small station that covers sports. Your assignment may be the rewriting of press releases and the results from the wire services. You may then progress to on-air sports reporting. If the station produces sports events, you may learn to do the background color, get a producing or directing assignment, or even do the play-by-play. There are also technical jobs in sports at the local level. It may be a long way to the Super Bowl, but it is still the best way to get ahead in TV sports.

CHAPTER 14

America's Love Affair
with the Soaps

What do Warren Beatty, Ellen Burstyn, Dyan Cannon, Robert DeNiro, Peter Falk, Dustin Hoffman, Kevin Kline, Bette Midler, Christopher Reeve, Tom Selleck, and John Travolta have in common? Yes, we gave you the hint. They are among the famous graduates of daytime drama—otherwise known as the soaps.

Twenty million Americans watch the soaps every day, fifty million watch at least once a week, and 25 percent of this audience are men. More statistics: Soaps sell almost $1 billion in advertising a year and they are purported to account for a third of ABC's profits.

The reason for this high profit margin is the relatively low cost of producing soaps. A sixty-minute drama costs between $150,000 and $200,000. A prime-time series costs many times that amount.

Radio soaps date from the mid-1920s. Our first TV station, Dumont's WABD in New York, experimented with soap operas in 1946. (Incidentally, they're called "soap operas" because the early radio dramas were sponsored primarily by soap advertisers. The "opera" comes from their melodramatic, larger-than-life plots and highly charged emotions.) NBC and CBS got into the soap act in the early 1950s. These shows were adaptations of radio soap operas. Of the shows now airing, NBC's "Days of Our Lives" was launched in 1965, CBS's "As the World Turns" got started in 1958, and ABC's "General Hospital" in 1963. The oldest soap still bubbling is CBS's "Guiding Light," which made it to TV in 1952. It broadcasts a fresh episode five times a week, fifty-two weeks a year.

Prime-time soaps made their TV debut in 1964. CBS's "Dallas" came along in 1979. It lavished audiences for eleven years. ABC's "Dynasty," a "Dallas" lookalike, hit prime-time in 1980 and lasted for ten years. Both shows went on to successful marriages in TV syndication. Although some industry mavens considered "Dallas" and "Dynasty" soaps, in terms of their use of name actors, high production values, and lush settings, they were a radical departure from their daytime compatriots. Their budgets ran about four times the cost of a similar daytime production.

In recent years we have seen few soap-type dramas on prime time. One reason may be that many working people tape daytime shows and watch them in the evening.

Although its audience has shrunk, daytime soaps are still profitable because of their low production costs. The medium takes in about $1 billion a year in advertising revenues. One top network executive recently declared that daytime is the one bright marketplace on his whole network.

As of this writing, the three largest networks are producing ten soaps:

CBS

The Young and the Restless
The Bold and the Beautiful
As the World Turns
Guiding Light

NBC

Days of Our Lives
Another World

ABC

All My Children

One Life to Live
General Hospital
Loving

By spring 1993, CBS had gone for 208 weeks in a row as the top-rated network in daytime TV, bolstered by the ratings of its soaps. ABC and NBC followed.

Among the soaps, the leader in the ratings was "The Young and the Restless," followed by "All My Children" and "As the World Turns."

LUST FOR LIFE ON VIDEOTAPE

Each week a column in the *Los Angeles Times* carries synopses of the story lines of the networks' soap operas.[1] Some examples:

"All My Children": Nick and Erica were relieved to learn Mona's cancer surgery was successful and her future looks bright.

"Days of Our Lives": Marlene is intent on helping Roger beat his booze problem.

"The Young and the Restless": Victoria and Ryan were about to make love when Nina arrived on their doorstep.

"The Bold and the Beautiful": Sally was livid when Clarke refused to have anything to do with their son.

Health, addiction, sex, family relationships, and murder—these are the subjects the soaps have been tackling for years, along with such old standbys as drugs, abortion, rape, and illegitimacy. These days, in an attempt to attract younger viewers, soap producers are introducing bolder themes like homosexuality, incest, sexually transmitted diseases, and AIDS.

Curiously, audiences become emotionally involved with soap characters. Eileen Fulton has been playing the role of the sexy, often-married (six times) Lisa on CBS's "As the World Turns" for thirty-two years. Years ago, her real life father, a Methodist preacher, got a letter from an irate viewer berating him for allowing his daughter to do the despicable things she does on the show. Her scheming fictional personality has resulted in hundreds of hate letters condemning her as a "horrible bitch" and even as a "baby killer."

Focus on "Days of Our Lives"

NBC's "Days of Our Lives" celebrated its twenty-eighth anniversary in 1993, having aired 7,000 episodes. Three members of the original cast, including the veteran actor Macdonald Carey, were still with the show. Its mix of adventure, romance, mystery and comedy have made it a consistent favorite with soap audiences. Let's examine the credits for this show.

"Days of Our Lives" is produced by Corday Productions in association with Columbia Pictures TV and NBC Entertainment. The producing end has an executive producer, a supervising executive producer, a supervising producer, and a senior and associate producer. The writing end calls for a head writer, a co-head writer, and three associate head writers. There are four directors for the show and three production associates. Four of the writers, one director, and two production associates are women. Although many soaps are shot in New York, "Days of Our Lives" is produced at NBC's studios in Burbank.

HOW A DAYTIME SOAP IS PRODUCED

It took about ten days and more than a million dollars to produce one episode of the prime-time soap "Dallas." The producers of "All My Children" do the entire one-hour show in a day on a budget of about $200,000.

Between 150 and 200 people are involved in the production of "All My Children," many working twelve-hour days. Taping goes on every weekday, including holidays. It has not had a hiatus or rerun for twenty years. The following is a brief account of a day in the life of "All My Children."

"All My Children" first aired on January 5, 1970. In 1993 it had a cast of thirty contract players, twenty-eight noncontract players who appear regularly on the show, and some extras who vary from show to show.

The work starts at 7:30 A.M. when the director gives the actors a run-through of the day's show. They study the script and decide exactly how to move on the set. The actors don't know their lines yet; they will start learning them later in the day.

The first rehearsal (conducted off the set) concerns just physical movement. The run-through ends at 10:00 or 10:30 A.M.; then the whole cast and directors go down to the set. There are generally about nine or ten sets in place for each show, every day. In "All My Children," they can include a dining room, the hospital room, a motel, a car, and so forth. The actors go through their prepared movements while the director gives instructions to the four camera people about the shots they will take during the taping. Using five cameras saves time because they can get all the different shots at once—close-ups, long shots, long views, and so on. The material is edited later.

At noon everybody breaks for lunch until 1:15, when dress rehearsal starts. The actors must be completely dressed and made up by 1:15. Most of them devote the lunch hour to this process. The dress rehearsal, however, is really for everybody except the actors. During the dress rehearsal, the producer and the director sit in the control room and review how the show will look through the camera. They shout out any immediate changes they want to the actors and crew on the set.

At 3:30 P.M. there is a break, and a light fruit snack is served for the actors. The director and the producer sit with the actors, exchange notes, and go over the show once again, pointing out changes they want made as they go along.

Taping usually starts anywhere from 4:00 to 5:00 P.M. It lasts about two hours, unless the script features scenes with many extras, or some great event like a wedding, a fantasy, or choreography. Then it can run one or two hours longer. The two hours of taping is edited and broadcast two or three weeks later as a one-hour show. Most shows are shot in studios, not on location, although much more location work is done these days than before 1980.

OPPORTUNITIES IN SOAPS

Soaps mean jobs for many actors, writers, and technical people. Because the networks are involved, all jobs are controlled by the various theatrical unions. The head writer of a week's worth of one-hour soaps will receive the Writers Guild minimum of approximately $20,000 for his or her efforts, but this work is limited to a select group of dialogue specialists.

The "bible," or general plot direction, of a soap is created months before taping, while individual episode outlines take much less time. Most soaps accept sample scripts. If you want to write for the soaps, call the network for the particular show you're interested in and get the name of the show's head writer and executive producer. If permission to submit a script is then given, those individuals are your best contacts.

Although there are some highly paid actors, most work for scale, and the regimen is very demanding. The American Federation of Television and Radio Artists (AFTRA) union scale is $402 a day for a half-hour soap and $536 for a one-hour. Actors in movies film about one page of dialogue a day. On prime-time serials, they do three pages a day, but on the soaps, the requirement is twenty-five to forty pages a day.

Most of the soaps are shot in New York City because of its abundance of stage actors. If the reader can break into the TV and film industry through soaps, it's a good beginning—and the work is steady.

NOTE

[1] Nancy M. Reichardt, "Sickness and Health, Plots and Tomfoolery," Los Angeles Times, September 14, 1992.

CHAPTER 15

Syndication: Mining for Gold

For the 1992–93 season, "Murphy Brown" was a leading comedy show, reaching an audience of about seventeen million households. In the fall of 1992, at the start of its fifth season, the show entered the syndication market. It will earn its production company a fortune. Here's how it works:

As we have already seen, a license from a studio or production company gives a network the right to show each episode twice, one in the first run and once as a rerun. The network is granted the right to order up to twenty-six episodes per season from the production company. The right to broadcast the original show includes the right for one rerun. Therefore, if the network orders twenty-six episodes, with reruns the show will make up a fifty-two-week schedule.

If the show has been in prime time for at least three years (the barometer of success, since it needs high ratings to last that long), the production company then syndicates the show to independent and affiliate stations, cable networks, and foreign TV. In 1993, "Cheers" completed an eleven-year run on prime time. By this time, almost 300 episodes were in syndication. Paramount, the producer of "Cheers," will earn hundreds of millions of dollars from this syndication. Bear in mind, however, that most studios initially lose money producing series, as explained in chapter 12.

Syndicated shows air on independent stations at various times of the day. To establish continuity with the audience, many independent stations air their syndicated sitcoms and drama shows five nights a week.

One profitable cable network, Ted Turner's TBS, runs very old shows like "The Brady Bunch," "Happy Days," "Three's Company," "The Andy Griffith Show," and "The Beverly Hillbillies" each weekday afternoon for three whole hours. Over all, syndication of TV programming in the U.S. and worldwide is a $5.5 billion-a-year business.

A NEW TWIST IN SYNDICATION

Production companies and studios like Lorimar, Warner Bros., Buena Vista (Disney), and Paramount are becoming involved in a variation of the syndication theme—first run. First run refers to original series that are produced for the syndication market. These original series have proven more popular than traditional syndicated fare, so stations can charge much higher prices for their commercials. One independent station cut its movie nights from six to three nights a week to make room for these new first-run syndicated series.

In January 1993, Paramount introduced a new series for the syndicated market, "Star Trek: Deep Space Nine" and a new version of "The Untouchables." Although in the past these shows would have gone the network route, Paramount has gambled that it will be more profitable to go directly into syndication. The studio produces the "Star Trek" one-hour shows for between $1.2 million and $1.5 million per episode; however, it sells the series to independent stations for first run, to other broadcast and cable stations for rerun, and to foreign TV. There is no waiting period.

Sitcoms and drama shows are not the only fare making the move into first-run syndication. Talk shows, game shows, animation, and fam-

ily and children's programming have long been produced and immediately syndicated to network and independent stations.

Talk shows have become increasingly popular as syndicated programming. The "Oprah Winfrey Show," for example, has consistent-
ly held a high rating, with an audience that averages eleven million.
In its first six seasons it generated cumulative revenues of $705 mil-
lion and annual profits approaching $100 million. With about half
"Oprah"'s audience, the "Donahue" and "Sally Jesse Raphael" shows
are nonetheless highly profitable. Add to this list "Geraldo," "Regis &
Kathie Lee," "Arsenio Hall," and "Entertainment Tonight," which is
owned by Paramount, the studio that also produces "Star Trek."

THE GAME SHOW MANIA

When Merv Griffin sold his two game-show creations, "Wheel of Fortune" and "Jeopardy," to Coca-Cola for $250 million, industry pundits
were not surprised. "Wheel of Fortune," TV's highest-rated game show,
has about twenty-seven million viewers tuning in every day, and "Jeopardy" is not far behind.

The success of these game shows reflects their syndication advantage. These shows are not reruns but first-run syndications. They're
produced to run daily on independent television stations and some affiliates. These stations prefer them to the more costly network reruns
that don't have the same audience appeal.

"Wheel of Fortune" now airs on about 200 television stations. Since
its prizes are donated by manufacturers as promotional considerations,
the show's annual production costs only run about $7 million. Its gross
revenues—$120 million. That's truly mining for gold.

Don't waste too much time thinking of game-show ideas. There are
probably not too many new ones. You may have more luck in trying to
become a contestant. There's a school in Los Angeles called (what else)
the Game Show Company that will teach you how.

BARTER AND OTHER GAMES

The simplest form of syndication is the straight sale of programs to stations for cash. At other times, a large advertiser buys a program directly and then purchases time on selected stations to air the program as its sole sponsor.

In a barter, an advertiser or agency buys a program from a production company and gives it to a station with two or three built-in commercials. These commercial spots replace payment from the station. The station then sells the remaining spots. There are also part-cash, part-barter arrangements.

THE COMING CRISIS IN SYNDICATION

We have seen that syndication is big business. In one recent year, advertisers placed $2.5 billion in advertising on syndicated shows. You can begin to understand why TV stations sell for so much money.

With the sale of ABC to Capital Cities, the sale of NBC to General Electric, and the reign of Laurence Tisch at CBS, the battleground is set for a war over syndication profits. With advertising revenues down in 1990, 1991, and 1992, syndication revenues have become increasingly important for the networks. The networks want revenues from syndication reruns to balance their losses from pilots and new sitcoms that don't work. The production companies as well are demanding revenues to cover the difference between what the networks pay and what the shows really cost. The networks are also troubled by affiliates that preempt network shows in favor of syndicated fare. An affiliate retains almost half the commercial time on a syndicated show versus only 10 percent from a network program.

Until 1991, FCC rules precluded networks from owning or acquiring a stake in any network-carried programming produced by an independent supplier. The regulations that bar networks from domestic syndicate distribution are called "fin/syn." Fin/syn refers to "financial interest" and "syndication rules." They were designed to limit the networks' influence over the entertainment industry by prohibiting them from producing their own shows and later syndicating them. Through this policy, the FCC seeks to prevent a monopoly practice in TV entertainment. Fin/syn rules were imposed in 1970, modified in 1991, and changed again in 1993.

Here are the new fin/syn rules:

1. The television networks can own rerun rights to the prime-time shows they carry.
2. The networks are no longer restricted from owning a financial stake in the programs they broadcast.
3. The networks can negotiate a financial position in shows developed by outside producers.
4. A network may syndicate, nationally and internationally, all in-house productions.
5. The networks are excluded from participating in "first-run syndications"—shows like "Star Trek," "Oprah Winfrey," and "Donahue."

The new regulations seemed favorable to the networks; however, syndicators and independent stations worry that if the networks produce more of their own programming they will use the output for the benefit of their O&Os and affiliates, and against the interest of independent stations and the cable market.

CAREERS IN SYNDICATION

As a career opportunity, syndication can be exciting. Primarily, it is a sales business; that is, the chief work for the fifty or more major syndicators is selling their programming inventory to independent stations, cable, and the foreign market. At any one point, these syndicators are offering more than 300 different programs. Arranging sales, which may run into the tens of millions of dollars, requires the services of business affairs people—lawyers and other financially astute people who draw the contracts and consummate the deals.

The syndication industry requires promotion and publicity people to help promote the product to the end user. Since more than half the syndicators' output is first run, there are jobs in all phases of production. At independent stations and cable networks, programmers help select and purchase syndicated programs.

There are syndication jobs at networks, ad agencies, production companies, movie studios, and organizations that do nothing but sell other people's products.

PART IV

The Cable
Revolution

CHAPTER 16

Hooked on Cable

The largest cable-television system in the United States is in Fairfax County, Virginia, near Washington, D.C. If you are a cable subscriber there, you are in the enviable position of receiving 103 channels on your set. This melange of cable programming might include:

* Travis Tritt strumming his guitar on CMT, Country Music Television
* a trip to the World War II memorial warship *Arizona* at Pearl Harbor on the Travel Channel
* the Chinese Channel and the Greek Channel
* six Christian channels
* nine public access channels
* four shopping channels

Cable TV offers diversity and choice. It is not just about selling Irish porcelain shamrock ducks on QVC, the shopping channel, and endless reruns of "The Brady Bunch." It is also the medium that offers such quality programming as a documentary about women's political opportunities on the Lifetime Channel, an environmental-music special hosted by Kenny Loggins on the Disney Channel, and an in-depth examination of how Japanese people seek out their individualism in a homogeneous nation on Ted Turner's TBS.

In this chapter we will explore the scope, components, and future of cable TV.

A SHORT HISTORY

In the late 1940s, in TV's infancy, some companies strung cable from antennas atop an area's highest point down to homes in the valley. That's how TV consumers could receive better reception on their tiny sets. They called this system CATV (community antenna television). Engineers also discovered that they could use this system with microwave relay stations to import TV signals from distant TV stations. CATV systems began sprouting up in areas already served by local broadcast stations. Cable television was on the way to communications glory, but there were obstacles.

Advancements in the 1970s increased the capacity of CATV systems beyond one hundred channels; however, major CATV companies found that it cost far more to lay coaxial cable in cities than they had anticipated, and there was not yet an overwhelming demand for their services. Then, in 1972, along came Time Inc.'s HBO (Home Box Office) which leased a transponder on RCA's Satcom 1 to distribute its "pay-TV" service. Its first programming day featured a hockey game from Madison Square Garden and a movie, "Sometimes a Great Notion," that it beamed to an audience of 365 cable subscribers in Wilkes Barre, PA. From this inauspicious start, HBO grew rapidly, and in a few years it offered subscribers more than sixty recently released motion pictures a month, sports events, and comedy specials. Soon others followed HBO's lead, distributing their own programming via satellite. This new programming dramatically increased the demand for cable.

Today there are two types of cable networks: basic and pay. A cable system has a franchise from a municipality or other local government to construct and install coaxial and fiber optic cable and to connect it to individual homes. In large cities like New York, there are several cable system operators. Most cable systems have monopolies in their areas. Contracts with a municipality run for a fixed term and are renewable, typically for eight years. Cable households pay the system owner a monthly charge for basic cable service.

The monthly subscriber's charge provides improved TV reception and a wide range of basic cable channels like Cable News Network (CNN), USA, Music Television (MTV), Entertainment Sports Programming Network (ESPN), Lifetime, and Arts & Entertainment (A&E).

These cable networks are ad-supported, meaning they derive most of their income from the sale of advertising. The cable system owner also pays each cable network a small per-subscriber monthly fee for the right to carry its programming. For example, the cable owner in Milwaukee pays ESPN thirteen cents per subscriber for this right. Similarly, Paragon, a cable system in upper Manhattan, pays CNN an agreed amount monthly per subscriber to carry its programming. Basic cable (no extra charge) is also called "first tier" programming.

Pay-cable networks, where the subscriber pays an additional monthly charge beyond the "basic" monthly cable fee, include HBO, Showtime, The Movie Channel, and Playboy. The pay-cable networks share part of their subscribers' fees with the cable system. Pay-cable is called "second-tier" service.

THE SCOPE OF CABLE TODAY

Cable has grown exponentially in the past twenty years. By 1993, over 12,000 operating cable systems served about 19,000 communities. America's sixty million cable households comprised 65 percent of all TV homes. Of these cable subscribers, about 44 percent have pay-cable penetration, meaning that they subscribe to one or more pay-cable networks. The largest pay-cable network, HBO, has at this writing more than seventeen million subscribers and enjoys an annual net profit of $200 million. By the year 2000 there likely will be one-hundred-million TV households with a cable penetration of about 70 percent.

The modest per-subscriber fee paid to cable networks adds up to billions of dollars. Cable's subscription revenues for 1992 were over $18 billion—more than the amount spent on movie attendance and video cassette rentals combined. Pay-cable channels like HBO, Showtime, and Cinemax receive additional revenues from subscribers for their service.

In 1980, the total amount of local and national advertising revenues on cable networks was $53 million. By 1993, that figure had vaulted to $3.9 billion, about 9 percent of all TV advertising volume. At this point, ESPN, the largest cable network in terms of advertising revenues, sold about $300 million worth of advertising, followed by USA with about $280 million.

Cable TV's top ten advertisers put only about 6 percent of their TV budget into cable. Procter & Gamble, the nation's largest advertiser, places about $1 billion in over-the-air TV, yet it only spends about $112 million in cable.

The hook for cable TV advertising is selectivity. National advertisers can eliminate waste and save money by running small targeted cable system buys instead of a single big network buy. A local advertiser can present a positive image by running inexpensive local spots on national cable networks like CNN and ESPN.

VIEWER PATTERNS

Prime-time ratings are important barometers of TV viewership. On some nights HBO has more viewers than any of the major networks, but that is not the rule. At the time of this writing, the average prime-time rating for the three major broadcast networks was about 42 (or about thirty-nine million TV households). All of cable had only an average of about 9.5 million households during this period.

Although it is a pay-cable service, HBO is the highest-rated cable channel. USA Network is the highest-rated, basic-cable channel. Ironically, USA is the one basic-cable channel whose programming emulates over-the-air broadcast channels.

Cable's top five is indeed a mixed bag of every taste and interest. In terms of subscribers, ESPN has fifty-nine million, USA has fifty-seven million, the Family Channel has fifty-four million, Lifetime has fifty-three million, and A&E fifty-one million.

Although the cable medium has chipped away at broadcast TV's audience, by early 1993 it still had not achieved huge ratings. Here, for example, are the prime-time ratings and shares of the top-five basic-cable networks:

	RATING	SHARE
USA	2.2	3.3
TNT	1.8	2.7
TBS	1.4	2.7
CNN	1.2	1.9
ESPN	1.2	1.8

CABLE SYSTEMS OPERATORS

The people who install the coaxial and fiber-optic cable, connect it to homes, maintain it, and send out a monthly bill for these services are called cable systems operators. Tele-Communications Inc. (TCI) is the largest cable systems operator. Its systems spread across the country. TCI has a financial interest in cable systems that reached a total, by 1993, of more than twelve million homes. TCI also has a financial stake in many of cable's important programming networks including The Discovery Channel, Prime Network, and the combined Turner network. In 1993 TCI provided some of the backing to QVC Network in its $1.16 billion acquisition of the rival Home Shopping Network.

American Television and Communications (ATC) and Continental Cablevision are the second and third largest cable systems operators with a total of more than seven million subscribers. American is a part of the Time Warner family. This extended family includes the cable networks HBO, Cinemax, Movietime, and the Comedy Channel.

WHAT'S ON CABLE

For years, the bad rap on cable by viewers and advertisers alike has been the quality of its programming. Not any more. Endless reruns have given way to original programming, much of it meeting a higher standard than broadcast TV.

One reason cable programmers can innovate is that they don't have to appeal to a mass audience. Rather, cable is a targeted medium, geared to a specific audience. As one cable-network programmer put it, "There's tremendous freedom in the fact that we don't have to try to catch all the fish every time we throw the net out."

For the 1992–93 season, for example, here are some of cable's shows and series:

* A&E: "Pole to Pole," an eight-part series by Monty Python veteran Michael Palin about his travels to the North and South Poles.
* The Discovery Channel: Alex Trebek of "Jeopardy" fame hosts a series called "Heart of Courage" that tells of everyday people who risked their lives to save others.
* Lifetime: A continuing series on issues of concern to women such as "Seize the Power: Challenge to the Women of America."

Yet, cable's programming has its low points as well, filling too many hours with ancient movies of the "Alexander Graham Bell" vintage. With hundreds of programming hours to fill, cable finds itself facing the same problems as its network counterparts.

THE LARGEST PAY-CABLE PROGRAMMING NETWORK

Home Box Office (HBO) is clearly the heavy hitter in the pay-cable league. In 1975, HBO became the first in the TV industry to use the satellite for regular programming transmission. By 1977, HBO had already turned a profit.

In the early 1980s, HBO, whose principal programming was one-year-old movies, became a powerful force in Hollywood because it bought rights to so many movies. At the time, HBO's audience was middle-aged, middle-class America, traditionally a group that doesn't go out to the movies. Why pay $5 (at that time) for a movie at a theater, when for $10 a month you can see twenty or thirty movies?

HBO's involvement in movies took many forms. It would buy rights to recently released pictures and would also make preproduction film investments with producers and studios, thus gaining certain exclusive rights. Then, in 1981, HBO produced its first made-for-pay-TV movie, "The Terry Fox Story." By 1993, the network had produced fifty feature films and was shooting on location throughout the world.

Although the budgets for films produced by HBO do not match those of the major Hollywood studios, they do use major stars. To increase its film business, HBO joined in 1981 with Columbia Pictures and CBS to form TriStar Pictures, a producing and distribution film company. TriStar was later acquired by Columbia's parent company, Sony. In November 1992, HBO subscribers viewed the network's most expensive movie production to date, the $10 million "Stalin."

HBO's subscriber base has increased rapidly. By 1982, it had eleven million subscribers, and by 1990 it peaked at 17.6 million, a figure it maintained into 1993.

HBO and other pay-cable services continue to face the problem of those unsightly futuristic backyard dishes, now euphemistically called "home satellite dishes." For an investment of a few thousand dollars, home owners can bypass cable services. Pay-TV countered this development by scrambling its signal so that dish owners couldn't receive cable's programming. HBO, in turn, made peace with dish owners by offering them a descrambler for a fixed monthly rate.

At this writing, HBO provides two twenty-four-hour, pay-cable services, HBO and Cinemax, and one ad-supported, basic-cable service, Comedy Central, that is jointly owned with Viacom.

HBO's basic programming formula rests on movies—more than sixty each month. It adds new entertainment specials, documentary and series programming, sports specials, big sporting events, and a wide range of family programming to the movie mix.

Another area of HBO's innovation is in making series for the commercial TV networks. By the end of 1992 it had three shows on the Fox network and one on ABC and was developing shows for CBS and NBC. In HBO's future are plans to offer its service on three channels instead of one, staggering the times for greater audience convenience.

HBO has an all-movie channel, Cinemax, that complements HBO's programming with about 135 movies per month. It goes to about 6.5

million subscriber homes, enabling viewers to watch back-to-back movies.

ABC'S CABLE OPERATIONS

ABC's parent company, Capital Cities/ABC, is actively involved in cable through its 80 percent ownership of ESPN, the premiere cable sports network, and one-third interest in the Arts & Entertainment (A&E) and Lifetime cable networks.

Launched in 1979, ESPN broadcasts for twenty-four hours a day and is a formidable competitor to the networks' sports divisions. By 1993, ESPN had sixty-two million subscriber households.

A&E is a profitable joint venture of Capital Cities/ABC, The Hearst Corporation, and NBC. It has been successful with a formula of comedy, dramas, and documentaries—all acquired at low cost. Lifetime began operations, in 1984 and continues to be successful with programming aimed at women, such as a reality series, "Unsolved Mysteries," and an original teleproduction, "Majority Rule," about a female, three-star general running for president.

USA: A CABLE HIGH-FLYING SUCCESS STORY

USA is the only network whose founder, president, and CEO is a woman, Kay Koplovitz. USA began operations in 1981, in partnership with Paramount, MCA, and Time Inc. (Time exited in 1987.) Its early programming included reruns of popular movies, wrestling, and trashy "sex-and-sin" series, earning USA a reputation as the "murder-and-mayhem network." It worked.

By 1992, USA had augmented its programming by producing, through its two movie company partners, Paramount and Universal, thirty low-budget films a year. In addition, Paramount and MCA (Universal) use the films in their home-video divisions.

In September 1992, the innovative USA kicked off the Sci-Fi Channel, reaching out for that audience's many devotees. At the time of this launch, USA was number one in cable ratings. It boasted sixty-million subscribers, revenues of $380 million, and a profit margin of almost $100 million, extremely high for the cable industry.

HOW ADVERTISERS LOOK AT CABLE

An advertiser will pay about $300,000 for a thirty-second commercial on the network prime-time series "Roseanne." That advertiser could buy an eight-spot package of thirty-second commercials on Turner Network Television (TNT) for about $40,000. Which buy is more efficient? Probably the one on TNT.

Cable viewing is increasing and ad dollars tend to follow viewing. In the years from 1989 to 1992, cable was the one place to show quantifiable viewing increases. Cable's share of advertising budgets, about 5 percent in the 1980s, has soared to 20 or 25 percent.

The reasons are many. Some advertisers could never afford network TV or they left the medium because of its ever-increasing costs. Also, cable offers greater selectivity than network TV. A beer advertiser on ESPN, the all-sports network, is reaching exactly the right demography for its product in a very cost-efficient way.

Because of more specialized programming, cable networks offer advertisers greater audience selectivity than broadcast TV. Cable TV allows advertisers to target customers with the least waste. An advertiser on CNN, for example, knows that the network will deliver a literate, serious-minded audience throughout its telecasting schedule. In addition, the average cable-TV subscriber tends to be younger, better educated, and more affluent than the broadcast viewer.

The declining quality of network TV programs has eroded its audience and given cable an opportunity to improve its numbers and prove to advertisers that viewers can no longer be defined simply by age or sex. Cable advertising's proponents project that by the year 2000, the medium's advertising revenue will exceed $10 billion. At that point, its viewership and advertising revenues should match network television.

PAY-PER-VIEW TV AND ITS POSSIBILITIES

If you live in New York's borough of Queens, your home may be one of 2,500 chosen for Time Warner's 150-channel Quantum system. By using fiber-optic transmission-lines and digital-compression techniques, Quantum offers three to ten programs on a single channel. For a fee of $3.95 these homes may access pay-per-view recent hit movies.

Consider the possibility of seeing a blockbuster movie at home on the same day it opens in theaters. That is one attraction of pay-per-view television. Also, the opportunities to present many sports events on pay-per-view will certainly increase once the technology is fully developed.

Cable is facing new challenges from many areas. New regulations permit the TV networks to own cable systems, a right previously withheld. Communities are asking the federal government to regulate cable rates. Telephone companies are competing with cable operators for control of the electronic highways of the future. The advertising dollar is up for grabs between the broadcast and cable networks. One conclusion is evident. By the year 2000 the cable business will be only a facsimile of what it is today.

In December 1992, Tele-Communications Inc. (TCI), the nation's largest systems operator, announced a revolutionary new video-compression technology that can bring more than 500 TV channels to subscribers. This digital system can deliver advanced services like interactive TV and high-definition television.

In April 1993, in yet another aggressive move, Tele-Communications announced a unique affiliation with Carolco Pictures, producer of the "Rocky" films and "Terminator 2: Judgment Day." In return for a $90 million investment by Tele-Communications, Carolco gave them the right to broadcast four of its movies on pay-per-view before they reached the theaters. Home viewers will likely pay about $30 per viewing. Of course, enough TV households must be capable of receiving pay-per-view for this revolutionary development to work.

NARROW-CASTING AND NICHE PROGRAMMING

Generally, narrow-casting and niche programming mean aiming programming at a specific limited audience or sales market. These developments clearly represent cable's path in the immediate future.

Some examples of recent narrow-cast cable channels are science-fiction, courtroom, and cartoon networks. In the planning stage are channels devoted to the golden-age set, a Romance Classics channel aimed at readers of romance novels, a Game Show channel featuring reruns of popular game shows and some original programming, and an all-purpose, How-To channel.

When most of the nation's TV sets have a capacity of more than a hundred cable channels, these and other innovative programming ideas will definitely be in our future.

YOUR FUTURE IN CABLE

Jobs in cable parallel those in broadcasting. At a cable TV network, there are jobs in programming, production, news, research, engineering and technical development, promotion and marketing, and airtime sales. The most difficult jobs to get are in programming and production. If you are seeking a spot as a play-by-play announcer at ESPN or as a VJ on MTV, your odds are slim indeed, primarily because of the few situations available. Try the big networks like HBO and Turner Broadcasting first. We discuss Turner and CNN in the next chapter.

Consider the area of time sales. As with the broadcast networks, salespeople call on ad agencies and advertisers to sell cable-network

---

CAREER TIP

HBO offers some paid internships, the number depending on the need of a particular season. There is a twelve-week internship for undergraduate students and a twelve-week internship for graduate students. Interested readers should write to HBO's Department of Human Resources, 1100 Avenue of the Americas, New York, NY 10036.

time. Local-cable sales, however, is an easier way to get started. You may also be able to sell local time in your own home area for a national cable network. Selling this advertising is similar to selling radio or newspaper space, but it can be more creative. Often the sales representative is involved in the creative preparation of the commercial, since he or she has experience with the medium. The successful, local-cable ad-salesperson, obviously, can rise to sell commercial time for a cable network on the national level. All the large networks have sales offices in the major cities.

For a cable systems operation, jobs are primarily in the technical, sales, and marketing areas. A systems operation emphasizes subscriber sales, particularly since 35 percent of the nation's homes have not yet bought cable.

There are even opportunities to start new shows. You can launch a show inexpensively on public access cable. If it succeeds, you can approach your local system or try to sell it to a cable network.

In terms of salaries, jobs in cable pay about the same as they do in broadcast TV.

For a listing of all the broadcast and cable networks and the names of their key executives, find a library that files *The Hollywood Reporter*. The listing appears each September in their annual Fall TV Preview issue.

CHAPTER 17

The Turner Broadcasting System

T he Persian Gulf War established the Cable News Network (CNN) as a truly international news network with extraordinary influence in the world's capitals. Indeed, among its regular viewers are world leaders like Boris Yeltsin, Fidel Castro, Yasir Arafat, François Mitterand, Muammar Qaddafi, and Saddam Hussein.

CNN's unprecedented coverage of the Persian Gulf War extended to Iraq's surrender in early March 1991. Along the way, it even drew criticism from the other networks. They claimed that CNN's Peter Arnett, who remained in Baghdad and transmitted reports censored by the Iraqis, was being used for propaganda.

CNN has more than its fair share of detractors. Some claim that what CNN provides is raw information, often unconfirmed, inaccurate, unedited, and uninterpreted. Perhaps some of these charges are justified, yet one can't deny its success as the preeminent, worldwide, news-gathering operation.

CNN is the most visible star in the Turner Broadcasting horizon. Now let's look at the Turner universe.

THE SCOPE OF THE TURNER
BROADCASTING SYSTEM

Turner Broadcasting was born in 1970 when Ted Turner bought WJRJ, a small UHF-TV station in Atlanta. In 1976, the renamed station, WTBS, was beamed via satellite to cable homes nationwide, becoming cable's first "superstation."

To help provide programming for the new station, Turner bought baseball's Atlanta Braves and a controlling interest in the National Basketball Association's Atlanta Hawks. That's entrepreneurship.

In 1980, Turner made news-broadcasting history when he launched CNN as the world's first twenty-four-hour all-news network. It had 1.7 million subscribers. In 1982, Turner introduced Headline News, a companion service to CNN's more in-depth coverage. Headline News draws upon CNN's resources to produce continuously-updated, half-hour newscasts twenty-four hours a day. By 1985, CNN, Headline News, and the Turner Broadcasting System's (TBS) television programming were transmitted on the Galaxy 1 satellite, where it enjoyed full-time access.

Widening its base, CNN introduced CNN International in Europe in 1985 and, in 1987, to the People's Republic of China. That year, Ted Turner sold 36 percent of the Turner Broadcasting System to Tele-Communications Inc., the giant cable operator, and Time Inc. (later to become Time Warner) for $560 million to finance the purchase of the MGM/UA film library.

By 1988, Turner was ready to introduce another cable service, Turner Network Television (TNT), which debuted in seventeen million cable homes, the largest network debut in cable history. In just two years it had fifty million subscribers.

After selling the 36 percent interest in his parent company to cable operators in 1987, Turner resisted further sales or threats of a takeover. Both NBC and CBS tried to purchase partial ownership, but were rebuffed.

For 1992's operations, Turner Broadcasting System had revenues of $1.77 billion and earned a record $78 million—this in a period of declining ad sales.

CNN

In 1980, when the indefatigable Ted Turner started CNN in Atlanta, his stated goal was to bring journalism into the space age by relying completely on satellites to gather and disseminate news, and to "deliver the most objective news to be found, live and around the clock." A lofty purpose, indeed.

CNN got off to a jump start in its very first year by covering such events as the first space shuttle launch, the two national political conventions, a royal wedding in Britain, and the shootings of a president and a pope. In the subsequent decade, CNN overpowered the established network news teams with its reporting of the 1987 New York Stock Exchange crash, the Pan American Lockerbie disaster, the Exxon *Valdez* oil spill, the Iran-Contra hearings, and its spectacular scoop in January 1986 when CNN alone carried live coverage of the liftoff of space-shuttle *Challenger*, which exploded in full view of its cameras.

The Numbers

When Turner launched CNN, he had only 1.7 million subscriber households, but CNN's reach grew rapidly. By the end of its first ten years, it had over fifty million U.S. cable subscribers and fifty-three million more abroad. Our use of subscribers here means that CNN is paid by cable systems operators to serve their cable TV households.

CNN lost $200 million in its first five years, but by 1985 it was breaking even, causing fits among its network competitors. Jack Welch, CEO of General Electric, NBC's parent company, is reported to have engaged in heavy table pounding at a staff meeting in December 1986, when he expressed his envy of CNN, which broadcast news twenty-four hours a day on an annual budget of only $100 million and made a profit, while his network had only four hours of news a day, spent $275 million a year and lost $100 million on its news operation.[1]

Maintaining a network with the scope of CNN requires more than just satellite time. At this writing, CNN employs about 1,700 people in twenty-eight news bureaus (nineteen outside the United States). Approximately 150 CNN staffers are on-air anchors or correspondents.

Besides broadcasting news on its cable network, CNN sells its news coverage to hundreds of independent and network-affiliate, over-the-air stations. For example, KCTV-5 in Kansas City, a CBS affiliate, pays CNN $700 a week for an hour of Headline News, which they carry at 5:00 A.M., and for the right to plug CNN stories into local newscasts. Many independent stations use CNN news to supplement their national and international coverage.

PROFILE: TOM JOHNSON

In 1990, when Tom Johnson came to CNN as president, at age 48, he had already had a long and successful career in broadcast and print journalism. His last job before moving to CNN was chairman of the Times Mirror Company, owner of the *Los Angeles Times*, a one-million circulation newspaper that he had published for almost ten years.

Johnson graduated from the University of Georgia, in his native state, majoring in journalism. He later received an MBA from Harvard. After working at the White House for a few years, first on a fellowship and then as a special assistant to Lyndon Johnson, he moved into broadcasting. In the mid-1970s, Johnson became editor, then publisher, of the *Dallas Times Herald*.

Tom Johnson came to CNN just before the Persian Gulf War and led his newsgathering troops to a creative and ratings victory. The CNN audience, which reached a peak of more than eleven million households during the war, didn't hold. CNN reverted to its average audience of about one million when the war was over.

But Johnson is determined that CNN succeed as a global news network and clearly has Ted Turner's mandate to accomplish it. The Persian Gulf War cost CNN about $30 million and required a staff of seventy-five people. No one complained. Johnson is committed to in-depth coverage of important events whether or not they result in an immediate payoff.

Johnson's mix at CNN includes live coverage and analysis of breaking news events, in addition to comprehensive newscasts and interviews. He introduced provocative talk shows like "Both Sides with Jesse Jackson" and continued to schedule the viewer favorites "Crossfire" and the two-million-audience "Larry King Live." By most standards, Tom Johnson has succeeded brilliantly at CNN.

Working for CNN

The bad rap about CNN in the broadcast industry goes back to 1980, the network's earliest days in Atlanta, when the newsroom was in the basement of an old deserted house.

When he first saw the place, one job candidate is quoted as saying, "Oh, my God, what have I done? I'm out of work. I've flown down here, and it turns out to be this old rickety house that Sherman forgot to burn."

These days CNN newspeople operate from a huge, high-tech movie set version of a TV newsroom where journalists and producers function in an atmosphere of controlled frenzy.

CNN is a nonunion shop. Employees at ABC, for example, have a NABET contract that guarantees them high salaries and a generous benefits plan. At CNN, the starting salary in the newsroom is about $16,000, the same as it is at ABC, but at ABC it automatically goes to $20,000 after eighteen months, not at CNN.

At the upper level, Bernard Shaw, CNN's highest paid anchor, earns about $500,000 a year, which doesn't approach the salary of fellow anchors Dan Rather and Peter Jennings. CNN replies, "We have scores of anchors, and our viewers expect to get news coverage, not anchor presentations of the news."

There are other considerations. An executive producer with a New York–based network makes more than an executive producer for CNN, but the New York executive is probably forty-five or fifty years old and must live in New York. At CNN, the executive producer is probably thirty-five and has been gaining important experience working for ten years in twenty-four-hour news production. He or she also lives in Atlanta, where living costs are a fraction of those in New York.

But even at penurious CNN, middle- and lower-level, employee salaries have increased in recent years and CNN has gone a considerable distance toward eliminating any remaining salary discrepancies at those levels.

Further, the people at CNN point out, "Salary structure and job security are sometimes inversely related. We continue to grow, with the security and upward mobility that that assumes, while our competitors are laying off people each year."

They Made It at CNN

As the new guy on the block, CNN has not always had the first choice of journalism graduates. Yet its reputation as a star-maker surpasses that of the three major networks. The reason: CNN gives new people the opportunity to establish their journalism credentials almost from the beginning of their employment. Here are a few typical success stories taken from an interview with their personnel chief and from information supplied by CNN:

Jeff Flock holds a B.S. in broadcast journalism from Boston University. After graduating, he worked for a radio station in Boston as an anchor-reporter. Flock came to CNN in 1980 at the news network's inception, training first as a video journalist before being named reporter-producer in the Southeast Bureau. A year later he became Chief Midwest Correspondent and covered such big stories as the Teamsters' bribery-conspiracy trial and the election of Chicago's first black mayor, Harold Washington. Today Jeff Flock is CNN's Chicago Bureau Chief.

Christiane Amanpour was born in London and moved to the United States, where she attended the University of Rhode Island, graduating summa cum laude with a B.A. in journalism. She began her broadcasting career in England as a reporter, producer, and researcher for "The World Tonight," BBC Radio's nightly news and current-affairs program.

Returning to the States in 1981, Amanpour spent a year as a reporter, anchor, and producer for WBRU-Radio in Providence. Later she moved to TV, working as an electronic graphics designer at WJAR-TV, also in Providence.

Amanpour began her CNN career in September 1983 as an assistant on the network's international assignment desk. In March 1984, she became a news writer and later produced, wrote, and served as the off-screen narrator for news packages. She also took part in the production of the 1985, four-week series "Iran: In the Name of God," which won CNN's first DuPont award.

Amanpour's next assignment, to CNN's Frankfurt bureau, placed her at the epicenter of the dramatic changes that took place in the late 1980s, with the breakup of communism in Eastern Europe.

In 1990, she was sent to the Persian Gulf, where she covered the Gulf War from Iraq's invasion of Kuwait to the Kurdish refugee crisis on the

Turkey-Iraq border. Her Gulf-War reporting won her the "Breakthrough Award" from an industry group, Women, Men, and Media.

As CNN's Paris-based correspondent since 1991, Amanpour has reported on the attempted Russian coup, the conflicts in Yugoslavia, and the African famine.

Charles Jaco's coverage of the events in Saudi Arabia during the Persian Gulf War made him a CNN star. Although media critics uniformly gave Jaco high marks for his reporting of the war, he was chided for his "gas mask dramatics," when he wrongly reported, along with another network, that one of the first Scud attacks on Israel contained chemicals.

Charles Jaco's journalistic credentials are a mile wide. He has won more than forty national and international awards, including the prestigious Peabody Award. He majored in English at the University of Chicago and received a masters in journalism from Columbia University in 1976. Jaco spent three years as news director and anchor for a Chicago radio station and has written for many national newspapers and magazines.

Jaco spent nine years with the NBC Radio Network reporting for and anchoring radio newscasts. He joined CNN in December 1988 as a correspondent in CNN's Miami bureau, where he covered many stories for the network, domestically and internationally.

As of this writing, Jaco is CNN's Miami Bureau Chief.

HEADLINE NEWS

The people at Turner Broadcasting refer to their second twenty-four-hour news-network as "Around the World Every Thirty Minutes." That's what it is. The Headline News format allows the viewer to tune in any time of the day, and in just thirty minutes receive the top national and international stories, along with business, sports, weather, entertainment, and informative features. Its thirty-minute structure serves as an alternative to CNN's more in-depth and diverse program schedule and news coverage.

Begun in 1982 with just 800,000 cable homes, Headline News now reaches over fifty-one million cable households and millions more via the more than 250 American broadcast affiliates that use the service to enhance their own news broadcasts. Headline News is also seen in more than 670,000 U.S. hotel rooms and is a major source of programming for CNN's international feed, which goes to 125 countries.

Headline News is headquartered at CNN's high-tech facility in Atlanta where it taps in to what they refer to as the most modern newsroom computer in the world. Nine anchors and 250 journalists, along with CNN's newsgathering resources, make up the staff of Headline News.

TNT

TNT stands for Turner Network Television, launched by the adventurous Mr. Ted Turner in October 1988. Its formula: a blend of high-profile sporting events, vintage motion pictures, and original programming.

TNT debuted with the first cable-exclusive telecast of "Gone with the Wind." At the time, it had seventeen million subscribers. By 1993, its subscriber count reached fifty-nine million.

Although pay-cable services like HBO and Showtime offer movie classics and recent films, no basic cable service gives viewers the variety and quantity of films of TNT. Its library contains more than 4,000 titles from MGM, RKO, Warner Brothers, and Columbia Pictures. For a movie junkie, TNT is Nirvana—vintage movies at the rate of nine or ten a day.

On one night, for example, TNT ran four back-to-back Spencer Tracy films, including the classic "The Last Hurrah" and "Edward My Son." Later the same week it featured a James Bond festival.

On another night, TNT programmed such classics as "Key Largo" (1948), "The Big Sleep" (1946), "Lassie Come Home" (1943), and the more recent "Urban Cowboy" (1980) and "Grease" (1978).

TNT soon realized that a formula of vintage movies alone would quickly bore its regular viewers, so it added some original programming to its schedule. One recent production, "The Last Elephant," with John Lithgow, Isabella Rossellini, and James Earl Jones was about elephant poachers in Africa. Another, "The Habitation of Dragons," was a two-hour Horton Foote drama.

In the sports arena, TNT has been active covering NBA basketball and NFL football. For football fans who don't get enough on Sundays with CBS's and NBC's coverage, TNT provides the only source for Sunday night games—ten each season. TNT also telecast the 1992 and will telecast the 1994 Winter Olympics.

TNT doesn't forget the kids. It offers a mix of pre-1948 cartoons: Bugs Bunny, Daffy Duck, Tom & Jerry, and Popeye.

TBS SUPERSTATION

As mentioned earlier, Ted Turner bought his first station in 1970, the rinky-dink WJRJ in Atlanta, later renamed WTCG. It was soon to become the TBS superstation when, in 1976, its signal was beamed to cable systems nationwide via satellite.

TBS broadcasts on a twenty-four-hour-a-day schedule. Here, as with TNT, the programming mix uses classic films, live sports events (domestic and international), and original films and documentaries. When TBS began transmitting via satellite in 1976, it was received by four cable systems with 24,000 households. By the end of 1992, TBS had fifty-eight million subscribers.

GOING TO WORK FOR
TURNER BROADCASTING SYSTEM

Ted Turner has a high-voltage personality and his networks are high-energy operations. With 1,800 employees worldwide at CNN alone, it presents a major job opportunity. By way of comparison, the news divisions of the three major networks employ only about 1,000 each. But is there a negative side to working for Turner and CNN?

As we have seen, CNN's fortunes can escalate during a temporary event like the Persian Gulf War and then drop precipitously when the crisis ends. A sense of jubilation can quickly turn to depression.

Clearly, another disadvantage of working for Turner is salary, particularly at the middle and upper levels. You will earn less than your network compatriots even if you become a rising news star like major anchor Frank Sesno. For example, the payroll of the thirteen-person Chicago office of CNN has a $1 million budget, less than the salary of CBS's Chicago anchorperson. And if you're thinking about your old age when you go to work for Turner, forget about a pension plan. On the positive side, talent is recognized at Turner Broadcasting and CNN and moves ahead rapidly, regardless of age.

THE FUTURE OF TURNER BROADCASTING AND CNN

A 1992 Advertising Age/Electronic Media survey of agency media buyers and marketing executives asked the question: "Which cable networks have the greatest growth potential?" Of thirty-five networks, CNN drew the largest response. Forty-four percent of the respondents said CNN had the greatest growth potential. TNT placed second, with a 33.5 percent response.

Former Secretary General of the United Nations Javier Perez de Cuellar has said, "TV is the town crier of the twentieth century, walking through the diverse neighborhoods of our global community." If this is the case, then Ted Turner is TV's Paul Revere. He has spread the word in this global village.

NOTE

[1] *Hank Whittemore*, CNN: The Inside Story *(Boston: Little Brown, 1990).*

CHAPTER 18

Trends in Broadcast TV and Cable

TRENDS IN VIEWERSHIP SIZE AND PREFERENCE

Communications Industry Forecast publishes an annual survey that includes noteworthy figures on the relative size of audiences for TV, radio, cable, and other communications areas. According to the 1992 survey, broadcast TV is losing viewers, primarily to videocassettes (see Table 7). Cable has grown while newspapers and magazines have not. Surprisingly few hours per year—twelve, in both 1985 and 1990—are spent going to the movies.

The same survey predicted viewership for network affiliates, independents, and cable (see Table 8). According to these figures, the affiliates will lose viewers while the others gain, but not by much.

TRENDS IN THE GLOBAL MARKET

We know that American TV programming is widely accepted in other countries. Successful prime-time programs are released to foreign

TABLE 7. NUMBER OF HOURS PER PERSON
PER YEAR SPENT USING MEDIA

MEDIUM	1985	1990
Television	1,530	1,470
Network-Affiliated Stations	985	780
Independent Stations	335	340
Basic Cable Programs	120	260
Pay-Cable Programs	90	90
Radio	1,190	1,135
Newspapers	185	175
Consumer Magazines	110	90
Movies	12	12
Home Video	15	50

TABLE 8. PREDICTED SHARES
OF TOTAL TELEVISION VIEWING

YEAR	NETWORK AFFILIATED STATIONS	INDEPENDENT STATIONS	BASIC CABLE	PAY CABLE
1989	56.0%	23.5%	14.1%	6.4%
1994	51.5%	24.0%	17.5%	7.0%

broadcasters at the same time or even earlier than they reach the U.S. domestic syndication market. Often these programs are dubbed in the language in which they are broadcast. Major U.S. television events like the Academy Awards and football's Super Bowl broadcast are transmitted via satellite to the global TV market.

Europe is the best market for a wide range of American TV programming, yet even Third-World countries buy U.S. sports and entertainment programs, news shows, and made-for-TV movies.

In terms of reciprocity, however, very little foreign-programming finds its way to American TV audiences. Notable exceptions are "Masterpiece Theatre," and other British properties that appear regularly on our public television.

How TV Is Distributed Globally

Once a year, in October, about 8,000 of the world's TV distributors and buyers convene in Cannes, France, for the International Film and Program Market for TV, Video, Cable, and Satellite (MIPCOM), the largest international TV program market. For American-TV-program distributors it is indeed a bonanza, generating an estimated $2.1 billion in sales of American TV-programs and feature films to international TV outlets. It is also an opportunity for foreign TV producers to distribute their output to other nations.

Here's an example of some offerings at the 1992 MIPCOM:

The Bulgarian National Network offered a series, "The Funny Adventures of a Bulgarian in Europe," the adventures of a middle-class hero in turn-of-the-century Bulgaria.

Poland's Film Polski offered "Franz Kafka," an animated special inspired by the diaries and novels of Franz Kafka.

Britain's Channel 4 International had a half-hour series, "Terry and Julian," in which a comedian moves in with a down-to-earth Londoner.

Britain's Granada Television was selling syndication rights to several series, five documentaries, and three telefilms.

The American TV distributor Warner Bros. International had almost one hundred properties to sell for foreign distribution rights. These included: "Batman: The Animated Series," "The Sports Illustrated Swimsuit '92 Special," a miniseries dramatization of the life and career of Frank Sinatra, and a group of TV series including "Knot's Landing," "Murphy Brown," "Night Court," and "Perfect Strangers."

At MIPCOM, the American sellers of TV product face many problems, not the least of which are currency fluctuations, the general state of the world economy, and the need to find time for the vast amount of programming offered. Besides, a foreign country's locally originated programs still dominate their prime-time scheduling.

Some U.S. production companies use a forum like MIPCOM to seek foreign financing or co-production deals for their projects. Typically, a foreign broadcaster or distributor who commits to part of a show's production costs retains a broad range of the production's foreign-broadcasting rights. U.S. production companies also produce some original programming for the foreign market. In these cases, the U.S. becomes an ancillary market.

While many countries are in the world-TV distribution game, U.S. fare is still the most widely exported of any nation's TV production.

The price range of TV shows sold abroad varies greatly. An animated half-hour show may sell for as little as $25,000 and as much as $250,000, depending upon subject and quality. These are typical figures for the total foreign market. An American two-hour, made-for-TV movie can sell in a range of $600,000 to a little over $1 million. At times, there may even be distribution in movie theaters for this product.

OTHER TRENDS

From Passive to Interactive

In January 1987, the then Warner Amex cable company introduced the first satellite feed of interactive programming in Columbus, Ohio. They called it Qube. Pundits predicted it would revolutionize TV. It didn't. It was too costly and of too little interest to viewers then. An interactive TV system requires viewers to use a laptop keyboard that connects to a central computer via modem.

Here's how the Qube experiment worked. Subscribers in Columbus had a unit installed on their sets with various buttons and keys. In one experimental football game, the audience was asked to select a play for the quarterback while he was in a huddle. The audience's choice fed through the computer in seconds and was relayed to the quarterback in time to call it as his next play. In 1987, Qube may have been ahead of its time, but by the early 1990s consumers had become more familiar with computers, video games, and interactive technology.

In an article in *Adweek*, Don Keefer showed how interactive technology was used six years after the Qube experiment.[1] Game shows, as of this writing, are major candidates for interactive TV participation. One company, Interactive Networks of Menlo Park, California, sells a $499 laptop keyboard that lets viewers play along with game shows like "Wheel of Fortune" and "Jeopardy." When the participant has finished with a game, the answers are sent to the company's main computer via modem. Prizes are then awarded to viewers at home, as well as to studio contestants.

Interactive TV is also useful in polling and conducting surveys. Viewers may be easily polled on the political and social issues of the day. In a lighter sense, in one new show, viewers at home join celebrities in trying to guess the results of surveys about situation ethics like, "Should a married man accept a dinner invitation from an old flame when she's visiting from out of town?" Futurologist James Naisbitt predicts that at least 40 percent of U.S. households will have some kind of interactive TV by the year 2000.

Advertiser-Produced TV Shows

For some time, advertisers like Hallmark cards have purchased the entire commercial inventory of a prime-time show and produced it as well. Procter & Gamble has also been involved in the production of soap operas to sell their soap. The trend is now broadening.

In December 1991, McDonald's and its ad agency, Leo Burnett, produced a half-hour animated Christmas special that ran on CBS. The same year, M&M Mars produced a half-hour special on CBS called "The Last Halloween." In October 1992, ABC aired a Chrysler-produced movie, "The First American Hero."

Advertisers see two reasons for assuming the expense and responsibility of producing their own shows. First, they can produce programming that will create a precise type of media environment for their product. Also, with declining network advertising revenues, the advertiser can make favorable deals with the network. Advertisers who own shows can also reap the benefit of an after-market, like foreign distribution. We may be seeing a growing trend in the direction of advertiser-produced shows.

TV News in the 21st Century

David Bartlett, president of the Radio & TV News Directors Association (RTNDA), makes intriguing forecasts about TV news.[2] In the future, viewer demand, he believes, for news and information will be limitless. News on demand will be the order of the day. Instead of watching a package prepared by a TV producer, viewers will put their own package together by issuing voice commands to a computer to retrieve the information they want.

According to Bartlett, it's already happening: "Viewers who once were willing to sit still for a half-hour and watch a carefully-assembled, TV-news program are now inclined to usurp the producer's role and switch around the dial, assembling a personal news package suited to their own interests and attention spans."

The Future Technology of Television

In terms of television technology, we can look forward to the following in the near future, according to writer Jonathan Weber:[3]

* High-powered satellites will send signals to small, cheap home dishes, bringing us a broad range of programming.
* Video compression will allow a single satellite channel to carry up to a dozen TV programs, thereby reducing costs.
* High definition TV will bring movie-theater quality pictures to wall-mounted, flat panel TV sets.

AT&T is entering the interactive TV fray, using its long-distance network to transmit video signals. With this new technology, the home TV set will serve as a computer. Armed with a remote control device, viewers will be able to order movies on demand, shop at home, and send voice- and video-mail messages.

In May 1993, one of the baby Bell companies, US West, paid $2.5 billion for an interest in Time Warner Entertainment. With the marriage of programming and telecommunications, and the rise of globalization, opportunities will increase dramatically for careers in these burgeoning industries.

NOTES

[1] Don Keefer, "You Can Touch This," Adweek, January 14, 1991, p. 20
[2] David Bartlett, "TV News in the 21st Century," Communicator, June 1992, p. 30.
[3] Jonathan Weber, "And Now a Word from Our Future," Los Angeles Times, October 19, 1992.

PART V

Radio

Courtesy Bettmann Archive

CHAPTER 19

A Short History
of Radio

THE ORIGINS OF RADIO

The scientific development that led to the invention of radio originated with a Scot, James Maxwell, who, in 1865, discovered that electrical impulses travel through space at the speed of light. Then, in 1888, the German physicist Heinrich Hertz proved the wave theory and established a relationship between electrical waves and light waves.

In 1895, putting all this together, Guglielmo Marconi developed the first wireless telegraph, and by 1901 he had sent the first transatlantic radio message, from England to Newfoundland.

In 1904, the English electrical engineer John Ambrose Fleming invented a vacuum tube that could detect radio signals. An American, Lee De Forest, developed the triode, or three-element vacuum tube, in 1907.

In 1918, President Woodrow Wilson became the first president to use radio when he broadcast from a ship to World War I troops aboard other vessels.

After World War I, manufacturers began to develop the new medium. American Marconi (a U.S. branch of a British company) held the patents, but Westinghouse, General Electric, and American Telephone & Telegraph (AT&T) bought out Marconi to form the Radio Corporation of America, the initials of which, you might notice, are RCA.

The career of radio pioneer David Sarnoff parallels the rise of radio. Sarnoff, an immigrant, taught himself Morse code and became a wireless operator with the American Marconi Company. He was at his post when the fateful message came through about the sinking of the *Titanic* on April 14, 1912. He was also there on May 7, 1915, when the *Lusitania* was sunk by German U-boats. The *Titanic* is considered electronic media's first scoop.

RCA formed the National Broadcasting Company, which was to become the first network, in 1926. It was joined in 1927 by the fledgling Columbia Broadcasting System, founded by William S. Paley. These commercial radio pioneers later became television pioneers and were moving forces in broadcasting for fifty years.

The earliest scheduled radio program aired on radio station KDKA in Pittsburgh. It aroused public interest by broadcasting, on the night of November 2, 1920, the returns of the Harding-Cox presidential election. The audience, a meager few thousand, listened on homemade sets. It marked the birth of scheduled broadcasting.

Following KDKA's auspicious debut, radio stations sprang up in every major city. By 1924, there were already 1,400 stations, many of which would later become the affiliates of the major networks. The audience for these stations zoomed as well. By 1923, 2.5 million radios had been sold.

THE ORIGIN OF "K" AND "W" CALL LETTERS

If you have ever wondered why some stations' call letters begin with "K" and others with "W," K's are west of the Mississippi and W's are east. These designations came about as a result of an early Federal Communications Commission (FCC) ruling. KDKA was named before this ruling.

The first use of telephone lines to connect two stations came in 1922. A New York and a Chicago station joined to broadcast a football game simultaneously. This development hastened the rise of the networks.

As early as New Year's Day 1927, David Sarnoff's NBC network broadcast the Rose Bowl game in Pasadena as the first coast-to-coast radio hookup.

The phenomenal expansion of radio in the early 1920s led many businesses to overextend themselves. Between 1924 and 1926 the number of stations shrank by half, to about 600. Radio company stocks worth $160 million in 1924 fell to $65 million in 1926.

RADIO IN THE 1930S

Radio bounced back in the late 1920s and early '30s, programming proliferated, and radio advertising became big business. Of course, radio commercials on small-town stations were cheap. Old-timers refer to those commercials as "a dollar a holler."

The names of radio personalities became household words. The list would include the first well-known radio reporter, Graham McNamee. Billy Jones and Ernie Hare, the Happiness Boys, were commercial pitchmen who plugged Interwoven Socks. "The Uncle Don Radio Show" was a family favorite. Parents would write to Uncle Don, telling him their kid's birthday and where the present was hidden. Then, if the kid was lucky, he'd be listening when, miraculously, Uncle Don would mention his name and the little secret that a pair of skates was hidden in the top drawer of his parents' dresser.

Many great entertainers of this period performed on radio. The great "Jazz Singer," Al Jolson, sang on NBC as early as 1928. Rudy Vallee charmed audiences with his "Maine Stein" song. "Amos 'n' Andy" was one of the first radio sitcoms. The family-oriented comedy-drama "Rise of the Goldbergs" ran for more than fifteen years. One family favorite was "The American Album of Familiar Music," starring Frank Munn and Lucy Monroe.

Advertisers went into radio in a big way beginning in the early '30s. Listeners associated a program with its sponsor much more than viewers do now with television. It was a kind of shared intimacy. So, even fifty years later, some of us still remember the "A&P Gypsies," "Amos 'n' Andy," sponsored by Pepsodent, Jack Benny, who came on the air with "Jell-O again, it's Jack Benny," and the adventure series "Death Valley Days," sponsored by 20 Mule Team Borax, whatever that was.

In 1938, in what some call radio's most famous program, Orson Welles panicked millions of Americans listening to his production of H.G. Wells's "War of the Worlds." "A late news bulletin" announcing that Martian spaceships had landed in New Jersey sent thousands of listeners calling newspapers and radio stations for news of the invasion. The military was alerted and people actually reported sighting the Martians. The program repeated warnings that the broadcast was fictional, but the damage had been done. The Federal Communications Commission (FCC) investigated and concluded that there would be no more fictional, scare-news bulletins.

The late '30s and early '40s was the era of the Big Bands. We became accustomed to listening to live music on a radio network. On Saturday night, a group might get together and dance to the music of Glen Gray and his Casa Loma Orchestra from the famous Aragon ballroom, high atop the Belvedere Hotel in downtown "Anywhere." The Big Bands died at about the same time television took radio's place as the nation's favorite broadcast medium.

Radio reigned in the period before World War II. Most families had only one radio, but as an entertainment medium it offered something for everyone. For the boys, it was "Jack Armstrong, the All-American Boy," for the girls, "Little Orphan Annie." "Just Plain Bill" appealed to Mom while the whole family loved Jack Benny, Fred Allen, and George Burns and Gracie Allen—studio audiences, laugh machines, and all. (Laugh tracks were introduced later to provide more consistent laughter.)

WORLD WAR II

On December 9, 1941, the largest audience in radio history, estimated at ninety million, heard President Franklin D. Roosevelt address the U.S. Congress two days after the Japanese attack on Pearl Harbor. Roosevelt, throughout his presidency, brought government to the people through his "fireside chats."

In Europe, Adolf Hitler and Benito Mussolini used radio to militarize Germany and Italy and later to soften up neighboring countries for conquest.

During the war, radio brought us reports from the fronts and news and commentary from the well-recognized voices of Gabriel Heatter, H. V. Kaltenborn, and Edward R. Murrow. Murrow was the only one in this group to make a successful transition to television.

THE END OF THE GOLDEN ERA

The "Golden Era" of radio ran from 1926 to 1940. By 1950, there were about forty million radios in U.S. homes. By 1957, almost that many radios were installed in automobiles. Yet, when television came along in the late 1940s, radio seemed doomed. Many in the media said it would become the networks' forgotten child. *Time* magazine opined in 1948 that TV "will eventually make radio as obsolete as the horse." *Newsweek* magazine maintained that "radio's days in the big time seem numbered." Others in the mainstream press delivered obituaries, but radio was not ready to be interred.

In the late 1940s, when these comments were made, the U.S. had about 2,000 commercial radio stations. Today there are more than 10,000 commercial stations and 1,800 noncommercial.

When TV scored its giant blows in the early 1950s, radio didn't take the ten count. It bounced back and took advantage of unchartered opportunities. Radio went from being a medium of programs like "The Lone Ranger" and "The Shadow" to a medium of formats, each finely tuned to a very specific audience—news, top forty, Big Band, talk, and so on. It experimented with new formats—all news, all music, interview shows. The term "deejay" entered radio language. Stations reached the vast car-radio audience with special "drive time" programming. If one format didn't work, the station changed to another.

In the early '80s, another phenomenon boosted radio listening—small, highly portable radios with lightweight headphones for personal listening anywhere, anytime. At this writing, more than twenty million people use these sets.

Today, seventy years after its commercial start, radio is far from dead. You'll learn all about it in the chapters ahead.

CHAPTER 20

The Scope of Radio Today

Radio is more than seventy years old, and despite cyclical problems that have affected all media in the early 1990s, it is still a plucky survivor.

In 1948, before competition from TV, radio's advertising revenues were $562 million. At this writing, radio's advertising revenues are more than $8 billion, less than a third of TV's, and the 1992 edition of *Communications Industry Forecast* projects them to be $11.4 billion by 1995. Radio's production cost and capital expenditures, however, are many times less than those of television.

Acquisition fever in radio remains brisk. Consider Gene Autry, America's original singing cowboy and an early investor in radio. KMPC in Los Angeles, purchased by Autry and a partner in 1952 for $800,000, is worth about $40 million today. Profits from the station paid for Autry's purchase of a Los Angeles TV station in 1964 for $12 million. He sold it in 1982 for $245 million—not bad for a movie cowboy.

In March 1986, in what is believed to be the largest sale ever of a radio station group, Metromedia sold nine of its eleven stations to an investor group and Morgan Stanley and Company for $285 million. The nine stations are in six of the nation's largest markets and have a collective audience of about forty-four million.

But records are made to be broken. In June 1993, KRTH-FM in Los Angeles was sold by its owner, Beasley Broadcast Group, to New York–based Infinity Broadcasting for $110 million in cash, the highest price ever for a radio station. At the time, Infinity already owned twenty-one stations in thirteen cities.

Even in smaller markets, broadcasting companies and other entrepreneurs have been paying the kind of prices for radio stations that used to be paid for TV stations. In Greenville, South Carolina, an AM/FM station was sold in 1990 for $7.25 million, and in a tiny market, Burlington, Vermont, a station was sold for $1 million.

Prices for radio stations rose sharply in the 1980s because of the relatively small number of licenses available from the FCC; however, except in major markets like New York and Los Angeles, where prices are still rising, radio entered a slump in the early 1990s. Lower advertising revenues caused the price of stations to drop by 30 to 50 percent. Until 1992, FCC regulations prohibited any company, of whatever size, from owning more than twelve AM and twelve FM stations. In 1993, the FCC revised its regulations so that one company may own as many as eighteen AM and eighteen FM stations. One company may not own more than two AM and two FM stations in a large market and a total of three stations in a small market.

Of all stations, about 5,200 are commercial AM, 5,700 commercial FM, and another 1,800 public FM. According to FCC regulations, an educational station must be operated on a nonprofit basis and may not accept paid advertising.

The FCC grants licenses for new stations, regulates changes of ownership, and mandates the amount of time stations devote to public service programming and announcements. License renewals for stations are considered every seven years.

Of the nation's approximately 12,700 AM and FM stations, about 6,000 are owned by one-city or one-station companies. As for the large companies, some of their multimillion dollar acquisitions may be at risk because of the FCC's licensing of 700 new FM stations in March

1985, primarily to individual owners. Industry experts predict that there will be more than 11,000 commercial stations by the close of the century.

And with all those stations, where are the radios? There are a half billion radio sets in the U.S., two for every man, woman, and child, or 5.6 radios per household. About 72 percent are in the home; the rest are in autos or in people's ears as radio headsets.

The owners of these 150 million battery-operated radios are called "walk-along" users—what else? Of this group, 48 percent are adults between the ages of eighteen and thirty-four.

Among "upscale" Americans, better than 95 percent listen to radio three or more hours a day. Between 10:00 A.M. and 3:00 P.M. radio reaches 163 million consumers each week, more than that time's TV audience.

The largest midday audience group is women, ages eighteen to thirty-four, but men in the same age group are not far behind. The lowest midday radio customer group is young men of twelve to eighteen.

RADIO STATIONS: AM AND FM

Technically, AM means amplitude modulation and refers to a technical characteristic of the radio wave. AM waves maintain a constant frequency while the intensity, or amplitude, of the signal rises and falls. This change, or modulation, puts the information (voice or music) into the signal. The AM broadcast band uses 117 frequencies beginning at 540 kHz and continuing at 10 kHz intervals to, and including, 1700 kHz. FM, or frequency modulation, refers to a system that keeps the amplitude steady while the frequency changes. FM broadcasts are less susceptible to atmospheric distortion than AM, but the signal does not cover as large an area. The FM broadcast band consists of the frequencies between 88 and 108 MHz. It is divided into 100 channels (channels 201–300) with a band width of 200 kHz each.

Because of its clearer signal, FM lends itself to the music format, while talk and news are most often broadcast on AM stations. At this writing, there are slightly more commercial FM than AM stations. The

New York radio market, number one in the U.S., has nineteen AM stations and twenty-five FM stations. With regard to audience, FM today leads AM 60 percent to 40 percent in share of listeners. Another consideration is a station's power, or range, expressed in watts (w) or kilowatts (kW). A kilowatt is 1,000 watts. A large station may have a range of 50,000 watts; a small one as little as 150 watts.

HOW RADIO MEASURES ITS AUDIENCE

The number of listeners, share of market, audience demography, listener loyalty—even attitudes of the audience—all add to a station's profile. This information guides radio stations in making programming decisions to increase both the number of listeners and the length of time they listen. Also, a station's advertising and promotion staff can use these estimates to plan on-air and off-air campaigns to garner a larger audience.

Two groups dominate radio research: Arbitron and the Scarborough Research Corporation. Arbitron concerns itself with the quantitative factors of radio audiences while Scarborough measures their qualitative and demographic aspects. Formerly separate entities, the two businesses joined in 1992 for what they said would be "a marriage made in audience-survey heaven."

How Arbitron Gets Its Information

On a leisurely Sunday morning, someone in your neighborhood pours a cup of coffee, tunes in a favorite radio station, glances at the clock and makes a notation of time and station in a booklet conveniently placed next to the radio. This booklet is a diary from Arbitron and the information provided may decide how your local radio station serves its audience.

Before Arbitron came on the scene, radio research was very different. In the 1930s, a telephone survey asked listeners to recount their previous twenty-four hours of radio listening time. In the '40s, with the proliferation of multiple sets per household and in-car listening, phone calls were not always consistent with listening habits, so a mechanical device, the audimeter, was attached to car radio receivers; however, it couldn't withstand the bumps and jolts of driving and was soon dropped. The 1950s brought both the birth of rock 'n' roll and changes in radio design. Smaller, less expensive radios helped move the focus of research from metering the set to monitoring the behavior of individual listeners. In 1964, a television research company called ARB (American Research Bureau) began measuring radio-listening habits by using a survey technique that had worked well for television. Each listener was mailed his or her own booklet, called a diary, to record listening habits. From ARB eventually evolved the name Arbitron. The company now measures 260 cities and towns, called "metro markets." Each of these markets is measured at least once, 130 markets are measured twice (in the fall and spring), and listeners in 79 markets are surveyed four times each year—in the winter, spring, summer, and fall.

Arbitron still uses the seven-day personal "diary" system as a measurement tool. It is sent to each individual twelve years of age and older in a randomly selected household that has agreed, by telephone, to participate. The diary provides space to note the time of listening, the call letters and frequency of the radio station, where the listener is situated, and any additional comments. Although identities are kept confidential, each diary-keeper is asked to provide basic demographic information. Arbitron receives 51 percent of all diaries back.

Scarborough's Qualitative Reports

Scarborough, Arbitron's new partner, is concerned with both the listening habits of and demographic information about radio audiences. It telephones one person, eighteen years or older, per household and asks that individual to fill a seven-day, personal diary and a questionnaire.

Scarborough uses this questionnaire to measure respondents' usage of the three prime local media: newspapers, radio, and television. Clients of Scarborough's service can receive brand information, besides learning the size and makeup of audiences listening to radio.

Radio station sales departments use Arbitron's and Scarborough's research as valuable marketing tools. The media departments of both advertisers and their ad agencies also use this material as a guide to placing their radio advertising.

CAREER TIP

Station managers and their advertising departments carefully study Arbitron and Scarborough data. Advertisers and agencies use this information as a guide for their radio-buying decisions. For readers with a degree in computer science and an interest in broadcasting, this phase of the business would make a good career choice. It pays well, and there are substantial employment opportunities in the media departments of advertising agencies.

Arbitron maintains executive and marketing headquarters in New York City and operations, production, and research facilities in Laurel and Beltsville, Maryland. It also has offices in Chicago, Atlanta, Dallas, Los Angeles, and San Francisco. Write for information on job opportunities to:

Arbitron Ratings Company
1350 Avenue of the Americas
New York, NY 10019.

The future of radio-listening measurement will tap into the most sophisticated high technology available, including electronic diaries, personal computers and data transmitted over satellites.

THE BROAD DIVERSIFICATION OF RADIO AND HOW IT AFFECTS CAREERS

Today, radio-station employment exceeds 125,000, with another 1,000 people employed at the major radio networks. As a positive career choice, radio has an advantage over a field like advertising, in which most of the agencies are located in three or four large cities. Radio stations are everywhere. Table 9 lists several cities and their station complement.

With more than 10,000 stations, radio offers excellent opportunity for the media novice. One can get started at a small, local station and move up the ladder in that city or take the riskier move of trying for a job at a big-city station.

TABLE 9. NUMBER OF RADIO STATIONS IN U.S. CITIES

CITY	POPULATION	RADIO STATIONS
Chicago	8,193,800*	38
San Francisco	6,073,900*	49
Detroit	4,661,700*	30
Dallas/Ft. Worth	3,776,000*	32
Seattle-Tacoma	2,500,000*	10
Portland (OR)	1,395,000*	25
Indianapolis	1,243,400	20
Salt Lake City	1,069,000	30
Providence (RI)	917,400	26
Tulsa	740,500	18

* Population of metropolitan statistical area

CHAPTER 21

Who Does What in Radio

WORKING IN RADIO

All those radios out there—in cars, bedrooms, living rooms, kitchens, offices, on wrists, and in ears—need radio stations. Radio needs good people who are flexible, creative, dynamic, and hard working. It needs people to create and implement the variety of program formats. It needs people to interpret and deliver the news. It needs announcers, technicians, administrators, and salespeople to sell the advertising.

A college journalism or mass-communications program is good training for a career in radio, especially in news. Many colleges offer two-year, four-year, and graduate programs in broadcasting. (See chapter 27.)

Most entry-level people start at small stations. Here, the station manager, who is often the owner, may act as sales manager or perhaps as program director, announcer, and copywriter. At small stations, announcers often do their own writing, operate the control board, and even sell advertising.

At large stations, tasks become more specialized. Typically, large radio stations have five major departments: news, programming, engineering, sales, and general administration.

Radio stations are more inclined to hire beginners than are TV stations. There is a downside, however. Depending on one's duties, hours worked in radio can be extremely demanding for the newcomer. While overtime is sometimes paid, especially at a station with a union contract, it does not always fully compensate a person who works a double shift, a six-day week, or a twelve-hour day. Although this type of schedule in not the norm, radio personnel must be ready to accept working holidays, weekends, and early-morning or late-night hours.

Although radio generally pays less than TV, a professional in a key talent or management position at a large-market station can earn a six-figure salary.

Because there is such a wide range in salary for each job described in this section, depending on the sales volume of the individual station, we list average salaries for both high- and low-volume stations. Jobs at midsized stations will have proportionate average salaries. For certain support staff jobs, many of which are entry level, we will list the average starting compensation. Salary levels are not given for every job described in this section because of the unavailability of data.[1]

A word about unions in the radio field: Union members generally make more money than nonunion employees. The American Federation of Television and Radio Artists (AFTRA) is the only union representing on-air employees. In New York City, this union has contracts with more than 90 percent of the major stations, which means these stations must hire union employees for all jobs covered by AFTRA.

Technical people belong to either the International Brotherhood of Electrical Workers (IBEW) or the National Association of Broadcast Employees and Technicians (NABET); however, radio now has substantially fewer technical jobs than it once did. Advances in technology are phasing out these jobs.

JOB CATEGORIES

At most stations, a table of organization contains five divisions. Following is a list of the divisions and their key job functions. (Bear in mind that at a small radio station one person may perform several functions. That means you will have more work—probably without more money—but it's a wonderful way to learn.)

GENERAL ADMINISTRATION

General Manager
Business Manager
Producer/Director
Announcer/Deejay
Public-Service/Community-Affairs Director
Various Freelancers
Music Director/Librarian
Traffic Manager
Promotion/Community Relations Director
Production/Traffic Assistant

PROGRAMMING

Program Director
Production Manager

NEWS

News Director
Assistant News Director/Assignment Editor
News Reporter
Business Editor
Sportscaster
Consumer Affairs Reporter
Sky Cop/Traffic Reporter
Weather Reporter
Desk/News Assistant

ENGINEERING

Chief Engineer
Studio Engineer
Transmitter Engineer
Maintenance Engineer
Contract Engineer

SALES
General Sales Manager
Local Sales Manager
National Sales Manager
Account Executives
Sales Assistant
Research Director

General Administration

General Manager In radio, the general manager—or station manager, as the position is often called—is the boss. He or she has authority over operations, programming, advertising sales, and personnel—the whole show. The general manager is usually a corporate officer reporting directly to the station's owner or board of directors. At a station with a sales volume of $250,000 to $500,000, the average salary is $43,000. At a station with a sales volume exceeding $2 million, the average salary is about $100,000. (These same sales-volume figures apply to all the salaries listed in this section.)

Business Manager This professional handles all financial transactions, develops business plans and goals, prepares statements and budgets, and supervises the activities of accountants, bookkeepers, and billing clerks. Business-administration courses in college are helpful preparation, as is an accounting or management degree. The average low-volume salary is $23,000, the average high-volume salary, $38,000.

Producer/Director The producer/director plans, rehearses, and/or produces live or recorded programs. This person works with music, voices, and sound effects to achieve the best possible presentation for a program. At talk show stations, producers choose and schedule interviews. A producer/director must have experience in announcing, writing, and production. A liberal arts degree with a major in broadcasting or communications is preferred.

Announcer/Deejay Announcers, deejays, and other on-air personalities introduce programs and recordings, read commercial copy (when they do, they are paid extra for it), give station identifications and recordings, and read promotional and public service announcements.

Announcers often have strong personal styles. They may host talk programs and deliver comments or information, often giving the show a distinctive tone. Some select the music played (at larger stations the program director selects the music) and operate some or all of the studio controls and equipment. (The word "deejay" stems, of course, from "DJ"—"Disc Jockey"—though the term is seldom used today.) On twenty-four-hour stations, announcers must be prepared to work odd schedules. A prime requisite for the job is a good, clear, well-modulated voice that conveys warmth and integrity, although some hard-rock stations seem to require a frantic personality.

An announcer on a talk or call-in show must be an informed generalist with an excellent educational background in the arts, history, and social and political science. There are now about 30,000 announcers in U.S. radio and, because supply far exceeds demand, beginning announcers work for low salaries (see Table 10). According to a 1992 report of the National Association of Broadcasters (NAB), news announcers, news reporters, and sports reporters receive lower salaries than the announcer/deejay. For example, a news reporter at the lowest-revenue station earns only an average of $12,000.

TABLE 10. SALARIES FOR ANNOUNCERS/DEEJAYS

STATION REVENUES	AVERAGE ANNUAL COMPENSATION	AVERAGE STARTING COMPENSATION
More than $2 million	$38,000	$23,000
$1 to $2 million	$22,000	$16,000
$500,000 to $1 million	$18,000	$14,000
$250,000 to $500,000	$17,000	$14,000

Source: National Association of Broadcasters, 1992

An announcer or deejay with a large following will either move into a prime-time slot at the station with a big salary raise or be wooed by another large station. There are even consulting and talent agencies that recruit for the networks and major stations.

Public-Service/Community-Affairs Director This person plans, writes, and produces the station's public service programs and is responsible for adhering to FCC requirements. The position exists primarily at large stations.

Various Freelancers Freelancers include traffic reporters, entertainment and arts reviewers, environmental specialists, financial commentators and analysts, cooking experts, psychologists, and medical doctors. These specialists offer regular news and commentary on their fields. Those syndicated to many stations are well compensated.

Music Director/Librarian A station with a music format needs a librarian to catalog and store the records, tapes, and CDs. The job requires familiarity with the field of music—popular or classical—broadcast by the station. Some librarians select the music for air play and may survey local stores and trade magazines to learn what is currently popular. This individual needs good organizational ability. There is clearly a difference between the compensation of a music director at a large station and a librarian at a small one. The music director may earn as much as $100,000 a year, while the small station librarian may earn a fraction of that amount.

Traffic Manager The traffic manager coordinates the station's programming with the advertising provided by the sales department. He or she works with the engineering department on the accurate placement of these elements. Computer training is an asset for this job.

Promotion/Community Relations Director At a large station, this position may be expanded to two separate jobs. The promotion director is concerned with image building, sales presentations, and relations with the local community. Public relations and advertising courses in college are good preparation for this job.

Desk/News Assistant and Production/Traffic Assistant These are the entry-level jobs at a radio station. Some are merely "gofers." Even so, one can obtain excellent experience from a year or so in either of these positions. The desk/news assistant works for the news department. The production/traffic assistant works for the production manager and, where the title exists, the traffic manager. If you're good, there is no place to go but up.

Programming

Program Director The program director is responsible for everything broadcast from the station. He or she works closely with the general manager, who runs the whole show, and the sales manager. (The station's owners, of course, will have a major say regarding the station's programming.) The program director plans the program schedule by considering the audience, the competition, the advertisers, and the budget. If shows are to be produced, the program director decides who will produce them. Many program directors start as announcers, some as deejays. At some stations, program directors also host shows and do special-event broadcasts. They know all the various radio formats and trends, and are prepared to make format changes when necessary. Program directors need long experience in radio. A liberal arts education, with courses in English, speech, and drama, is a plus. The average salary at a low-volume station is $25,000, the average high-volume salary, $77,000.

Production Manager The production manager is involved in assigning announcers, newscasters, and producers. He or she also arranges schedules and recording sessions. The job requires broadcast experience, especially an understanding of the physical limitations of the medium. The ability to supervise and organize is a *sine qua non* for this function. This position exists only at larger stations where original programs are produced.

News

News Director The news director sets the station's news policy. Obviously, at an all-news station this function assumes greater importance than at a station with five-minute, hourly news breaks. The news director supervises reporters, monitors news printers (or computer screens), and takes telephoned news tips. Some stations take their news from wire services' reports, news network services, and their own staff of reporters in the field. Good preparation for this job comes from college-level courses in journalism, political science, and social studies. A person usually moves into the news director's job after years of reporting experience. The average salary for a low-volume station is

$18,000; the average for a high-volume station is $46,000.

Assistant News Director/Assignment Editor This individual helps the news director with reporters' assignments. These positions exist only at larger stations with heavy- or all-news coverage.

News Reporter The news reporter gathers the news through journalistic efforts in the field and studio. He or she then edits and produces taped segments for on-air presentation. The news reporter may broadcast the report or the station's announcer may present it. The job requires good vocal delivery and journalistic experience. A degree in broadcast journalism is a distinct advantage for this job. An all-news station has many reporters on staff. The average low-volume salary is $15,000, the average high-volume salary, $28,000.

Business Editor Stock market reports, financial news stories, and financial forecasts are the province of this reporting job. Often a freelancer handles this function. One needs a thorough grounding in business administration and economics as preparation for this job.

Sportscaster Ronald Reagan began his career as a sports announcer. With the increased interest in sports, the role of a sportscaster today is far removed from that of his time.

The sportscaster gathers and reports the local and national sports news, often gives the play-by-play, and conducts interviews with athletes, managers, and coaches. Former athletes often do well at this job. Journalism courses at college and speech training are good preparation for this position. The average low-volume salary is $14,000, the average high-volume salary, $36,000. A local station's sportscaster who does play-by-play of home and away events will receive a far higher salary than one who merely reads the sports news. Syndicated sports personalities like baseball's Vin Scully, whose play-by-play accounts are broadcast on many stations, earn high six-figure salaries.

Consumer-Affairs Reporter This reporter helps listeners with shopping, health, and environmental news. In recent years, with growing consumer awareness, the job has become important in radio and TV. The job of consumer-affairs reporter is a specialized version of news reporting. Educational and occupational requirements are thus similar to those of the news reporter and announcer, and college courses in marketing are good preparation.

Sky Cop/Traffic Reporter Large stations with extensive traffic coverage use helicopter, sky-cop companies to monitor and report traffic conditions. Some stations have their own helicopters and employ reporters specifically for this function.

Weather Reporter At small stations, the weather report is read by the announcer. At large stations, the weather report is often combined with the traffic report.

Engineering
Readers interested in radio's engineering function should realize that, although broadcasting is technically complex, changes and improvements in the technology have reduced engineering staff sizes. Many job categories now double up.

Chief Engineer Sometimes called director of engineering, this individual heads the department and supervises the technicians. Small stations may have a one-person department. A chief engineer needs at least five years' experience as a broadcast technician. The chief engineer and the technical staff install and maintain studio and portable equipment and the station's transmitter. This person generally has an engineering degree and a thorough understanding of the principles of electronics, as well as an FCC license.

The FCC no longer conducts examinations for broadcast engineers and a license is needed only for transmitter operation and maintenance. Technical certification has replaced the license examination and comes from membership organizations like the Society of Broadcast Engineers. For these engineering jobs, however, many employers prefer to hire technicians with an FCC license and technical certification. The average low-volume salary is $22,000, the average high-volume salary, $45,000.

Studio Engineer This job exists only at larger stations. The studio engineer analyzes the technical requirements of studio programs and operates the control room during a broadcast to feed the program to the transmitter. During a broadcast, the studio engineer controls the microphones, plays the records and discs, incorporates the remote feeds (material originating outside the studio), monitors the sound levels, and communicates with the producers and performers via headphones while the show is on the air. This position requires at least a high school diploma. Since competition for this job is so keen, however, candidates with a college degree plus courses in electronics have an advantage.

Transmitter Engineer The transmitter engineer cares for and monitors the transmitter. He or she tests the performance of and makes technical adjustments and repairs to both transmitter and tower. The position also entails maintaining records and logs of tests and repairs.

Maintenance Engineer The duties of the maintenance engineer include installation of and preventive maintenance on control consoles, boards, recording equipment, microphones, intercoms, two-way radios, remote facilities, and a variety of other station equipment and electronic systems. When systems fail to operate, the maintenance engineer repairs them.

Contract Engineer The contract engineer regularly inspects and maintains the equipment of several small stations in an area. Large stations have on-staff contract engineers. This engineer is on call for emergencies.

Sales

As with television, airtime sales pay for a commercial radio station's costs and ultimately account for its profits. This advertising revenue comes from two sources—local and national sales. The local sale is made by the station's own sales force. Large rep firms that work on a commission basis usually handle national sales (see page 212). If a local station is a network affiliate, the network may sometimes compensate the affiliate for advertising revenues earned by the networks.

General Sales Manager The general sales manager directs the station's sales force and sells airtime. He or she works closely with the program director and the general manager to evaluate the total amount of available airtime and to pinpoint those programs able to attract the highest-paying advertisers.

In directing the sales force, the sales manager must set sales goals, supervise sales presentations, and thoroughly understand the local business market. Often the sales manager will go on sales calls with the station's salespeople.

Sales managers usually rank just below the general manager in a station's pecking order. They often succeed to the top spot at their own station. Training for this job comes from working at radio sales. A successful salesperson in any field, however, can make the jump to radio sales. An undergraduate degree in advertising or marketing is a good door-opener. The average low-volume salary is $35,000, the average high-volume salary, $93,000.

Local Sales Manager The local sales manager supervises the local salespeople, assigns accounts, and goes along on sales calls.

National Sales Manager The national sales manager works with the station's national sales rep firm to solicit national advertising. The rep firm may have regional sales offices in key cities across the country.

Account Executives The soldiers out on the line selling those ten-, thirty-, and sixty-second commercials are the account executives. These people must know the audience and match them with a particular program daypart (as in television, a particular segment of a broadcast day). Often salespeople help an advertiser prepare commercials. Account executives earn reasonably high salaries, especially as commission is a factor. A degree in marketing or advertising helps land a first job.

Sales Assistant This employee tracks the activities of the sales staff, writes orders, maintains a schedule of available airtime, and often acts as the department's "gofer." This is an entry-level job that requires at least a high school diploma. Successful assistants often move into advertising sales jobs. The average salary for this job is low, about $13,000 to $15,000, but it's a foot in the door.

Research Director The research director works for both the sales and programming departments, collecting information about a station. Researchers study programming effectiveness and popularity, commercials, and the relative strength of the competition. The job requires a college degree in business administration, advertising, accounting, or mass communications in addition to computer and statistical skills. Average salaries range from $17,000 at a small station to about $32,000 at a larger station.

NOTE

[1] *The source for all salary data given is a study by the National Association of Broadcasters.*

CHAPTER 22

Programming Formats in Radio

FUN WITH FORMATS

Arbitron charts the listening of adults age twelve and older, Monday to Sunday, 6:00 A.M. to midnight, in the top 200 measured markets of the country. In the spring of 1993, the Arbitron survey revealed the top five stations in each of the top five markets:

STATION	FORMAT
NEW YORK	
WRKS-FM	Urban (music)
WLTW-FM	Soft AC (adult contemporary music)
WCBS-FM	Oldies (music)
WBLS-FM	Urban
WINS-AM	News

STATION	FORMAT

LOS ANGELES

KLAX-FM	Spanish
KOST-FM	Soft AC
KPWR-FM	CHR
KFI-AM	Talk
KIIS-AM/FM	CHR

CHICAGO

WGCI-FM	Urban
WGN-AM	MOR/Talk (middle of road music)
WUSN-FM	Country
WBBM-FM	CHR
WHT-FM	AC

SAN FRANCISCO

KGO-AM	News/Talk
KMEL-FM	CHR
KCBS-AM	News
KNBR-AM	Talk
KFRC-AM	Nostalgia

PHILADELPHIA

KYW-AM	News
WWDB-FM	Talk
WIOQ-FM	CHR
WYSP-FM	Classic Rock
WYXR-FM	AC

Now, what does all this jargon mean?

Radio stations operate with a basic format, but one format is not always exclusive. A news station like KNX-AM Los Angeles will carry a food-news hour, classic radio programs, and play-by-play sports besides regular news coverage; however, to attract and keep an audience, a station will not break its programming into disparate elements. News and talk go together; big band and hard rock are an unlikely combination.

Radio programming is broken down into more than sixty different formats that break down into further subcategories. For example, the black category includes black oldies, black adult contemporary, and black rock. Here is a short description of some of the most popular formats:

Adult Contemporary (AC): AC includes soft rock, light rock, recent popular forms, and a few oldies. AC stations play the likes of Phil Collins, Whitney Houston, Natalie Cole, Huey Lewis, Robert Palmer, Bonnie Raitt, James Taylor, and Elton John.

Beautiful Music: Beautiful Music is also known as Easy Listening or, to its detractors, as elevator, shopping-mall, or dentist-chair music. One Beautiful Music program director says of his station's format, "Yes, we're Easy Listening. But no, we won't put you to sleep." Barbra Streisand, Mantovani, and semi-classical selections are the proven fare of this format.

Black: This genre includes Urban Contemporary and Disco. Stations with this format program dance music, rap, and music from such black artists as Vanessa Williams, Luther Vandross, and Regina Belle. When black stations go in the direction of rap, playing artists like Hammer and Paula Abdul, they lose the over-twenty audience. Black stations that appeal to the very young are often designated Urban.

Classic Rock: Classic Rock plays popular rock music of the '60s, '70s, and '80s. Folk heroes of this classification are Mick Jagger, Van Halen, Peter Gabriel, and Eric Clapton.

Contemporary Hit Radio (CHR/Top 40): The staples of CHR are hot-selling records. CHR stations have a limited playlist of twenty to forty rock hits that are repeated throughout the day. This format's roster includes Guns N' Roses, Skid Row, Bon Jovi, and Madonna.

Country: Country music is sweeping the nation. By the early 1990s it had become the most popular format programmed on U.S. radio stations, according to the *1993 Broadcasting & Cable Market Place*.

Country-formatted radio stations have benefited from a wealth of new artists and new country music styles, making such performers as Garth Brooks, Wynnona, Randy Travis, and Hank Williams, Jr., household names across the United States. Country's big appeal is among the twenty-five to fifty-four age group. It has its greatest popularity in the South and West; two of the very best stations are in Fargo, North Dakota, and Waco, Texas.

Middle-of-the-Road (MOR): MOR stations feature a traditional AM format of music, news, and talk. The songs played are the popular standards. These stations sometimes cover sporting events.

Oldies: Oldies programming, sometimes known as "Golden Oldies," appeals to the twenty-five to fifty-four set. This format includes anything from tunes from the late '50s to songs of the mid-'80s. Its selections differ from AC and might include Joannie Mitchell, the Beatles, Elvis Presley, and Motown favorites.

Rock/AOR (Album Oriented Rock): This cousin of Classic Rock features music from the '60s to the present, often played in "sweeps" or uninterrupted sets of entire albums.

Talk: The talk format often combines with the news format. A talk station typically includes interviews and listener call-ins. Many of these stations air national, satellite-delivered talk programs.

Other popular radio formats include Big Band, Classical, Foreign Language, New Age, Progressive, Religious and Gospel, and Urban. By the way, although there is no major trend in radio for polka music, six FM stations, all in Wisconsin, include polka music in their formats.

We should also point out that many classical stations are either public radio stations or subscriber-supported. Foreign language programming is usually carried by small FM stations, some of which run more than one language in a day.

According to the 1992 edition of *Broadcasting & Cable Market Place*, the radio programming formats in order of number of stations is as follows:

FORMAT	NUMBER OF STATIONS
Country	2,603
Adult Contemporary	2,347
Religious/Gospel	1,104
Oldies	1,020
CHR/Top 40	845
MOR	550
News	530
News/Talk	530
Classical	429
Jazz	368

An examination of the top ten formats in all the 100 leading markets (metropolitan survey areas) shows no clear-cut domination of a particular format, although music formats remain the most popular.

Further, in major markets with ten or more stations, the share for the tenth-highest-rated station may be half, or less than half, of the highest-rated station. Shares are what make the difference in advertising rates. Simply stated, WRKS-FM in New York, with 150,000 listeners and a 5.6 rating, can charge much more for its commercials than the twelfth station, WQHT-FM, with 96,000 listeners and a 3.6 rating.

The variety of radio station formats should encourage those with a particular interest in radio programming because it proves there's a format for every aspiring radio professional.

THE STARS OF TALK RADIO

Industry watchers estimate that about fifteen radio talk stars across the country earn more than $1 million a year. The acid-tongued syndicated talk show host Howard Stern is, no doubt, the leader in this select circle. His station, WXRK-FM, is number one among morning shows in the New York market.

In June 1992, superstar talk show host Don Imus reportedly signed a five-year, $15 million contract with WFAN-AM in New York. At the time of the signing of this contract, the station was only in tenth place in the New York ratings. Yet, the station management justified the huge salary for Imus, since his show brings in about $8 million to $10 million in yearly sales.

ALL-SPORTS RADIO

There is a trend toward all-sports programming. As of this writing, there are all-sports stations in San Diego, Denver, Philadelphia, and New York. The sports station in Denver, KYBG-AM, carries University of Colorado basketball and live reports of events like the French Open and the Indianapolis 500.

If this trend continues, it will mean jobs for new on-air people with sports expertise. It also opens up opportunities in the marketing and promotional areas of sports programming.

WHO LISTENS TO WHAT

The nation's largest radio market, New York City, boasts fifty AM and sixty-seven FM radio stations. This mix offers a bit of everything, including two all-news stations, two all-classical music stations (one owned by The New York Times Company), a station owned by the City of New York that carries public-radio programming, a number of college stations, and stations for call-ins to psychotherapists, psychologists, financial advisers, real estate experts, and sports editors. There are also foreign language stations, featuring Spanish, Greek, Russian, Yiddish, Polish, and Italian, and stations with every possible format of popular music.

Seattle is generally considered an upscale market. It has twelve radio stations. The format mix breaks out as follows: Golden Oldies, CHR, Easy Listening, Classical, News, Sports and Information, AOR, Adult Contemporary, and Adult Rock. Can we make a conclusion here? Not really. Most cities of Seattle's size would have a similar breakdown of formats.

Many young people probably think that their elders listen exclusively to Beautiful Music. Not so. Most men and women fifty-five and older are fans of news and talk stations.

Men aged forty-five and older often select the Big Band/Nostalgia stations that feature performers like Patti Page, Billy Eckstine, Helen O'Connell, and Rosemary Clooney, as well as the major bands of the '40s.

CHAPTER 23

Syndication
and the Networks

R adio syndication and radio networks are not the same as in television. Radio syndication sells or barters a particular entertainment or information program (or segment thereof) to radio stations. In essence, the syndicator puts together a network of stations that carries its programming. The station doesn't necessarily use this syndicated programming for its entire broadcasting day, but rather for periods of anywhere from thirty seconds to a few hours. In television, a syndicator sells or barters a particular series, for example, "The Cosby Show," no longer running on television.

In radio, there are two kinds of networks. A network may be a group of stations owned by one company, or it may be an affiliation of stations that receive programs created by a syndicator. Sometimes, a network syndicator supplies programming; in return, the station gives the syndicator some free commercial spots to sell to advertisers for cash. In other situations, the syndicator makes a straight sale of the programming to the affiliated stations.

Some examples of programs offered by syndicators in 1993:

Adventures in Good Music
A Bit about Computers
Soap Opera News
Detective Theater
Health Care Tips
Investor's Guide
American Time Capsule

Two of the three largest television networks, ABC and CBS, own several radio stations and supply programming to many affiliated stations. The networks are connected to these affiliated stations by satellite. Whereas a television affiliate usually carries at least 70 percent of its network's programming, a radio affiliate has greater autonomy.

ABC, for example, has seven satellite-delivered radio networks that provide programming to more than 3,200 affiliates nationwide. ABC, in this relationship, functions as a syndicated programmer to these stations. The term "network" as it is used here refers to stations that receive ABC's special programming under certain financial arrangements.

Let's take a closer look at the major networks in radio.

ABC

ABC owns and operates ten AM radio stations and seven FM stations, all located in major markets. Its roster includes two stations in each of the top two markets, New York and Los Angeles, and one in Chicago.

ABC's seven satellite-delivered networks provide up to 3,200 affiliated stations with special programming.

ABC Information
ABC Entertainment
ABC Direction
ABC Contemporary
ABC FM
ABC Rock
Satellite Music

These affiliates also broadcast programming other than that supplied by ABC.

In July 1989, ABC bought the Satellite Music Network, a producer of satellite-delivered live music formats, for $45 million in cash. SMN has more than 1,000 affiliates for whom they provide ten radio formats from twelve to twenty-four hours in length. ABC Information offers the resources of ABC News and ABC Direction as a nonmusic, spoken-word format.

CBS

CBS divides its radio operations into two areas. The CBS Radio Division consists of eight AM and twelve FM stations, including two each in New York, Los Angeles, and Chicago. The specialty format of the Radio Division's AM stations is news and news/talk. The format is music on its FM stations. The stations also broadcast live college and professional sports events, including major league baseball and the National Football League.

CBS Radio also has four syndication networks. CBS Radio Network provides news, sports, and information programming to 440 affiliated stations, mostly AM. CBS Spectrum provides stations with brief newscasts and an audio feature package. The CBS Hispanic Radio Network provides Spanish broadcasts of various U.S. sports events to Latin American stations. CBS Radio Programs provides music programming to a variety of FM stations.

WESTWOOD ONE

A profile of Westwood One is a profile of its dynamic founder, Norm Pattiz, the Ted Turner of radio. Pattiz built an empire from an investment of $10,000. Though jobless at the time, he ignored the classifieds, setting his sights instead on going into business for himself.

In 1974, Pattiz was listening to a local Los Angeles station's fifty-two-hour blitz of Motown music. Why, he reckoned, couldn't he package this music and syndicate it to radio stations? He spent a whole year creating a twenty-four-hour "Sound of Motown" special that he sold to 200 stations. He made some mistakes but fixed them before they were terminal and he wound up bringing in about $200,000 on the transaction.

Soon, Westwood One was outshining the major radio networks with a formula of syndicated concerts for which it bought broadcast rights, and regularly scheduled programs that it packaged and produced. His basic formula: Trading programs to radio stations for blocks of commercial spots that he then sold to national advertisers—the barter system at its simplest.

In 1985, Westwood One moved into the big time with the purchase of the fifty-two-year-old Mutual Broadcasting System syndication network, for a price of $30 million. Mutual's News, Sports, and Talk network increased Westwood One's programming inventory and broadcast capabilities while complementing the company's successful entertainment lineup.

A second major acquisition came in 1987, when Pattiz's company bought NBC's three syndicated radio networks for $50 million in cash. The sixty-two-year-old NBC Radio Networks included The Source, a leading young adult programming network, and Talknet, the most listened-to radio talk show network in the country. As though this was not enough for one year, Westwood One purchased *Radio and Records*, an important radio and music industry trade publication, for $20 million.

Among the programs Westwood One syndicates are:

"My Side of the Story" featuring Larry King
"Casey's Biggest Hits" and "Casey's Top 40," with Casey Kasem
"The Countdown with Walt Love" (urban contemporary music and interviews with personalities in this field)
"Money Magazine Business Report"
"On the Garden Side" with Jerry Baker
"Don Criqui on Sports"
"The Rock Report"
"Dr. Joyce Brothers"
"MTV News"
"The Beatle Years"

Although Westwood One's syndicated programs are primarily music, it increased emphasis on news, sports, and talk formats in the 1990s. By 1992, Westwood One's programming orbit extended to a global audience of sixty million listeners a week on about 4,000 stations.

Headquartered in Culver City, California, with offices across the country, Westwood One employs more than 500 people.

CHAPTER 24

Radio News and Talk Radio

Radio news was once the backbone of electronic journalism. It was often the first source of reporting. Now all that has changed, with television taking over the live-news-reporting function. The reason: cost cutting by radio stations whose listeners demand more entertainment and less news.

Although almost every radio station broadcasts news, in this chapter we will deal primarily with all-news stations.

Washington, D.C., had three all-news stations in the 1970s; now it has two. Stations in New York, Chicago, and San Francisco that formerly devoted a great deal of airtime to news have reduced this programming drastically. New York has only two all-news stations, as do Chicago, Los Angeles, and San Francisco. We must conclude from this that while TV news is a growing market, radio news is on the wane.

Another factor in the reduction of news time is the decreasing audience of AM stations, traditionally the source for much news broadcasting. Nevertheless, there are still approximately 380 all-news stations in the U.S. and about 20,000 people earn their living in this field.

The all-news radio stations that have survived the video news upsurge are, for the most part, profitable enterprises. Let's look at one such station, KNX Newsradio in Los Angeles.

PROFILE OF AN ALL-NEWS STATION

KNX is owned by CBS. It is a twenty-four-hour, 50,000-watt station that covers Southern California. As with any network-owned station, KNX generates its own local news and features, but draws upon its parent, CBS News, for national and international coverage.

The station's focus is Los Angeles, but its reach extends some 200 miles above Bakersfield to the north and below San Diego to the south. In the nation's second-largest market, KNX competes head-on with another news station, KFWB. The ABC network's station, KABC, with a talk formula, ranks sixth. Eight of the others in the top ten have music formats.

In terms of billing, for 1992 KNX was thirteenth in the U.S. with $21 million. Four Los Angeles music stations were also in the top ten nationwide.

A look at KNX's program schedule shows more features than news, although news is broadcast twenty-four hours a day. From 10:00 A.M. to 11:00 A.M. (not drive time), the station runs a Food News Hour that features food tips and call-ins for recipes and information. From 9:00 P.M. to 10:00 P.M. and again from 2:00 A.M. to 3:00 A.M. it broadcasts the KNX Drama Hour with classic (meaning old) radio series like Gangbusters, Sergeant Preston, The Lone Ranger, and Jack Benny.

KNX devotes considerable airtime to sports. Besides broadcasting scores and sports developments every hour, the station carries play-by-play of University of Southern California football and basketball, NFL football, major league baseball games and playoffs, the World Series, and major horse racing events.

Since KNX is a station owned by CBS, it receives many features from the network and carries network-originated pieces like "Dr. Joyce Brothers," "Dan Rather Reporting," "Speaking of Health," "On Fitness," and the inimitable "Charles Osgood File." This is in addition to the CBS network's "World News Roundup" in the morning and "The World Tonight" at 6:00 P.M., both of which cover national and international news.

For an interview with two KNX veterans, see page 295.

THE ROLE OF THE ASSOCIATED PRESS IN BROADCAST NEWS

The Associated Press (AP) is the largest news gatherer and provider for both radio and TV. Few news stations can support extensive news gathering for anything but local news. Other stations with music formats allot only a limited amount of airtime to news. About 1,000 stations subscribe to the services of AP Broadcast News. This may take the form of packaged newscasts or live special reports. AP's flexible programming covers many areas:

AP News
AP Sports
AP Business
AP Lifestyle Features
AP Public Affairs
AP Agriculture

Variety is the keynote of AP's programming. In Lifestyle Features, for example, there are special reports called Consumer Watch, Chip Talk (about computers), Health & Medicine, The Hollywood Report, Home Entertainment Update, Kid Stuff, and Pets and People.

CAREER TIP

It is particularly difficult to launch a career in radio news at the station level unless you are willing to work in the boonies. Try instead to make it with the AP. See page 116 for information on how to apply for a job with this organization.

CNN GETS INTO THE RADIO ACT

Ted Turner is a world class seizer of opportunities. With a vast news-gathering organization of nine domestic and nineteen international news bureaus and broadcast affiliates in the United States and abroad, CNN Radio is an obvious adjunct to the company's TV news network. CNN Radio provides radio stations in the United States and overseas with top-of-the-hour and half-hour newscasts and closed-circuit news-feeds throughout the day.

CNN Radio's station subscribers receive live coverage of breaking stories. These may then be aired live or tape-delayed for programming flexibility. Besides hard news, CNN also supplies its 500 affiliates with business briefings, sports updates, economic and health reports, human interest stories, entertainment news, and lifestyle features.

RADIO NEWS AS A GROWTH AREA

If you plan to go to work at a small-market radio station, you should know that there are few opportunities in the news area. A 1993 study by Professor Vernon Stone of the University of Missouri found that these small stations average one full-timer, a news director who is assisted by one part-time employee. In larger markets, the average commercial radio station has a news staff of one to two full-timers and one part-timer. About a third of the stations in large and major markets have three or more full-time news staff.

The study estimated that of approximately 16,000 people working in radio news in 1993, about 9,000 worked full-time and 7,000 part-time.

CHAPTER 25

Radio Sales

THE STRUCTURE AND SCOPE OF RADIO SALES

In 1992, the total spent on radio advertising was $8.77 billion, about one-third of the amount spent on TV, and about 7 percent of the total for all advertising spending.

Radio's advertising is divided into three categories—network, spot, and local. For 1992, the respective breakdowns in advertising revenues were as follows:

Network	$388 million
Spot	$1.48 billion
Local	$6.9 billion

Let's define each category.

Network In chapter 23 we discussed networks. In radio, a network may be a group of ABC's seventeen owned and operated (O&O) stations, or it may be one of the same company's seven satellite-delivered networks, like their Satellite Music Network that has 1,000 affiliated stations.

Since a company's O&Os have different formats and different audiences, it is rare for an advertiser to buy a campaign in all these stations; however, a network like Satellite Music can aim for an audience composition of a particular age, sex, and income, and can target a company's advertising to this group. An example would be a campaign by Levi's to reach males and females between the ages of eighteen and twenty-five.

Spot Advertising Spot radio advertising pinpoints a particular market (population survey area) or demographic grouping. An advertiser like American Express may buy spot ads in a dozen large cities to encourage use of its charge card and to support local retailers and restaurants that accept the card. The ad buy might specify that the commercials run once an hour during morning and evening drive time, five days a week.

Another typical spot radio campaign is the Florida Citrus Commission's October drive to place ads in thirty to thirty-five specific markets and promote the health benefits of citrus products.

Spot radio advertising is also an accurate, measurable means for testing a new product. An example is Xerox's spot radio campaign for a new copier that was tested recently in Phoenix. Listeners were asked to call an 800 number for further information about the equipment. Of these callers, 25 percent then bought the product. On the strength of this test, the campaign was extended nationally.

Local Advertising Local advertising accounts for almost 80 percent of all radio advertising. Some examples might be two thirty-second spots a day for a local pizzeria on a Top-40 station or a campaign for a local auto dealer on an all-news station. The amount spent on local radio advertising comes to $6.9 billion a year.

THE TECHNIQUES OF SELLING RADIO TIME

Commercial radio stations live and profit from the sale of commercials. Selling this advertising effectively is the formidable task of a corps of local, regional, and national salespeople. Here are some challenges they face:

* Many competitive forces are at play. Advertisers in a local market can buy TV time, newspaper and magazine ads, space in shoppers (advertising circulars), and on billboards.
* Effectiveness of advertising is often difficult to prove.
* Radio is not always the most efficient medium on a "cost-per-thousand" basis, the standard used in broadcast and print to evaluate the efficiency of advertising dollars. This standard measures the cost of reaching a thousand people. For example, if a commercial costs $100 and the show has an audience of 10,000, the cost per thousand is $10.00. If, however, a newspaper ad in the same market can reach these 10,000 people for $80.00 (cost per thousand: $8.00), it is considered more "efficient" on a cost-per-thousand basis.
* Agencies prefer television because it represents a bigger profit potential for them than radio.

The radio salesperson must overcome these obstacles with creativity and high energy. One advantage of radio advertising is its ability to target advertisers more efficiently than TV. While TV can sell an audience composition of, say, eighteen to forty-nine, or twenty-five to fifty-four, radio can target its listeners into smaller segments.

Two important tools the radio salesperson must use are ratings and rating points. Ratings measure the audience of a radio program as estimated by survey. Radio time is also sold on its cost-per-rating point. If a radio network, for example, charges $2,000 per thirty-second commercial and attains an average quarter-hour rating of 1.0 percent among the target population group, its cost-per-rating point is $2,000 ($2,000 divided by 1.0).

WHO SELLS RADIO ADVERTISING

Each of the three principal categories of radio advertising—network, spot, and local—is sold somewhat differently.

Network Radio Advertising

ABC, CBS, and Group W own many stations. Westwood One sells advertising on behalf of its networks. They each maintain staffs of sales representatives to sell advertising for their O&O stations and their networks. For example, word goes out to the advertising trade publications that a major marketer, say, PepsiCo, has made successful tests of a new product and wants to reach teenagers via a radio campaign. ABC, CBS, Group W, and Westwood One have affiliated networks that reach this audience. To gain this new business, the sales staffs of these networks will pitch the client, PepsiCo, and its advertising agency, to win this substantial piece of business. The winning networks will carry PepsiCo's commercials on all their stations that have teenage audiences.

Network sales organizations have offices in many major cities. These sales groups can coordinate their efforts so they can cover an agency in one city and a client in another.

Spot Radio Advertising

Spot radio is sold by the networks' sales organizations, by two large rep firms, InterRep and Katz Radio, and by several smaller rep firms. These reps have offices in major metropolitan centers and sell their clients' commercial time to advertisers and agencies. Stations pay an agreed rate of commission. Since few radio stations are large enough to support a staff of advertising salespeople, most use rep firms to handle ad sales for them.

Here's how sales reps operate for a radio station. Let's say that Procter & Gamble is test-marketing a new soap product in the South Florida area. Rather than contacting the stations in that market individually, P&G's ad agency calls the national sales reps, InterRep and Katz, and buys time on the stations they represent, based on efficiency, audience ratings, and other criteria. The rep firms provide these data about their South Florida stations.

Similarly, suppose a national brokerage company, Merrill Lynch, wishes to inaugurate a radio advertising campaign in fifteen major cities. They decide that classical and news stations in these markets are the best medium to target their message to upscale audiences. Merrill Lynch and its agency call on the radio sales reps to make presentations for their individual station clients.

The rep firms that sell spot radio are substantial organizations within themselves. InterRep employs more than 100 sales people in forty-five offices across the country and sells about $600 million of radio advertising a year.

About 1,500 radio salespeople sell network and spot radio. Four times as many salespeople sell TV time.

Local Radio Advertising

Local radio is by far the largest source of advertising for the medium—$6.9 billion in 1992. This figure includes only the advertising sold by local radio stations' staffs to local advertisers. It is estimated that large stations employ about twelve people in this role and small ones about three, for an average of seven. It is estimated that there are about 70,000 sales jobs at local radio stations.

Work in local radio sales is painstaking yet creative. The salesperson must sell against other media, and is often asked to contribute in the preparation of a local advertiser's commercial.

WOMEN IN RADIO SALES

In at least one creative area of broadcasting, women have achieved parity with men—radio sales. InterRep has a sales force that is three-quarters female. Women traditionally came into this field as secretaries but have moved up as sales assistants or researchers, and from there into sales.

A study conducted by the Radio Advertising Bureau in early 1991 showed that women held 48 percent of all broadcast sales jobs, up from 37.5 percent in 1981. Minorities hold 7 percent of these jobs. Women account for 27 percent of all management jobs at the stations, versus only 7 percent in TV.

INTERVIEW: ELLEN HULLEBERG ON A DAY IN THE LIFE OF A NATIONAL SALES REP

We asked Ellen Hulleberg, former president of McGavren Guild (now a part of InterRep), about the life of a national radio rep salesperson.

We start at 8:30 A.M. with a sales meeting. Salespeople discuss techniques and opportunities, or a station person discusses qualitative data on a particular station. Then our people make calls at advertising agencies and, occasionally, at advertiser clients. On another typical day we will fly out to visit a station we represent for a day or two. When in their home office, salespeople make several agency calls per day.

There is no fixed number of calls per day or week that must be made; it's up to the salespeople themselves. Their compensation is based on sales results, so they have to hustle. In New York, each salesperson is a specialist for some of the stations he or she represents so they will spend a lot of time camping out at an agency. This "specialist" will necessarily develop personal relationships with every radio decision-maker at that agency.

The radio reps' tools of the trade are up-to-date data on the stations they cover. Our firm uses a research memory system. New data, including the latest station information, goes into our computer. We receive mail every day with all the changes in the marketplace.

Most of our time is spent going after existing radio dollars. We don't sell against TV or newspaper advertising, although our firm has six people calling on advertisers to interest them in radio as a vital medium. Radio selling requires a lot of paper work. We try to take care of the paper work for the customer.

Another problem we face is that creative directors at ad agencies are interested in getting recognition by winning awards for TV ads. We are starting to develop awards in radio, but TV still has that area locked in.

Network radio is growing tremendously, and sales representation for this field is doing very well, but local radio sales is probably the best area overall because it is growing even more rapidly than national, and more emphasis is being placed on local business. A local radio advertiser is better able to track the success of a campaign than a national advertiser.

Our advice for people eager to get a job in radio sales is to contact a company like InterRep or to try for an internship program at another rep company. Also, they should try to get their schools to give credit for internship work. More and more colleges are doing this.

THE COMMITMENT OF
NATIONAL ADVERTISERS TO RADIO

In 1992, radio advertising revenues hit $8.77 billion. As a group, the top five advertisers in radio were the following:

Sears, Roebuck & Co.	$68 million
AT&T	$36 million
General Motors	$26 million
Philip Morris Cos.	$26 million
Anheuser-Busch	$25 million

Source: LNA/Arbitron; Radio Advertising Bureau

Many national advertisers use radio for specific marketing purposes. Others buy radio as a hedge against the spiraling cost of TV advertising. Two beer companies, Miller and Anheuser-Busch, spend a total of about $60 million a year on network and spot radio advertising.

THE COMMITMENT OF
LOCAL ADVERTISERS TO RADIO

Many local businesses rely on local radio advertising to peddle their wares. Who spends the most? Here's a list of the leading categories for 1992 in order of their total spending.

Retail
Services (mostly financial)
Automotive
Drug Products
Food (includes restaurants)
Travel
Entertainment and Amusement
Beer and Wine

Source: LNA/Arbitron; Radio Advertising Bureau

THE TOP-BILLING RADIO STATIONS

While not even approaching the revenues of big-city network TV stations, big-city radio stations generate respectable revenues. Table 11 lists the top ten for 1992.

TABLE 11. TOP-BILLING RADIO STATIONS

STATION	FORMAT	TOTAL BILLINGS IN MILLIONS
1. WGN-AM Chicago	MOR/Talk	$40.4
2. KABC-AM Los Angeles	Talk	$31.0
3. KOST-FM Los Angeles	Soft AC	$30.5
4. WINS-AM New York	News	$30.0
5. WFAN-AM New York	Sports/Talk	$29.0
6. KLOS-FM Los Angeles	AOR	$28.1
7. WLTW-FM New York	Soft AC	$25.4
8. WCBS-FM New York	Oldies	$25.3
9. KGO-AM San Francisco	News/Talk	$25.0
10. KIIS-AM/FM Los Angeles	CHR	$24.0

Source: Duncan's Radio Market Guide, *1992 Edition*

(Note that the list of top-billing stations is different from the list in chapter 22 of the highest-rated stations. Advertisers will often pay a high rate for advertising on a low-rated station in a market because of the quality of its audience. They will also pay higher rates to reach the upscale audiences of talk and news stations.)

About a dozen other stations do over $20 million in advertising billings. Los Angeles is the nation's second-largest radio market, not surprising considering drive time. It has four of the top-ten billing stations.

As TV prices itself beyond the range of many advertisers, the radio market expands, offering a healthy opportunity for aggressive new salespeople to sell radio advertising, particularly at the local station level.

THE RADIO ADVERTISING BUREAU

The industry founded the Radio Advertising Bureau (RAB) in 1951 to increase radio's share of advertising revenues by designing, developing, and implementing appropriate programs, research tools, and activities.

RAB serves as the sales and marketing arm of America's commercial radio broadcast industry. In pursuing this objective, the group's literature emphasizes radio's advantages, like high listenership, the effectiveness of daytime and weekend radio, and the medium's dominance with the "auto audience."

RAB functions in many different areas. Their Sales Education Program, for instance, offers courses called For Rookies Only, For the Journeyman, For Specialization, For the Highly Skilled, and For the Sales Executives. The Rookie program is conducted as an intense weekend course taught by veteran radio sales managers.

In what RAB calls their "Fort Knox of Radio Creativity," they house an extensive sound library of classic and current radio commercials (more than 1,000 tapes containing more than 320,000 commercials).

Ten times a year RAB publishes a magazine for marketing professionals called *Sound Management*. Written for radio professionals, it also contains information of value to those entering the field such as marketing techniques, employment practices, success stories, and business trends. For information write to:

Radio Advertising Bureau
304 Park Avenue South
New York, NY 10010.

WHAT WILL YOU EARN SELLING RADIO?

According to a 1991 study conducted by Charles Warner of the Journalism School of the University of Missouri, the average compensation for a radio station's top salesperson in the 99 largest radio markets is $70,000. Average compensation for the top salesperson, whatever the market size, was $56,000.

The average radio salesperson earns $32,000, while a station's lowest paid salesperson earns $20,000. Nationwide, the average general sales manager earns $66,000; markets 1 through 99 average $83,000, according to the study. The study has not been updated, but traditionally radio sales compensation increases about 4 or 5 percent a year.

These are not huge salaries by TV standards, but the jobs are easier to get and, as we have pointed out, represent prime opportunities for women.

Radio sales is a growing field. Successful salespeople make almost as much money as their TV counterparts. Local sales jobs are not difficult to find and afford a good training ground for big-city sales jobs.

CHAPTER 26

Public Radio

EARLY HISTORY

One of the first broadcast stations in the United States, 9XM, was built in a University of Wisconsin physics laboratory. Renamed WHA-AM, it remains a major station in the public radio system.

By 1925, colleges and universities had 171 AM licenses; however, with the increased competition from commercial broadcasting, most of these stations were off the air by 1934, when the FCC was started.

In 1941, when regular FM broadcasting began, five channels were authorized for noncommercial educational use as a substitute for AM allocations no longer in place.

In 1948, the FCC authorized ten-watt operation on educational FM channels. This enabled schools and colleges to broadcast to a limited area of two to five miles for an outlay of a few thousand dollars. By 1978, 973 educational FM stations were on the air. At this writing, that figure reaches 1,900.

Public broadcasting in its present form emerged with the passage of the Public Broadcasting Act of 1967. That act authorized the establishment of the Corporation for Public Broadcasting (CPB), whose primary function is to funnel federal funds to qualified noncommercial licensees.

THE SCOPE OF PUBLIC RADIO TODAY

The Corporation for Public Broadcasting uses the designation "CPB-qualified stations" for those stations eligible for CPB financial support. The criteria cover facilities, funds, staff, and the quality of programming. In 1970, there were 96 CPB-qualified stations, in 1985, 275 stations, and by 1990, more than 350 stations receiving this support.

Subscriber support for public radio has grown as well. The average subscriber contributes over $40 a year to public radio. The number of subscribers grew from a mere 64,000 in 1973 to 850,000 in 1983, and to well over 1,000,000 in 1990. In the same period, listenership increased from 2.6 million weekly cumulative audience in 1973 to 13 million in 1990.

In the late '70s, when the privately chartered Carnegie Commission made its report on public broadcasting, the largest station in the public radio system had a budget of approximately $1.2 million, and the smallest had $100,000. By 1993, many of these stations had budgets in excess of $1 million.

PROGRAMMING AND AUDIENCE

The programming mix of public radio is eclectic and informed. Here is the breakdown from CPB's 1992 Annual Report:

Music	68.6%
News and Public Affairs	19.3%
Information	7.7%
Spoken Word/Performance	3.8%
Instructional	0.6%

The average local public radio station broadcasts for about twenty-two hours a day, although nearly half the stations broadcast twenty-four hours a day. Classical music and the National Public Radio "News Magazines" are the dominant formats.

As we have already noted, there are more than thirteen million weekly listeners to public radio. Yet this medium serves only a small portion of American radio listeners—about one out of every sixteen adults or teenagers. Although its audience cuts across most demographic lines, public radio appeals to an educated and loyal group. About one third of an average listener's total radio listening is to a public radio station. Per week, the average listener spends seven hours and fifty minutes with public radio.

NATIONAL PUBLIC RADIO

National Public Radio (NPR) was established in 1970 to link various public radio stations and provide them with programming service.

NPR is a network of about 450 noncommercial, nonprofit stations. The individual stations create their own programming to supplement that provided by NPR. The network's most important programs are "Morning Edition," "Weekend Edition," and "All Things Considered." The three programs have a news-and-information format that includes the independent journalism and political observations of analysts like Nina Totenberg, Kevin Philips, and Daniel Schorr. The shows have an average weekly listenership of about five million. These NPR radio programs provide in-depth story coverage and emphasis on the arts, along with headline stories and interviews—all without commercial interruption.

With a reduction of federal funding in the early '80s, NPR sought revenues through commercial ventures. These efforts almost forced the network into bankruptcy. Fortunately, a $9 million loan from CPB bailed them out.

NPR member stations are independent, autonomous broadcast entities. Each station bases its own programming format on the needs of the audience it serves. The network distributes its programming through the public-radio satellite system.

NPR operates with a monthly program budget of $1.7 million that seldom covers its eighteen-hour programming schedule. Support usually comes from its more affluent member stations, those that raise the largest sums from the public and are the recipients of the highest grants from the CPB.

AMERICAN PUBLIC RADIO

In public radio, unlike commercial broadcasting, stations may be part of more than one major network. American Public Radio (APR) is an independent, nonprofit program distribution company with more than 315 affiliate stations. APR develops, funds, acquires, and distributes public radio programming from independent and international producers. It distributes 200 hours of programming weekly. Most APR affiliates are also member stations of National Public Radio, and vice versa.

CAREER TIP

Gain your experience as a volunteer in public radio, particularly when you're in college. You probably won't get paid, but at least you'll accumulate on-air or technical experience that may help you land a commercial radio job.

PART VI

Pursuing a Career in Broadcasting

Courtesy Viacom International Inc.

CHAPTER 27

Colleges and Universities Offering Programs in Television and Radio

The Broadcast Education Association (BEA) publishes an annual *BEA Membership Directory and Guide to Broadcast and Telecommunications Departments in Colleges and Universities*. It lists more than 950 BEA member departments and individual members, arranged by state, that award two-year undergraduate and graduate degrees in communications, television, and radio around the United States. It is available for $20, plus $2 for shipping and handling. Order from:

Broadcast Education Association
1771 N Street, N.W.
Washington, DC 20036-2891.

The American Film Institute (AFI) also offers a comprehensive list of hundreds of colleges and universities with programs in this specialty—*The American Film Institute Guide to College Courses in Film and Television*. It is available for $20. Order from:

The American Film Institute
2021 N. Western Avenue
Los Angeles, CA 90027-1625.

Many schools offer undergraduate programs in film, television and broadcast journalism. There are also about two dozen colleges that offer graduate programs in these disciplines. Students often ask, "Should I go to graduate school, or can I achieve the same training through internships and work experience?"

The answer, of course, is complex. Here are some advantages of attending graduate school:

* Exposure to a faculty with field experience.
* Availability of professional technical facilities.
* Lectures by guests from the industry.
* Participation in the programming and production of material for on-campus, closed-circuit television, and cable.
* Opportunities for off-campus independent study.

If you attend a college with undergraduate majors in News Editorial, Broadcast Management, and Production, you may not need graduate school. Summer internships, free or paid, and the training you will receive at a small station may be as rewarding as graduate school.

You should ask some basic questions before making a commitment to a graduate school. Does the school place many of its students in internship programs? Does the school have an active placement service, and what is its record? What has been the career path of recent graduates?

Although there have not been any official evaluations of graduate programs in broadcast or broadcast journalism, the most highly regarded in film and television include:

University of California (Los Angeles) (UCLA)
University of Southern California (USC)
American Film Institute (Los Angeles)
Temple University (Philadelphia)
Syracuse University
University of Texas

The largest undergraduate program in this discipline is conducted by Temple, which has 1,500 students. USC has 700 undergraduates in its film and TV program and 700 graduate students. UCLA has 355 graduate students and offers six masters programs with various specializations. The university also maintains the largest extension program in the nation, with dozens of courses in broadcasting.

In the field of broadcast journalism education, Columbia University, New York University, and the University of Missouri are outstanding. Here is a capsule of the unique program at Missouri:

The School of Journalism at the University of Missouri (Columbia) offers a Master of Arts in Journalism. Students in this program prepare for careers in both print and broadcast media. The program is based on (1) a core curriculum, (2) an optional area of emphasis, and (3) a capstone experience in which the student writes a thesis or produces a professional project.

Students at the University of Missouri's graduate programs participate in the operation of the school's daily newspaper, Sunday magazine, commercial TV station, and public radio station. In one radio course, for example, Radio News Reporting and Editing, students prepare newscasts for the college's station, KBIA. In Television News Reporting and Editing, students report, write news stories, record and edit videotape for news broadcasts on the school's commercial TV station, KOMU-TV.

With the obvious benefits of undergraduate and graduate programs to broadcasting careers, readers may wisely consider planning to include this specialized education.

INTERVIEW: ANNA CARR

Anna Carr, a 1987 graduate of the University of Missouri's undergraduate broadcast sequence and now Assistant Promotion Manager of KOMU-TV, offers a perspective on this specific program and information on preparation for entering the field of broadcasting. Here are some of Carr's comments about the school and working at the station.

* * *

We do have something I would consider special in terms of preparing graduates for the "real world" of broadcasting. I recently had a conversation with a friend of mine who graduated from the program a year earlier than I did. She remarked how after working with people who had graduated from other programs, she could really see the benefits of her "Mizzou" education. While she could go out, report, write, shoot, and edit a story for the evening newscast, her colleagues were better at debating the fine points of ethics. They didn't know which end of the camera was up! Please don't think I'm belittling the ethics training, as we also include courses in legal issues and ethics in broadcasting. I still feel her point is valid. We send people out who can actually start working at a station, knowing a little something about putting together a newscast, either as a reporter, an anchor, or a producer. KOMU-TV is licensed to the curators of the University of Missouri. We were first on the air in mid-Missouri in December 1953. We are the NBC affiliate for mid-Missouri, and our market is Columbia and Jefferson City, Missouri. At last report, we were listed as the 150th market.

Generally, for the first two years at the University students take liberal arts courses fulfilling some pretty strict requirements, including thirteen hours of a foreign language. They are also required to take courses in math, English, science, and the humanities in an attempt to give the students a wide basis of information. As sophomores, the students petition to enter the broadcast program. Only the cream of the crop are accepted. They must have at least a 3.5 g.p.a., and have fulfilled all the lower-level course work. For those accepted, the journalism training begins in their junior year.

I won't pretend that it's easy to get in. It isn't. When I applied to the broadcast sequence, there were over 120 applicants for 60 slots. The school looked at everything from how we did on freshman placement tests, to g.p.a., to an essay we had to write. I was one of the students chosen and it was a real thrill. Of those original 60, I would guess that half graduated with me. Others took extra semesters; others didn't make it. At the station, we have recently started some other opportunities for students. I now have an internship program for interested students from any department, and we have an excellent placement record for those graduates. We even helped one of our interns create a new position in promotions at a station. We have students working on special series and projects, like KidsCenter 8. That particular student coordinates with local schools and shows the children how to report and write a story. We then send a crew in to shoot the piece with the children. We edit it and run it. It has been very successful, and the student involved has gained invaluable experience.

The journalism course work includes the basics, such as how to write for broadcasting, shooting, anchoring, reporting, and editing. We also include classes on communication law, history and principles of journalism, and mass media. In addition to our TV station, the students have an opportunity to work at the public radio station that we own, KBIA, or at the commercial newspaper, *The Missourian.*

CHAPTER 28

Internships in Broadcasting

INTERNSHIP PROGRAMS

Broadcasting offers interesting and often dynamic careers for increasing numbers of talented and creative people. It is a challenging industry that seeks individuals who possess imagination, initiative, sound judgment, and an understanding of communications in general and broadcasting specifically. For those with ability and determination, the rewards can be great.

Student and postgraduate internship programs provide valuable training for broadcast careers. Wisely, many students participate in these programs while still at college. Others pursue internships after graduation. Of course, a paid internship is desirable, but the amount of nuts-and-bolts training given is equally important. We have often heard of unpaid interns distinguishing themselves so much that they are offered a paying job at a station or network.

Public TV stations, by the very nature of their operations, are a good training ground. Internships at these stations may be easier to come by than at commercial stations.

Before signing up for an internship, ask about the duties and training opportunities. Even if you accept the role of gofer, you will want to know if you will have a specific mentor. Further, if you go to work for a TV station, will you get a chance to go into the field with camera and reporting crews and learn about the entire production process?

Academy of Television Arts & Sciences

A coveted internship in television is the one conducted by the Academy of Television Arts & Sciences. It offers twenty-eight internships in Los Angeles in an eight-week summer period. The program includes on-the-job training in twenty-four areas of the TV industry. Among these are:

Animation Production
Casting
Children's Programming/Development
Cinematography
Daytime Programming
Film Editing
Movies for Television
Network Programming Management
Public Relations
TV Directing
TV Scriptwriting
Videotape Post Production

Interns are assigned to industry professionals who serve as mentors and supervise their work. Their host employers cover a broad range of the industry, including the networks, TV stations, production houses, studios, and ancillary companies. The experience and exposure students gain through this direct contact with high-level professionals is unmatched among student internship programs in the communications field.

Posters and flyers go to 900 colleges and universities to announce the competition for the Academy's internship program. An applicant enters the competition by sending the Academy a resume, a transcript, letters of recommendation, and an essay. More than 900 students apply each year for the 28 openings.

Once accepted, each intern receives a stipend of $1,600 for the eight weeks and a $300 travel/housing allowance. Many graduates of the Academy's program stay on in Los Angeles to work in the TV industry.

For information, write to:

The Academy of TV Arts & Sciences
5220 Lankershim Blvd.
N. Hollywood, CA 91601-3109
(818) 754-2800.

The Academy of Television Arts & Sciences Foundation Annual College Television Awards

The Academy sponsors an annual student film/video competition for college students. Categories for submission are: Comedy, Drama, Music, Documentary News and Public Affairs, and Education. First prize in each category is $1,000, second prize, $500.

For entry forms and information, see your college's TV and film department or write to:

Academy of TV Arts and Sciences
5220 Lankershim Blvd.
N. Hollywood, CA 91601-3109.

The International Radio and Television Society's College Conference and Summer Fellowship Program

The International Radio and Television Society (IRTS) is a membership organization of 1,600 professionals in broadcasting. Each year the group sponsors the nine-week College Conference and Summer Fellowship Program. Out of 600 applicants, 23 full-time undergraduates are selected for an educational and work fellowship program in New York.

For one week, industry professionals give the fellows a comprehensive orientation in broadcasting, cable, and advertising. Then comes an eight-week fellowship working for the four major networks, national rep firms, ad agencies, or cable operators.

Those selected for the program receive air or train fare, housing at a local college dormitory, and a small stipend to defray the cost of food, commuting, and personal expenses. IRTS also provides supervision and counseling to insure that each student makes the most of this New York experience. For information on this outstanding program, write to:

Maria DeLeon
IRTS
420 Lexington Ave., Suite 1714
New York, NY 10170-0101.

Applications must be received by the third week in November.

Capital Cities/ABC Student Internship Opportunities
Capital Cities/ABC has a program for minority students that begins after their junior year in high school and runs through college graduation. They receive a salary and compensation to help pay college tuition. After completing this course of work and training, interns are eligible for full-time positions at the company.

Capital Cities/ABC's television, radio, and publishing properties offers internship opportunities for other college students too.

Between 1988 and 1992, the company's largest broadcast station, WABC-TV in New York, accepted about 250 juniors and seniors from some forty area colleges and universities. Each semester, the station places interns in four-month slots. They work in departments such as news, programming sales and research, creative services and on shows like "LIVE! with Regis and Kathie Lee," "New York Views," and "Tiempo."

For information on this program, contact:

Capital Cities/ABC
77 West 66 Street
New York, NY 10023.

NBC Internship Program
NBC conducts an internship for college students seeking course credit. Students must participate at least three days per week. For the summer program, applications must be received by April 11, and for the winter program by September 11.

For information on this program, write to:

Internship Program Coordinator
Human Resources Department
NBC
30 Rockefeller Plaza
New York, NY 10112.

Turner Broadcasting System's Internship Program

One of the most attractive internships available in broadcast journalism is at Turner Broadcasting. That's the good part. The bad part is you don't get paid. Yet each year hundreds of college students vie for the opportunity of interning at this dynamic company.

Turner Broadcasting accepts college juniors, seniors, and graduate-level students for unpaid internships at over thirty different departments of the network, including such high-profile shows as "Crossfire," "Larry King Live," and "CNN Headline News."

Assignments may be served at Turner's headquarters in Atlanta, in Washington, D.C., or in New York City. Interns are responsible for their own housing, but Turner helps in the search. The program accepts about 400 interns a year, 100 for each quarter. Generally, the internship program is designed for student volunteers who will receive academic credit from their colleges and universities.

Turner's program offers a good way to gain on-the-job experience and the opportunity to obtain important recommendations for future employment.

CNN's Internship Program

CNN's Video Journalist (VJ) program is a paid, entry-level, apprenticeship program that has grown increasingly competitive for the nation's top journalism graduates. It lasts six months and offers experience operating studio cameras, ripping scripts (separating six individual scripts that are distributed to anchors and producers), logging and editing tapes, and the like. Interns learn editing, writing, and producing skills, and then enter either operations or editorial jobs as their skills and training dictate.

For information on the Turner and CNN internship programs, write to:

Jackie Trube, Intern Coordinator
Turner Broadcasting System
One CNN Center
PO Box 105366
Atlanta, GA 30348-5366
(404) 827-2490.

Writer's Digest

Writer's Digest Books, located in Cincinnati, Ohio, publishes an annual listing of internships. The 1992 Internships contains 34,000 on-the-job training opportunities for all types of careers. Included are about one hundred TV internships and fifty in radio. The listings give the name of the company, the number of internships offered, whether they are paid or unpaid, and a job description.

19— Internships is available in most college, university, and large libraries.

Voice of America and USIA

The U.S. Information Agency and its broadcast arm, the Voice of America, are headquartered in Washington, D.C. These agencies employ broadcast technicians, writers, and producers who work in Washington and overseas. These jobs require an appropriate degree from an accredited institution or the equivalent in education and experience.

To keep you aware of openings, the agencies provide recorded numbers that are updated weekly. For openings at VOA, call (202) 619-0909; for openings at USIA, call (202) 619-4539.

To apply for one or more positions mentioned in the recordings, send one (or more, if needed) SF-171 forms (application for federal-government employment) to:

Voice of America
Room 1543, Cohen Bldg.
330 Independence Ave., S.W.
Washington, DC 20547

U.S. Information Agency
Room 518
301 Fourth Street, S.W.
Washington, DC 20547.

The National Association of Broadcasters

The National Association of Broadcasters (NAB) is the broadcasting industry's largest association. Its members include all the major TV and radio networks and nearly 5,000 radio stations and 950 TV stations.

NAB's activities encompass legal and regulatory affairs, human-resources development, public service and public affairs, research and planning, and science and technology services.

NAB's Human Resource Development Department maintains an Employment Clearinghouse that processes more than 2,000 resumes yearly in twenty-six job-skill categories, affording prospective employees a free resume bank.

NAB Human Resources Development also conducts workshops and seminars to provide students and industry professionals with information and advice on jobs and career strategies.

For information on the NAB Employment Clearinghouse, write to:

NAB Employment Clearinghouse
1771 N Street, N.W.
Washington, DC 20036-2891
(202) 429-5498.

NAB also publishes two booklets of interest to those planning careers in broadcasting: *Careers in Television*, Item #3012, and *Careers in Radio*, Item #3011. Each booklet costs $3.50; all orders and payment should go to:

NAB Services
Dept. 391
1771 N Street, N.W.
Washington, DC 20036-2891.

International Alliance of Theatrical Stage Employees (IATSE)

The important TV and film industry union, IATSE, offers apprenticeship programs of two to four years' duration through its various local unions. Those interested should contact the main office in New York to find local unions in their area of interest. The address:

IATSE
1515 Broadway
New York, NY 10036
(212) 730-1770.

The Walt Disney Company's Summer Intern Program

Disney runs a three-month internship program in various departments of the company. Interns are given a small stipend. Send a resume and cover letter stating your area of interest—TV, film, animation—to:

Brenda Vangsness
The Walt Disney Studios
500 S. Buena Vista Street
Burbank, CA 91521
(818) 560-1807.

The American Film Institute Television Writers Summer Workshop

The AFI conducts an advanced training program for writers. The program consists of seminars, case studies, individual work, and staged readings. Leading figures in the industry serve as faculty and mentors. Ideal candidates for this program are new writers with media or theater backgrounds who have no major commercial TV writing credits. For an application, write to:

The American Film Institute
Production Training Division
2021 N. Western Avenue
Los Angeles, CA 90027.

Corporation for Public Broadcasting's Employer Outreach Program

The CPB serves as a resource center that aids in affirmative action recruiting and hiring in public TV and radio. It runs an open job-line listing various opportunities in this field (1-800-583-8220). Their address is:

Employer Outreach Program
Human Resources Department
Corporation for Public Broadcasting
901 E Street, N.W.
Washington, DC 20004.

IMPORTANT ADDRESSES IN BROADCASTING

If you are considering a career in TV or radio, contact the following networks, unions, and industry organizations about internships and employment opportunities. For interviews with any of these organizations it is best to apply through the human resources departments.

The Broadcast Networks

Capital Cities/ABC Inc.
77 West 66 Street
New York, NY 10023

CBS Inc.
51 West 52 Street
New York, NY 10019

Fox Inc.
10201 W. Pico Blvd.
Los Angeles, CA 90035

NBC
30 Rockefeller Plaza
New York, NY 10112

NBC
3000 W. Alameda Ave.
Burbank, CA 91523

Public Broadcasting Service (PBS)
1320 Braddock Place
Alexandria, VA 22314

PBS
1790 Broadway
New York, NY 10019

The Studios and Production Companies

ABC Productions
4151 Prospect Ave.
Los Angeles, CA 90027

The Cannell Studios
7083 Hollywood Blvd.
Hollywood, CA 90028

The Carsey-Werner Co.
4024 Radford Ave.
Studio City, CA 91604

CBS Entertainment Productions
7800 Beverly Blvd.
Los Angeles, CA 90036

Children's TV Workshop
One Lincoln Plaza
New York, NY 10023

Columbia Pictures Television
3400 Riverside Drive
Burbank, CA 91505

King World Productions
1700 Broadway
New York, NY 10019

Lorimar Television
300 S. Lorimar Plaza
Burbank, CA 91505

MGM Worldwide Television Group
10000 W. Washington Blvd.
Culver City, CA 90232

MacNeil/Lehrer Productions
1775 Broadway
New York, NY 10019

MTM
4024 Radford Avenue
Studio City, CA 91604

NBC Productions
330 Bob Hope Drive
Burbank, CA 91523

Paramount Television Group
5555 Melrose Avenue
Hollywood, CA 90038

Spelling Television
5700 Wilshire Blvd.
Los Angeles, CA 90036

Twentieth Television
P.O. Box 900
Beverly Hills, CA 90213

Universal Television
70 Universal City Plaza
Universal City, CA 91608

Viacom Productions
10 Universal City Plaza
Universal City, CA 91608

Walt Disney Television
500 S. Buena Vista Street
Burbank, CA 91521

Warner Bros. TV
4000 Warner Blvd.
Burbank, CA 91523

Witt/Thomas/Harris Productions
846 N. Cahuenga Blvd.
Hollywood, CA 90038

The Cable Networks

Arts & Entertainment
235 East 45 Street
New York, NY 10017

CNBC
2200 Fletcher Avenue
Ft. Lee, NJ 07024

CNN
One CNN Center
P.O. Box 105366
Atlanta, GA 30348-5366

Comedy Central
1775 Broadway
New York, NY 10019

The Disney Channel
3800 W. Alameda Avenue
Burbank, CA 91505

ESPN
605 Third Avenue
New York, NY 10158

HBO
1100 Avenue of Americas
New York, NY 10036

HBO
2049 Century Park East, Suite 4100
Los Angeles, CA 90067-3215

Lifetime Television
36-12 35th Avenue
Astoria, NY 11106

MTV Networks
1515 Broadway
New York, NY 10036

Nickelodeon
1515 Broadway
New York, NY 10036

Showtime Networks
20 Universal City Plaza
Universal City, CA 91608-1097

USA Network
1230 Avenue of Americas
New York, NY 10020

The Unions

American Federation of TV & Radio Artists (AFTRA)
National Office
260 Madison Avenue
New York, NY 10016

AFTRA (West Coast)
6922 Hollywood Blvd.
Hollywood, CA 90028

Directors Guild of America (DGA) East
110 West 57 Street
New York, NY 10019

DGA West
7950 Sunset Blvd.
Los Angeles, CA 90046

National Association of Broadcast Employees &
Technicians (NABET)
7101 Wisconsin Ave.
Bethesda, MD 20814

Screen Actors Guild (SAG) East
1700 Broadway
New York, NY 10019

SAG West
7065 Hollywood Blvd.
Hollywood, CA 90028-6065

Writers Guild of America (WGA) East
555 West 57 Street
New York, NY 10019

WGA West
8955 Beverly Blvd.
W. Hollywood, CA 90048

Industry Associations and Trade Groups

Academy of TV Arts & Sciences
4605 Lankershim Blvd.
N. Hollywood, CA 91602

American Film Institute
J.F.K. Center for Performing Arts
Washington, DC 20566

American Women in Radio & TV
1321 Connecticut Avenue, N.W.
Washington, DC 20036

Broadcast Education Association
1771 N Street, N.W.
Washington, DC 20036

Cable TV Information Center
Mark Center Office Park
1500 N. Beauregard St.
Alexandria, VA 22311

Corporation for Public Broadcasting
1111 16th Street, N.W.
Washington, DC 20036

International Radio and TV Society
420 Lexington Avenue, Suite 1714
New York, NY 10170-0101

National Association of Broadcasters
1771 N Street, N.W.
Washington, DC 20036

National Cable TV Association
1724 Massachusetts Ave., N.W.
Washington, DC 20036

Radio Advertising Bureau
304 Park Avenue
New York, NY 10010

Radio-TV News Directors Association
1735 DeSales St., N.W.
Washington, DC 20036

Television Bureau of Advertising
477 Madison Avenue
New York, NY 10022

CHAPTER 29

Opportunities for Women in Broadcasting

DO WOMEN STILL DO "WOMEN'S" WORK IN BROADCASTING?

In 1989, funded primarily by the Gannett Foundation, the Communication Consortium, a Washington-based communications-consulting firm, conducted a comprehensive study called "Women, Men and Media." It concluded that women have not yet achieved parity with men in broadcasting.

Only traditionally female departments such as administration, data processing, promotion, and community service are dominated by women. Women are still underrepresented in such important jobs as technicians/engineers, production workers, news staff, and anchors.

Here are some highlights of the study:[1]

* In the media, in general, including broadcast and newspapers, women are paid sixty-four cents for every male employee's dollar.
* The media fails to promote women. Only 25 percent of those climbing the ladder to higher jobs are female.

* A woman executive earns significantly less than a man doing the same job at the same-size TV or radio station with the same number of years of experience, supervising the same number of employees. On average, a woman executive in TV receives approximately $9,000 a year less than a man and about $3,300 less in radio.
* Only 3 percent of TV presidents and vice presidents, and 8 percent of radio presidents and vice presidents, are female. Women lack control over content, policy, money, and direction. Men choose the messages; men decide what is news and what is entertainment. The message the American public receives passes through a male filter.
* In TV, only traditionally female departments have 50 percent or more women—the departments that are peripheral to the main business of the station. Even in on-air jobs women are relegated to co-anchor and weekend anchor slots.
* The 1989 study of nightly network newscasts found that women reported 22.2 percent of the stories on CBS, 14.4 percent of the stories on NBC and 10.5 percent of the stories on ABC.
* Beyond reporting stories, women were rarely the subject or focus of interviews. By network, the percentage of stories in which women were the focus was 13.7 percent at ABC, 10.2 percent at CBS, and 8.9 percent at NBC.

Upward Mobility

Yet change is clearly in evidence, even in the few years since this study. In 1993, at the three largest networks' entertainment divisions, where programming originates and develops, women held 43 percent of the top executive positions. At NBC, for example, there were women in eighteen out of the thirty-eight top slots. Ruth Slawson held the important post of senior VP, miniseries and motion pictures for television; Charisse McGhee was VP, current drama programs, and Linda Mancuso was VP, Saturday morning and family programs.

In that same year, Mary Frost became VP and general manager of ABC Television's network operations, East Coast, and Laurie Goldstein was made senior VP of operations at MTV Networks, New York.

Women, today, are making it in every area of broadcasting—as station managers in TV and radio, as sales managers, and in the top on-air jobs. They are being hired on an equal basis with men and they are moving to the top just slightly more slowly than men. Perhaps by the turn of the century any imbalance in their status in this medium will have been erased.

PROFILE: LUCIE SALHANY—TV'S TOP-
RANKING WOMAN

In April 1992, Lucie Salhany was appointed chairman of Twentieth Television, Fox's production and syndication arms. In January
1993, Salhany assumed the even more daunting responsibility of chairman of Fox Broadcasting Company, the first woman ever to head a
U.S. broadcasting network.

Salhany started her broadcasting career at age twenty-two, as an
entry-level secretary at a TV station in Cleveland. From there, she
edged up the career ladder as program manager of a TV station in
Boston, program director of a station in Cleveland, then VP-televi-
sion and cable programming for Taft Broadcasting, a major player
in the TV business.

In 1985, she joined Paramount Television as an executive involved
in the syndication efforts of the company. Paramount is a leading
supplier of programming for the networks. Before she left Paramount
for Fox, in July 1991, Salhany had advanced to the position of president of domestic television.

Salhany is part of a small, elite group of women who have reached
the top in this field. Kay Koplovitz heads the USA Cable Network;
Mary Alice Dwyer-Dobbin is a senior vice president at ABC; Jennifer
Lawson is executive vice president, national programming and promotion services at PBS; and Bridget Potter is the senior vice president of original programming at HBO. If Lucie Salhany succeeds at
Fox, many more opportunities will arise for women in this male-dom-
inated field.

CAREER HELP FOR WOMEN

American Women in Radio and Television (AWRT) is an outstanding
organization dedicated to improving the standards in radio and TV for
women. It holds both national conventions and regional conferences
and has forty-five local chapters that coordinate the group's participation at colleges. The organization publishes a national bimonthly
newsletter and conducts an awards program.

AWRT joined forces with the Women's Bureau of the U.S. Department of Labor to produce a publication for women considering careers in the electronic media. It is called "Women on the Job," and is a generally upbeat appraisal of the opportunities for women in the electronic media. It concludes that more women are currently employed in higher paying categories in broadcasting and cable than ever before, and that this is an excellent time to consider a career in the electronic media.

The book defines about seventy broadcast jobs and their responsibilities. Copies are available free. Write to:

Women's Bureau
U.S. Department of Labor
200 Constitution Ave., N.W.
Washington, DC 20210.

To help women in their job search, two national, broadcast-skills banks offer guidance and leads to available positions. American Women in Radio and Television operates Careerline, which aids any woman looking for a position in broadcasting. This service is free. For more information, contact:

Careerline
AWRT
1011 Connecticut Ave., N.W., Suite 700
Washington, DC 20036
(202) 429-5102.

WICI

Women in Communications, Inc. (WICI), is an organization of 12,000 members whose primary purpose is to advance women in all fields of communications.

Here are a few of WICI's activities:

* WICI's Membership Directory is a resource for establishing contacts and support for those entering the communications field or changing careers.

* WICI's national CLARION Awards recognize excellence in print and broadcast journalism, PR, advertising, and photography.
* WICI's national Job Hotline lists communications positions nationwide and most local chapters offer job services to members.
* WICI publishes an outstanding quarterly magazine, *The Professional Communicator*.

WICI has three categories of membership: Professionals in creative professional communications; Associates, individuals employed in communications less than two years; and Students, those working toward a degree and committed to communications as a career.

For more information about WICI membership and activities, write to:

Women in Communications, Inc.
National Headquarters
2101 Wilson Blvd., Suite 417
Arlington, VA 22201
(703) 528-4000.

NINE TIPS ON BREAKING IN

* Although broadcast TV is still by far the dominant medium in broadcasting, there are more entry-level jobs for women in radio and in cable-TV programming.
* In the news field, women are gaining as news directors. By 1993, they held almost one third of these top assignments in radio—fewer in TV.
* The median age of a woman news director in radio is 29.1, compared to men who were 35.0, according to a recent RTNDA survey. Unfortunately, women in news are still paid less than men for the same jobs.
* Public TV and radio do not seem to discriminate against women, either in hiring or promoting. At PBS, thirteen of the top twenty-four executives in the organization are women.
* Try to find a mentor to help guide your career. You probably can do this on the job or through a local chapter of AWRT or WICI.
* Consider the area of radio sales, where more women are employed than men.

* Be prepared to take your first job in a small market. Salaries are low, but it's a way of getting started. Last week's general-assignment reporter at a TV station in Nampa, Idaho, may be next week's assistant news-director at a TV station in Springfield, Massachusetts.
* Working at one of the TV production studios in Hollywood may seem glamorous and exciting, but jobs for women are more difficult to get than for men, particularly on the technical side. Take a job as a gofer just to get started, then network with the women you meet. Don't try to make it as an actor. The odds are against you.
* Consider graduate school if you are still in college. It may offer the competitive edge a woman needs to make it in broadcasting.

NOTE

[1] Women, Men, and Media. *Communications Consortium, March 1989.*

CHAPTER 30

Important Broadcasting-
Industry Publications

Y ou can probably learn more about an industry by reading its leading trade publications than from any other source. This is especially true in television and radio.

BROADCASTING & CABLE

Broadcasting & Cable, a weekly magazine, was established in 1931, back
in the early days of radio. Sixty-two years later, it has a paid circulation of 28,000 and a total readership of 100,000, a high pass-along figure for a business publication. Its readers are advertisers, ad agencies,
engineers, sales reps, TV and radio general managers, network executives, students, and teachers in communications.

Broadcasting & Cable publishes special reports throughout the year.
In 1992 and 1993, special reports covered such subjects as "Annual Radio Forecast," "The Changing World of Hispanic Media," and "Tight-
ening Times for Broadcasting."

Besides its dozen or more articles, *Broadcasting & Cable* runs short news items, notices of stations sales, classified ads, and a "Fates & Fortunes" column about promotions and job changes.

Those aspiring to careers in broadcasting will find a year's subscription ($85) to *Broadcasting & Cable* a worthwhile investment. The address:

Broadcasting & Cable
1705 DeSales Street, N.W.
Washington, DC 20036-4480.

Broadcasting & Cable also publishes the *Broadcasting & Cable Market Place* ($115), a complete guide to information about radio, TV, cable, and satellite. Some libraries keep *Broadcasting & Cable* on file. In May 1991, *Broadcasting & Cable*'s owner, The Times Mirror Company, sold the publication to Cahners Publishing Company for $32 million, in cash.

ELECTRONIC MEDIA

Crain Communications is the successful publisher of twenty-three business magazines, including *Advertising Age*, *Automotive News,* and *Crain's New York Business*. In 1982, Crain launched its formidable competitor to *Broadcasting & Cable*, the weekly *Electronic Media*. The publication covers not only broadcasting and cable, but also all other electronic media, including video and satellite communications.

A recent issue of *Electronic Media* contained in-depth coverage of the National Association of Broadcaster's convention, a special report on the Cabletelevision Advertising Bureau's (CAB) annual conference, a technology report on digital TV, and various standard features and columns.

A year's subscription to *Electronic Media* is $79. Write to:

Electronic Media
Subscription Department
1965 East Jefferson
Detroit, MI 48207-9969.

VARIETY

Published since 1905, *Variety* is to many in the industry the bible of show business. It publishes daily and weekly editions and is read by show biz buffs and professionals alike.

Both *Variety* and its rival, *The Hollywood Reporter*, offer comprehensive and knowing coverage of every phase of show business. One need only have breakfast at the coffee shop of cinemaland's Beverly Wilshire Hotel to observe a local ritual: the show biz professional at the next table invariably scans both "trades" before taking his first sip of coffee.

Variety's language in particular is explicitly "show-businessese." The publication has coined *feevee* for pay TV and *kidvid* for video cassettes for children. Headlines frequently call for translation: "Multimedia Buyers Blitz Boffo Mifed," for instance, refers to Mifed, a giant convocation of film, TV, and video executives held each year in Milan, where business was terrific ("boffo"), with sales made in many media and in many countries.

Many large libraries file copies of weekly *Variety*. For those who can afford it, a subscription is a worthwhile investment. A subscription to weekly *Variety* is $149 a year. Write to:

> *Variety*
> P.O. Box 6400
> Torrance, CA 90504.

A subscription to *Daily Variety* is $145 a year. Write to:

> *Daily Variety*
> P.O. Box 7550
> Torrance, CA 90504.

THE HOLLYWOOD REPORTER

In 1993, the highly respected trade publication *The Hollywood Reporter* celebrated its sixty-third anniversary. Its influence on the entertainment industry has grown in recent years, particularly since its acquisition in the mid-1980s by the BPI Entertainment Communication Network, a company that also publishes *Adweek*, *Billboard*, *American Artist*, and *Interiors* magazines.

The Hollywood Reporter is published daily on weekdays, 252 issues a year, and has a paid circulation of 23,370 at this writing. Special issues are the lifeblood of entertainment trade publications like *The Hollywood Reporter* and *Variety*. The *Hollywood Reporter* does about sixty of these special issues a year, covering such subjects as MIPCOM (an annual convention held in Cannes for the international TV program market), the NATPE (National Association of TV Program Executives) convention, Paramount's seventy-fifth anniversary, "Roseanne"'s one hundredth show and the annual Cannes Film Festival. Special issues generate a great deal of advertising revenue while offering readers an in-depth look at specific topics and phases of the entertainment business.

A one-year subscription to *The Hollywood Reporter* is $142. Their address is:

The Hollywood Reporter
P.O. Box 1431
Hollywood, CA 90099-4927.

The weekly international edition of this fine publication bears a subscription price of $75 a year. It is available in some large libraries.

ADWEEK AND ADVERTISING AGE

Although *Adweek* and *Advertising Age*'s readers are predominantly advertisers and advertising agencies, these two excellent publications offer extensive editorial coverage of broadcasting. We recommend them both to those pursuing a career in TV and radio.

CHAPTER 31

Getting the Job

THIRTEEN STEPS TO A JOB IN BROADCASTING

No job is harder than finding a job, particularly your first. Success requires planning, preparation, energy, and enthusiasm—all in large quantities. Here are twelve suggestions on how to pursue the job search.

1. Educate yourself about the business. Research the field of broadcasting. Read everything you can find about it. Most colleges and other libraries will have a collection of books on TV and radio. (See Recommended Reading, page 307.) Read the important industry trade publications. (See chapter 30.)

2. Pursue internship programs. Try to get an internship, free or paid, while you are in college or after your graduate. Your local TV or radio station may be a good place to start. (See chapter 28.)

3. Network. Talk to people who are already in the field. Learn from professionals where your talents and interests will best serve the industry. Research the alumni lists of your college for graduates who have gone into broadcasting. A letter or phone call to these people may turn

up good job leads. The networking process snowballs very quickly—the more you do it, the easier it is.

4. Create a good resume. Dozens of books have been written about how to write a resume. Read some. Highlight your relevant skills. Your resume should reflect your talents, interests ,and the benefits you will bring to the potential employer. Keep it neat, clear, concise, and free of typographical errors, and fit it on one page. Tailor your resume to each position for which you apply. Don't waste space on clubs you belonged to in high school. Punctuation, spelling, and production of the resume must be perfect.

5. Read the want ads. Want ads in trade publications are a good source for job information. See chapter 30 for specific information on these publications.

6. Consider postgraduate education. Graduate school in broadcasting or broadcast journalism may be a valuable educational experience and give the edge you need to get the right job. However, you may want to postpone this option until you have worked in broadcasting for a year or two. In fact, it may be easier to gain admission to a school after some work in this field.

You should also take advantage of the excellent extension courses offered by some colleges. These high-level courses may offer a practical alternative to graduate school and give you a professional education while you are on the job.

7. Take pains with each cover letter. Don't blow the impact of a good resume with a bad cover letter. Together they create a first impression of you. Stay clear of the form letter. Let your potential employers know why you think you are right for them. Pay special attention to spelling, typos, and grammar. Cover letters should be short. Say just what you want—an interview.

8. Use business directories for leads and company names. The annual MIPCOM Market Guide issue of *The Hollywood Reporter*, for example, lists the names and assignments of hundreds of broadcasting executives.

9. Prepare for an interview. Learn as much as you can about the organizations you are visiting. Read articles about them in trade journals. If you are in a school that has a good placement department, find

out if they can set up some role-playing situations with specific advice on handling an interview.

Just getting an interview is a foot in the door. Once you've secured an interview, prepare for it carefully. Organize your thinking and review the information you have on the company. Be articulate, self-confident, and enthusiastic. Talk about yourself—what you've learned, what you offer, and what you can do for Company X. Don't try to recite everything you know. Selectivity shows you are thinking. The well-known media specialist Roger Bumstead contributes these additional thoughts on what "turns him off" in an interview: "Candidates without a career focus . . . Candidates who want me to do the talking . . . Candidates who 'laze' in their chair across from me . . . Candidates who are either boring or arrogant . . . Candidates who don't dress properly because they think it doesn't matter when they're seeing a recruiter. Wow, are they wrong!"

10. Make sure you are adept at cold calling and letter writing. This may be a tedious and frustrating procedure, but it is probably the way you will get your first job.

11. Target your prospects. Decide for yourself whom you want to work for and where.

12. Meet the recruiters. If recruiters from the broadcast industry visit your campus, be sure to attend. Ask questions and try to learn their hiring practices, interview systems, attitudes about requirements for graduate work, and so forth.

13. Gain experience at small stations. Be prepared to go to work in the boonies to get started. Some students expect to graduate to jobs paying $50,000 in New York, Washington, or Los Angeles. You may have to face the reality that the only job you can get is one for $10,000 a year in the 200th market. This may be a wise option if you want to make it in broadcast news.

At a small TV station, a reporter right out of college might get to cover a story, carry the camera, tripod and recorder, shoot the pictures, edit the tape, write the story and voice it. That's hands-on broadcast journalism. One young journalist was given this opportunity only three weeks after he was hired for his first TV job.

Other recent grads who went to work at small stations were given shots as producers, co-anchors, and assignment editors.

WRITING A RESUME THAT ATTRACTS ATTENTION

A good resume should sell you. It should clearly state what you bring to the job. Be career-specific and include the exact dates you held any interim employment. See the sample below and on page 280 as a good example of an entry-level resume and cover letter. It exudes confidence, energy, and leadership. If you've won any awards for educational excellence or leadership, detail them.

Sample Cover Letter

Emma C. Pitt
330 Palmetto Street
Anytown, CA 00000
(714) 555-1234

September 25, 1994

Ms. Iris Forbes
Vice President, Human Resources
Capital Broadcasting Company
950 Third Avenue
New York, NY 10023

Dear Ms. Forbes:

As my enclosed resume shows, I am a recent broadcast journalism graduate of the University of Southern California. My experience includes internships with two Los Angeles broadcast stations. My educational background in broadcast news journalism and practical experience in field news reporting qualifies me for the video journalist training program at Capital Broadcasting.

I would like to meet with you to discuss a job with your network and I will call Monday, October 3rd, to arrange an interview.

I look forward to meeting you.

Sincerely,

Emma C. Pitt

Enclosure

Sample resume

EMMA C. PITT
330 Palmetto Street
Anytown, CA 00000
(714) 555-1234

OBJECTIVE: To obtain employment in broadcast journalism with a television station, a radio station, or a network that allows me to use my communications skills.

EDUCATION: B.A. Journalism with an emphasis in Radio/Television, University of Southern California, Los Angeles, May 1994. Courses included Introduction to Telecommunications, Basic Principles of Broadcast Production, Radio/TV Programming, and Broadcast Newswriting.

Summer courses at UCLA Extension, 1993, in Job Search Strategies in Broadcast News, TV Reporting and Production, and Delivering the News: On-Camera Techniques for Television Journalists.

EXPERIENCE: Public TV station KCET-TV: Los Angeles, Calif. Unpaid internship, May through August 1993. Aided the program director in screening program proposals. Typed and helped prepare copy for TV promos. Attended staff meetings on programming. Assisted fund-raising director in planning for fall campaign.

Radio station KNX-AM: Los Angeles, Calif. (a CBS O&O) Unpaid internship, May through August 1992. Assisted the news director in coordinating coverage and rewriting wire service copy. Accompanied reporters to on-street assignments. Attended mayor and police-chief news conferences.

Professional references available.

FINDING A JOB IN HARD TIMES

Getting a job any time is difficult. When times are bad and companies are cutting staff—or even worse, going out of business—finding a job is a Promethean task. Besides applying all tips suggested above, there is some additional advice that may help the cause:

* Beware of phony employment agencies that promise jobs but can't really deliver. Check them out with the local Better Business Bureau or the State Attorney General's office.
* If you're a recent graduate or an out-of-work professional, be willing to relocate.
* Organize a letter campaign to potential employers. Read the industry's trade publications to find out the companies who are engaged in acquisitions and expansion. Direct your letters to these organizations.
* Do not show dissatisfaction with an interview itself. Make it as productive as possible and evaluate it afterward.
* Do not plead for a position.
* Do not discount what reliable executive-search companies or human resource departments can do for you.
* Accept a lesser-paying job than you expect, especially if it increases your broad knowledge of the whole field of broadcasting.
* Use networking to widen your scope and increase your job sources.

CHAPTER 32

From the Horse's Mouth: Interviews with Industry Insiders

AN INTERVIEW WITH A TELEVISION ENGINEERING SPECIALIST

Bruce Sidran went to work at ABC in July 1978 as a junior engineer. His first assignment was the expansion of the main technical facilities in central switching, the very heart of the TV network in New York. In January 1979, he was promoted to full engineer. In 1980, he assisted with the captioning of the Sugar Bowl, the presidential inauguration, and several presidential press conferences and speeches. From 1981 to 1985, Sidran was the project manager for ABC's O&O station in San Francisco, and from 1985 through early 1989, he held the position of manager of engineering for all of ABC's O&Os. In 1989, he left ABC to work in electronics and computer technology.

Sidran received his bachelor's degree in electrical engineering from the City College of New York in June 1975. While working for ABC, he attended the Polytechnic Institute of New York and earned a master's degree in computer systems in January 1981.

What type of training did you need for your job at ABC?

I have a bachelor's degree in electrical engineering and a master's degree in computer systems, but what I know about television I basically learned on the job. When I was going to college, there were very few college-level courses in television engineering, so my background is generally in electrical engineering. And you learn specifics on the job as you go. Most people who worked for me had been trained in electrical engineering.

Is it essential to have a background in electrical engineering, or can you pick that up on the job, too?

To work in TV, it's possible to pick it up on the job, but I'd say it's more difficult that way. Operations and engineering is a technical field that requires someone with technical acumen. However, there were people in my department at ABC who were self-taught. One of the most talented people who worked for me had a background in general studies—no engineering courses at all. He taught himself everything. My boss, who was the general manager of engineering, never went to college. He was completely self-taught and one of the brightest engineers I know, so it's definitely possible to work in the field without formal training.

Do you need an FCC license to work at a TV station?

No. The FCC has relaxed its requirements considerably. The only person required to have a license is the actual operator of the station's transmitter—and that's usually just the chief engineer.

What engineering jobs are available at a typical television station?

There is really no such thing as a typical station, so I'll describe a large one. A large one—say, an owned-and-operated station, or one in any of the top fifty markets—would be run almost like a network facility. It would have anywhere from 300 to 700 employees, of which half would be technical. It would employ people who are mostly operators to run various equipment on a day-to-day basis—transmission operators, camera people, people to do the switching from on-air shows. At a small station, a handful of people are responsible for the engineering and camera chores.

Are those union positions?

It depends on the station. At the larger stations, yes, but at smaller stations, usually not. Each station, except for the ones owned by the networks, is really a separate entity unto itself. It really depends on the particular facility.

How would someone who wanted an engineering job at a unionized facility get into the union?

There are two major broadcast unions: One is called NABET, the National Association of Broadcast Employees and Technicians; the other is IBEW, which is the International Bureau of Electrical Workers. It has a subsection that deals with broadcast television. Getting into either of those unions is not a problem. The problem is getting a job. Once you get a job, you have thirty days to join the union. And there's no problem getting into the union once you have a job.

What about jobs at smaller stations?

Most stations, even very small ones, have ENG—electronic news gathering—teams, who go out into the field and gather footage for the local news using mini-cams. And those are usually NABET and IBEW positions. Then there is a group of jobs for quasi-technical people: stage managers, floor managers, people who interface with the on-air talent. They require some technical expertise, but not at the same level as the actual operators. At most of the ABC stations, these people belong to the DGA, Directors Guild of America, or IATSE, International Alliance of Theatrical Stage Employees, and Moving Picture Machine Operators of the United States and Canada, known in the industry as IA. This union has incorporated television, film, and video over the past few years.

What about the engineers who do need an FCC license? What do they do, and why do they need a license?

One person at a station has to have the station license. The one person with the FCC license is supposed to oversee the operations of the station to be sure that all FCC regulations are being adhered to. Bascially, the license allows you to transmit. The FCC gives you a piece of paper called a license, which says you can have this spectrum of space—this frequency—to broadcast on. You're very limited as to the geographical area and about the power you can transmit. There are a lot of other requirements to fulfill in order to comply with an FCC license.

And that's the responsibility of the person who holds the license?

Yes. Typically, it's the chief engineer. At some stations, it might be the owner of the station if he has a technical background. It could also be the general manager of the station, but it's usually the chief engineer. In days gone by, up until 1980, anybody who had anything to do with the transmitter was required to have a first-class FCC license. That's not the case anymore. You just need one licensee for the station, and that person can designate other people to operate under his authority. The licensee has the responsibility to adhere to all of the FCC's rules and regulations. But his staff actually handles the day-to-day work.

What are the direct responsibilities of the person holding the FCC license?

If, say, the station has interference problems with other stations in the area, the FCC will come to the person at the station who has the license to settle the problem.

What are some of the entry-level positions in TV operations and engineering?

A very typical entry-level position is the videotape operator; somebody familiar with various formats of videotape who can work videotape machines, play back, and record.

And where would that lead to in, say, two years?

He or she could become a videotape editor, and that's a well-paying, respected job. Another entry-level position is that of a Chyron operator—that's electronic character generation for the words that appear on the screen.

Whom do you contact about getting these jobs?

At a small station, the chief engineer. At a larger station, the manager or director of operations, or the director of engineering.

How have the advancements in technology affected jobs in this area of broadcasting?

Most of the jobs in engineering have not been changed by technological innovations. The tasks are the same; only the knowledge that it takes to operate some equipment has been altered. A standard format of videotape is standard for all modes of transmission, whether by microwave, satellite, fiber optics, or telephone lines.

What role does engineering play in the transmission of a sporting event or a news event?

The network has a division with mobile field units. There are large trucks, actually tractor-trailers forty-five to fifty feet long, that have the same equipment found in a typical television studio—except it's mobile, on wheels. In the case of ABC, for example, the truck was owned by the broadcast operations and engineering division and was, essentially, rented out to a customer—in their case, the customer was ABC Sports. The sports department would decide if it needed one, two, three, or perhaps four trucks to do the job. The producer would decide how many cameras were needed, as well as what other items, such as tape machines, editing facilities, and communication setups. And then it would be up to us, to engineering, to provide those facilities and to actually run them during the event.

The same sort of thing goes for news events, although they tended to be more impromptu, so typically there would be one or two mini-cam crews assigned. A mini-cam crew gathers the information and either records it on videotape or transmits it back to the studio for live transmission.

So, is operations and engineering really a service division?

Yes. And most networks and most stations work the same way. Operations is a service group, aiding the production people, as well as serving as "in-house" consultants on an ad hoc basis for specific projects—like the Super Bowl.

How does the a news story happening in France find its way onto ABC Evening News that same night?

ABC maintains news bureaus in various areas around the world; Paris is one of them. If a major event happens in France, an assignment editor in that office sends a mini-cam team, or a stringer team, to cover the story. An assignment editor finds out about stories via the wire services, press releases, and so forth. Also, all the news bureaus communicate with one another. Sports use stringers a lot more than news, because sporting events need more people, while a news event can usually be covered by a staff mini-cam crew.

How does the footage get from Paris to New York?

There are a couple of different ways. One scenario is to edit the videotape locally—if facilities exist nearby—and transmit it in any number of ways directly to ABC News in the United States. But usually in London ABC will gather all the stories from Western Europe. And then all the stories, fully edited and with voice-overs, are transmitted as a package directly to New York, which is where ABC's "World News Tonight" with Peter Jennings is done. London time is five hours ahead of New York so there is an advantage in doing that. ABC can gather stories all day and then transmit them later in the afternoon.

Is it prestigious to work in the operational aspects of a news department?

Yes. News and sports are equally prestigious. News is a very exciting place to work because of the immediacy of the events. The length of assignments is short—one to three days—so someone in this area is going to see a wide variety of tasks. Different places, different people, and there's a lot of travel involved; it's an exciting place to work. When I worked for CBS News, we would, on a day-to-day basis, never know whether we'd be sent to Boston or the Bahamas. Sometimes I'd have fifteen minutes to get ready if it was a fast-breaking story. Usually we got a day or two's notice. We were on call twenty-four hours a day. When Son of Sam was terrorizing New York [in the 1970s], I got a call at 2:00 A.M. to go down to the courthouse; I was working audio on a mini-cam crew at the time. David Berkowitz had been caught, and he was going to give a statement to the press. I ended up literally camping out at the courthouse for two-and-a-half days waiting for something to happen. That's what it's like—long periods of intense boredom punctuated by short bursts of intense activity. It's an interesting place to work. You need to be the type of person who can handle sitting outside someone's front door for three days in case he decides to come out and make a statement. And the next day you could be on a plane for God-knows-where.

Is there an element of danger?

One of the big drawbacks about working on a news crew is that there is danger present at various times. Often you're assigned to cover trouble spots, and by virtue of their being "hot," you're exposing yourself to a dangerous situation. Many of the people who have worked on news crews have at some point covered riots, or scenes of hostage takings, or war zones. There were crews that were assigned to transmit pictures from Beirut. They were shot at, beat up. Several news people have been killed; there is an element of danger involved. For some people, that adds excitement to the job.

What words of advice can you offer someone who considers operations and engineering as a possible career?

It is extremely interesting and rewarding work. It is typically very well paying, and because it is interesting, rewarding, and well paying, it's historically difficult to get jobs. Someone just starting out has a much better opportunity at a small station, away from the major markets. It is extremely difficult to get work in New York with no experience. Los Angeles, Chicago—the same story. But for someone who is really dedicated to the field, I would suggest going to a small-market station or a nonunionized facility, or starting out at a production company and gaining experience in production and engineering; then one could approach a larger station or a network. Three to five years of experience is reasonable dues with which to approach a bigger operation.

In summing up, I can only say that there isn't any area that's more exciting or gratifying than the technical and engineering area of television.

AN INTERVIEW WITH A RECENT JOURNALISM GRADUATE WHO MADE IT AS AN ANCHORPERSON

Leah Sanders was born in San Leandro, California, in 1968. By the time she enrolled at Loyola Marymount University in Los Angeles, in 1986, her family had already moved around the country nine times, but her peripatetic schooling did not impede her academic achievements. At Loyola, Sanders received a BA in media studies/management, with a minor in political science.

Upon graduation in 1990, realizing that her primary focus was broadcasting, she enrolled in the University of Missouri's acclaimed master of arts program in journalism, with a broadcast emphasis. While at graduate school, she participated in a number of internships; one was at the University of Missouri's own TV station, KOMU-TV, an NBC affiliate. Within months of her graduation from Missouri, Leah Sanders landed a job at an ABC affiliate TV station in Palm Springs, California. We asked her about her college background and her present job.

How do you feel your graduate education prepared you for your present work?

My graduate education put the finishing touches on my liberal arts education. Since I wanted to go into broadcast journalism, the program at the University of Missouri allowed me to focus on the practical side of this field. Hands-on experience—reporting, writing, producing, and anchoring at a network affiliate and at a National Public Radio station—enabled me to get right into the broadcast work force right out of school.

The University of Missouri owns a TV station that is a network affiliate. How did students use the station as a training ground?

After taking two classes that involved newswriting and production for radio and TV, I enrolled in a third broadcasting class that I took while starting out as a reporter and morning anchor at KOMU-TV (NBC). At the station I had a reporting shift in which I would work as a reporter on my own story, and as a photographer on a partner's story in the field. My stories filled the "Today" show cut-ins [local fillers], a noon-hour talk show, and a daily 6:00 P.M. and 10:00 P.M. newscast. There was also the opportunity to anchor the "Today" show cut-ins, the two seven-minute news blocks during the noon hour and the Saturday and Sunday 6:00 P.M. and 10:00 P.M. newcasts. Competition was tough for the weekend shows, but it prepared us to compete for jobs out of school. Finally, there was also the opportunity to take a course in which we produced daily shows.

While at college, you interned at two TV stations. How long were your internships, did you receive compensation, and how valuable was the training in getting you started?

I interned at KCBS-Action News in Los Angeles and at the Los Angeles bureau of CNN. I spent six months at each internship. The internships were unpaid, but I received college credit. This training allowed me to witness the day-to-day pressure and cutthroat nature of this business, and to see if I really wanted to become a broadcast journalist. Some days I worked just a few hours; on others I worked more than eight hours. It was an excellent way to start "paying those dues," as they say.

How did you get a paid job at a TV station within months of graduating from the University of Missouri?

I paid for a job service called *Media Line* that has daily listings of jobs open in broadcast news. The listing at KESQ-TV in Palm Springs, California, was for a photographer-reporter. I responded by telephoning the news director and asking if I could come by for an interview. An interview was set up and within one week I had the job.

At your station in Palm Springs, which ranks as the 170th market, you mention that there are seventeen staffers in the news department. Briefly, what are their assignments?

Our station has 98 percent cable penetration (about the highest in the U.S.). Our shows compete with the Los Angeles stations. As for the staffers, here are the assignments:

News Director: Oversees the product and the staff and is the manager of the newsroom.

Producer/Managing Editor/Anchor (5:00 P.M., 6:00 P.M. newscast): Along with the news director, oversees the content of the show, including the writing and choice of stories.

Producer/Co-Anchor (5:00 P.M., 6:00 P.M. newscast): Writes and aids in getting the shows ready for airing.

Assignment Editor: Responsible for finding stories for the daily newscast, setting up interviews, and keeping up with current events.

Three Anchor/Producer/Reporters: Same function as producer/co-anchor, but also reports.

Cut-ins Anchor Reporter: Same as previous listing, but not as much producing skills required.

Sports Director/Anchor: Responsible for sports content of newscasts, producing, writing.

Sports Anchor/Reporter: Produces and anchors weekend shows and is a news reporter during the week.

Photographer-Reporter: Shoots video during the week and reports on stories on the weekend.

Two full-time photographers: Shoot video during the week.

Two part-time photographers.

Midday News, Associate Producer: Books guests for the show, as well as writes.

Weathercaster: Reports the weather.

All employees are responsible for editing their own videotape.

Within a few months of working at your station you became a weekend anchor and producer. Do you write your own material? Please tell us in some detail what this job encompasses?

As a weekend anchor/producer I write all my own material, except for stories written and delivered by reporters. As the producer, I look for the most important news of the day, starting with local news and going international. The newspapers, AP wire, and the ABC network newsfeed provide the stories. Once I choose the ones I want to use, I put them in order and write the copy. I also must make sure satellite feed tapes are running on time, so that we cover all of our national and international news. Calls are made to local law enforcement agencies to check for stories. I also monitor the activity of photographers and reporters out in the field to make sure everything is finished on time. I edit videotape, as well as make sure the show is timed out for allotted time.

What do you think audiences look for in an anchor?

I believe the audience looks for honesty, trustworthiness, friendliness, and at the same time, someone who makes them feel at ease, even if the news is bad.

Finally, the pressing question: What advice can you give budding broadcast journalists?

Internships, internships, internships—to make sure this is the profession for you. Know what's going on in the world. The technical part of the business will come, but you need to have some sort of understanding of the mixed-up world we live in. Be patient, but persistent, and perfect all your skills. A liberal arts education opened my mind up to the world we live in and the graduate program gave me the technical skills.

AN INTERVIEW WITH A NOVICE
CNN VIDEO JOURNALIST

Amy Coe had worked for CNN in New York for one year and in Atlanta for six months at the time of this interview. Of her background, she said, "I grew up in New York City and attended Professional Children's School. While there I studied dance and theater and did television commercials. I majored in English at Barnard College and had internships at PMK Public Relations and CBS Daytime TV. After college I backpacked in Europe for two months before I started working at CNN." We spoke about her job at the network.

What is a typical day like for Amy Coe at CNN?

My typical day at work begins at 4 A.M. I grab some breakfast and "read-in" on CNN's computer system. I read the wires and look over the plans and outlines for the programs I work on. I speak with the producers and writers of the shows (they're in New York and I'm in Atlanta). Then I gather video, edit videotape, work with graphic artists, and keep an eye on any video coming in by satellite to make sure it arrives without any technical flaws. I speak with our New York staff several more times to keep up with the changes in the shows' structures. By 6 A.M., the first show is ready to go and I double-check that all the video is ready for air. Once the show is on, I'm in the control room making sure that everything is airing as planned. The producer in New York calls the shots and my function is to carry out her requests. I'm also ready for quick changes in case a news story breaks while our show is on air. The routine is the same for the later show which happens at 7:30.

After a lunch break (at 8 A.M.!), I get to work on another show that airs every weekday on CNN International. My function on this show is similar to what I do in the morning, but the procedure is different because this show is taped, not live. I speak with the producer and reporters in London, and gather and edit video according to their requests. I work with graphic artists and prepare Vidifont and Chyron information . (This is all the typed info in the show; for example, people's names and titles that appear on the screen.) Elements of the show are fed from London to Atlanta by satellite and then edited by a high-tech computerized system here. I work with the editor and an associate producer on editing the show. We edit anchor reads, reporter pieces, music, and special effects in one hour. Then we put the show on the air through an automated "playback" system. Once the show is on the air, my work day is over (at 2:00 P.M.).

The pace is, no doubt, frenetic at CNN these days. How does that manifest itself?

The pacing gets frenetic when news breaks. The newsroom runs at double its usual brisk pace and everyone works twice as hard and fast. The challenge is in communicating quickly and effectively with co-workers so that the information airs accurately and quickly.

What was your major at college? Did it help to get your first job, and has it been relevant to work at CNN?

My college major was English and it didn't help me in breaking into broadcasting. However, I do think it will serve me in the long run. Through my major I learned to read critically, write well, and ask a lot of questions—definitely vital skills for a journalist.

As a New Yorker, what do you think are the basic differences in working there or in Atlanta?

Working in Atlanta and New York are extremely different. Atlanta is an easier place to live. There's less crime and the city moves at a far less hectic pace. Atlanta is affordable; even people on entry-level salaries live well here. New York, on the other hand, is prohibitively expensive. Life there is harder, too. The weather is cold and the rush hour is merciless. But New York is much more exciting. It's a far more diverse city.

If you had it to do over again, what would you have majored in at college?

If I had to do it over again I would still major in English. A broadcasting-journalism major is not necessary for a successful career in the industry. A broadcasting major would have made my job easier initially but, in the long run, I don't think it matters. Most entry-level positions offer opportunities to learn the basics of the business.

What do you think is the best growth area of people choosing to enter the field of broadcasting?

The growth area in broadcast journalism is the electronic media. Satellite and cable television offer the widest range of opportunities since these areas are expanding rapidly.

How did you get your job at CNN?

I got my job at CNN by networking with a Barnard alumna. She was working at CNN's New York bureau. I called her through Barnard's Career Counseling Office and she informed me of a job opening in Atlanta.

AN INTERVIEW WITH EXECUTIVES AT A TOP ALL-NEWS RADIO STATION

We interviewed George Nicholaw, KNX's general manager, and Bob Sims, its news director, for insight into the Los Angeles radio station's management.

To George Nicholaw: Is KNX a union station?

Yes, there are three unions involved in the KNX newsroom—AFTRA, for those who speak on the air; WGA, for those who write on-air material for others to read; and IBEW, for those who maintain and operate the transmitter and other technical gear at the station. [AFTRA is the American Federation of Television and Radio Artists; WGA the Writers Guild of America; IBEW the International Brotherhood of Electrical Workers.]

What is the total number of full-time personnel at the station and how does this break down to the various departments?

There are about fifty-five full-time people in the news department, and another twenty of thirty part-time people. We have nineteen people in sales including traffic and sales assistants. There are seven in administration, five technical and engineering people, three in promotion, and three in community services.

In a twenty-four-hour day, how much of the time is devoted to straight news?

On a typical weekday, KNX fills twenty-two hours with news. In each hour, there will be national and local news interspersed with traffic, weather, business reports, sports, and, of course, commercials to pay the rent.

To Bob Sims: As news director, what is your day-to-day function?

A short answer. I oversee the news personnel and the product of the station.

What was your career path on the road to this job?

I worked my way through various colleges. The emphasis was on engineering, which evolved into science writing with an interest in journalism.

The station, no doubt, subscribes to AP, UPI, and, of course, CBS News. What other services do you use?

KNX subscribes to and uses the services of all AP wires and audio services, UPI, Reuters, CityNews Service, CBS News, Sportsticker, Metro Traffic Service, CHP, Computerlink, Byline Feature Service, and many local daily and weekly newspapers and magazines. [CHP is the California Highway Patrol.]

How many reporters are in the field?

On weekdays between 5:00 A.M. and 12:00 midnight there are between ten and thirteen full-time reporters on duty (plus many stringers in outlying areas). On weekends there are four to five reporters plus stringers.

How do you handle the flood of press releases you receive?

We are swamped with press releases daily. We cull through them the same way any news operation does. We look for stories that are interesting and significant to our listening audience.

Drive-time is a most important factor in the Los Angeles area. KNX maintains a twenty-four-hour traffic service. How do you handle it?

For the key traffic period morning and evening we use our own traffic reporters who report on traffic and weather about six times an hour. We also subscribe to Metro Traffic Service for interim traffic reports. They service a number of other stations in this area with reporters and a traffic helicopter.

To what extent do you use stringers? Are they on air, or do they just do the reporting?

We use stringers for stories from areas where it is impractical to establish bureaus or send staffers. KNX stringers are used on the air.

How do you mobilize your forces in a crisis such as the Los Angeles riots following the decision in the Rodney King beating trial?

On truly major stories we pull out all the stops. All the on-duty reporters are dispatched to the scene. Other reporters are called in on an overtime basis. We call in our own helicopter and alert any appropriate stringer and bureau personnel for sidebar material. Writers and editors work the telephones to get information and/or witnesses. Both are used on the air as part of the coverage. Commercials and normal programming are preempted.

With whom does KNX compete in the competitive L.A. radio market and how do you fare?

Our primary competition is with another all-news radio station, KFWB, which is owned by Group W. Secondary competition is with all the remaining stations in our Metro Rating Area of Los Angeles and Orange counties, with whom we compete for audience and advertisers. KNX and KFWB are usually neck-and-neck in the ratings. In the total survey area, all of Southern California, KNX dominates.

Radio is known as a low paying field, particularly at the small station level. Is this the case at a large station such as KNX?

Generally speaking, salaries in radio are lower than in TV. CBS policy forbids discussing dollar figures, but many large market radio stations pay very well . . . although usually less than large market TV stations.

Does KNX have an internship program, and if so, for how many people, and are they paid?

Yes, we have an intern program. Five people on weekends year-round and two summer intern positions on a forty-hour per week basis. These are paid internships.

Does your station have a training program?

We have no formal training program in the newsroom. We usually hire people who are already skilled and can pick up how we do things fairly quickly.

Final question. What advice would you give people intent on breaking into radio?

Go to college. Take some journalism courses but not necessarily as a journalism major. Learn to write. Writing is the key to this business. Look for work in a small market where you can practice what you ultimately want to be very good at. Be prepared for disappointment, but be persistent. There are few good jobs in radio news and plenty of competition for them.

IMPORTANT ADDRESSES IN RADIO

If you are considering a career in radio, you'll want to contact these networks, unions, and trade organizations. You will probably have to apply through the human resources or personnel departments for interviews with the networks.

CALIFORNIA

American Federation of Television and Radio artists (AFTRA)
1717 North Highland Avenue
Hollywood, CA 90028

Capital Cities/ABC
2040 Avenue of the Stars
Los Angeles, CA 90067

CBS
7800 Beverly Boulevard
Los Angeles, CA 90036

National Broadcasting Company
3000 West Alameda Avenue
Burbank, CA 91523

NEW YORK

American Federation of Television and Radio Artists (AFTRA)
1350 Avenue of the Americas
New York, NY 10019

Capital Cities/ABC
1330 Avenue of the Americas
New York, NY 10019

CBS, Inc.
51 West 52 Street
New York, NY 10019

National Broadcasting Company
30 Rockefeller Plaza
New York, NY 10020

Radio Advertising Bureau
304 Park Avenue South
New York, NY 10010

WASHINGTON, DC

Corporation for Public Broadcasting
901 E Street, N.W.
Washington, DC 20004

GLOSSARY OF
BROADCASTING TERMS

Affiliates: stations that have agreed to carry a network's programming and commercials in exchange for money.

AM broadcast: amplitude modulation system of radio transmission using power of twenty-five watts to fifty kilowatts, the maximum power permitted by the FCC.

Anchor: in news broadcasting, the principal face on camera. In a sense, the central core to which remotes from reporters and correspondents are directed.

Arbitron: a major, research and ratings organization.

Area of Dominant Influence (ADI): mutually exclusive television marketing areas defined by Arbitron. Each county is assigned to the market that accounts for most of its total viewing hours.

Audience: the persons (or homes) listening to or viewing a particular program.

Average Quarter-Hour Ratings: a measure of viewers who watch or listen for at least five minutes during a quarter-hour period.

Barter: the trading of a TV or radio show to a station by an advertiser or agency in return for commercials.

Basic cable: service that provides improved reception for local stations, and programming specially designed for cables that are available at no additional charge to subscribers.

Cable system: a distribution service designed to deliver programming from broadcast TV stations and other programming services via cable connection to TV households.

Cable TV: a communications medium that transmits TV signals by wire. Subscribers normally pay a monthly fee for the service.

Continuity writer: a job at a radio station that may involve writing commercials for advertisers without agencies.

Cost-Per-Rating Point: the cost of buying a single percentage point of TV home or individual-viewer audiences for a given program type or period.

Cost-Per-Thousand (CPM): a standard industry measure of how much it costs an advertiser to reach 1,000 persons or homes.

Coverage: the number of different people (homes) exposed and reached by a TV or radio station or broadcast.

CPB (the Corporation for Public Broadcasting): a private, tax-exempt corporation that supports the activity of public radio and TV stations.

Crawl: lettering that moves vertically or horizontally across the television screen and provides information (as performer credits and news bulletins).

Cume ratings: the number of different people who listen to a particular radio program for at least five minutes during a week. It is expressed as a percentage of the total radio audience for that market.

Daypart: a segment of a broadcasting day.

Designated Market Area (DMA): a mutually exclusive TV market area defined by the A.C. Nielsen Company. Each county is assigned to the market that accounts for most of its total viewing hours.

Diary: a daily record kept by survey respondents to show their viewing and listening habits. Research services use it to report demographic ratings.

Drive time: the most popular radio listening period, from 6:00 A.M. to 10:00 A.M. and from 3:00 P.M. to 7:00 P.M.

ENG (portable Electronic News Gathering): camera used to transmit videotape from the field to the station.

Equal time provision: a ruling of the FCC that grants equal TV time to all legally-qualified candidates for public office.

FCC (the Federal Communications Commission): an independent federal agency created in 1934; it regulates TV, cable, and radio.

First-run syndication: original shows produced specifically for the syndication market.

FM broadcast: frequency modulation method of radio broadcasting; it produces a clearer signal than AM.

Frequency: number of cycles per second in a broadcast signal; by broadcasting on different frequencies many radio and TV stations can serve a single area.

Ghost: results when two or more versions of the same TV signal reach a TV receiver at different times. This occurs when TV transmissions bounce off nearby buildings, towers, hills, etc., and travel over separate paths to reach a receiver.

Gross Rating Points (GRPs): the sum of the individual ratings in a media schedule. A measure of the total intensity of a media plan. See Media Plan.

Homes passed: the number of homes that are or could be connected to a local cable system.

HUT (Households Using Television): the percentage of all households in the population using television sets at a particular time.

Interactive TV: two-way services provided over broadcast and cable TV, but not including pay-per-view.

Interconnected networks: stations connected to receive programming by satellite from a central source. Programs may be carried live or on a delayed basis by local stations.

Lead-in: the portion of a program or script that precedes or introduces a commercial; a program that precedes a hit show (as on television).

Media plan: a recommendation from an ad agency to a client that details media and budget allocations to reach target buyers.

Metro survey area: a region generally corresponding to the definitions of a metropolitan area set by the U.S. Government's Office of Management and Budget (OMB).

NPR (National Public Radio): a network of about 325 noncommercial nonprofit stations.

Off-network syndication: the after-market for network TV series; that is, the running of hit series on independent stations, cable, and in foreign markets.

O&O: a station that is owned and operated by a TV or radio network.

Opposite programming: running against another network's show on the same day and in the same time slot.

Pay-TV (subscription TV): programming on specific broadcast and cable channels that subscriber households must pay extra to watch. A pay-TV channel transmits scrambled signals that are then unscrambled by a decoder box in the subscriber's home.

People meter: an electronic device for collecting TV-rating information; individuals record their viewing by entering identifying numbers when they start and stop viewing.

Playlist: the list of the recordings to be played during a particular radio program or time period.

PBS (the Public Broadcasting Service): an independent affiliation of the nation's public TV stations.

PUR (Persons Using Radio): the number of people listening to radio at any particular time.

RAB (Radio Advertising Bureau): the sales and marketing arm of America's commercial radio-broadcast industry.

Radio's dayparts: Morning Drive-6:00 A.M. to 10:00 A.M. Monday through Friday; Midday-10:00 A.M. to 3:00 P.M. Monday through Friday; Afternoon Drive-3:00 P.M. to 7:00 P.M. Monday through Friday; Evening-7:00 P.M. to Midnight Monday through Sunday; Weekend-6:00 A.M. to 7:00 P.M.

Rating: the audience of a radio or television program as estimated by survey; listeners divided by population equals Rating percentage.

Reach: the estimated number of different people or households who saw or heard a broadcast, or are exposed to a commercial schedule.

Satellite: a device launched into orbit around the earth.

Satellite station: a station that has made a rebroadcast arrangement with a primary broadcaster to service an area not normally reached by the parent station.

Scatter market: the buying of TV commercial time after a season begins, as distinguished from up-front buying.

Share: the percentage of households using TV or radio tuned to a specific station or network.

Shoulder programming: programming before and after a major event like the Super Bowl, and designed to take advantage of that event's large audience.

Spot sale: commercial time bought in specific markets only, rather than along the whole network.

Superstation: a station whose programming is carried by satellite to cable households outside its local market.

Sweeps: seasonal periods when the size of TV and radio audiences are used to establish a base for the price charged for commercials or individual shows.

Syndication: the after-market for a TV show or movie originally run on a network and then sold or bartered to individual stations across the country. In first-run syndication, shows are produced specifically for the syndication market.

Telestrator: a video chalkboard device used in sports broadcasting to explain plays or sequences.

Transmitter: a tall tower that sends a radio station's signal to its listening area.

Transponder: a radio, radar, or sonar transceiver on a satellite that automatically transmits a signal upon reception of a designated incoming signal. It then receives, amplifies and transmits the signals back to earth. Stations receive these signals at satellite earth terminals and send them via cable to subscribers' homes.

TSA (Total Survey Area): an area including all countries where there is important listening to radio stations located in the metro survey area.

TV's Dayparts: the separation of a broadcasting day into nine segments.

UHF (Ultrahigh Frequency): the TV band in the electronic spectrum from 470 to 890 megahertz, encompassing channels fourteen through eighty-three in the United States and Canada.

Upfront: a period of a few summer days when advertisers buy 60 to 90 percent of a network's entire commercial-time inventory in return for network guarantees that the advertiser will reach a specified minimum audience and agree to commit to an annual spending schedule. If the network fails to meet these audience guarantees, they usually give the advertiser extra commercial spots known as make-goods.

VHF (Very High Frequency): the TV band in the electronic spectrum from 30 to 300 megahertz, encompassing channels one through thirteen in the United States and Canada.

Videotape: a magnetic tape on which the electronic impulses produced by the video and audio portions of a TV program or motion picture are recorded. Use of this tape allows for speedy playback and editing of film.

Voice-over: a recorded voice (also called a "tell") that describes or interprets the video portion; an off-camera announcer.

Zapping: TV-commercial avoidance accomplished by channel switching—generally via remote control. Zapping also refers to deletion of commercials during VCR recording.

RECOMMENDED READING

BOOKS

Agee, Warren K., Philip H. Ault, and Edwin Emery. *Introduction to Mass Communications*. 9th edition. New York: Harper & Row, 1991.

Arbitron Cable Dictionary. New York: Arbitron Co., Inc., 1981.

Auletta, Ken. *Three Blind Mice*. New York: Random House, 1991.

Bagdikian, Ben H. *The Media Monopoly*. Boston: Beacon Press, 1983.

Beville, Hugh Malcolm, Jr. *Audience Ratings: Radio, Television and Cable*. Hillsdale, NJ: Lawrence Erlbaum Associates, 1985.

Blair, Gwenda. *Almost Golden: Jessica Savitch and the Selling of Television News*. New York: Simon and Schuster, 1988.

Bliss, Edward, Jr. *Now the News: The Story of Broadcast Journalism*. New York: Columbia University Press, 1991.

Blum, Richard A., and Richard D. Lindheim. *Inside Television Producing*. Stoneham, MA: Focal Press, 1991.

————. *Primetime: Network Television Programming*. Boston: Focal Press, 1987.

Bone, Jan. *Opportunities in Cable Television*. Lincolnwood, IL: VGM Career Horizons, 1993.

Book, Albert C., and Norman D. Cary. *The Radio and Television Commercial*. Chicago: Crain Books, 1978.

Boyer, Peter J. *Who Killed CBS?: The Undoing of America's Number One News Network*. New York: Random House, 1988.

Brenner, Alfred. *The TV Scriptwriter's Handbook*. Cincinnati: Writer's Digest Books, 1985.

Broadcasting & Cable Market Place. New Providence, NJ: R.R. Bowker, Annual.

Brooks, Tim, and Earle Marsh. *The Complete Directory to Prime Time Network TV Shows: 1946–Present*. (3rd rev. ed.) New York: Ballantine Books, 1985.

Brown, Les. *Les Brown's Encyclopedia of Television*. New York: Zoetrope, 1982.

Burrows, William E. *On Reporting the News*. New York: Simon and Schuster, 1985.

Castleman, Harry, and Walter J. Podrazik. *Watching TV: Four Decades of American Television*. New York: McGraw-Hill, 1982.

Christiansen, Mark, and Cameron Staith. *The Sweeps: Behind the Scenes in Network TV*. New York: William Morrow and Company, Inc., 1984.

Cleary, Beverly. *Ramona Quimby: The Making of a Television Film*. New York: Dell, 1988.

Coleman, Howard W. *Case Studies in Broadcast Management: Radio and Television*. (2nd ed. rev. and enl.) Mamaroneck, NY: Hastings House, 1978.

Craft, Christine. *Too Old, Too Ugly and Not Deferential to Men*. Rocklin, CA: Prima Pub. and Comm., 1988.

Ellerbee, Linda. *"And So it Goes": Adventures in TV*. New York: G.P. Putnam's Sons, 1986.

Ellis, Elmo I. *Opportunities in Broadcasting Careers*. Lincolnwood, IL: VGM Career Horizons, 1992.

First 50 Years of Broadcasting, The. New York: Broadcasting Publications, 1982.

Fornatale, Peter, and Joshua E. Mills. *Radio in the Television Age*. Woodstock, NY: The Overlook Press, 1980.

Gitlin, Todd. *Inside Prime Time*. New York: Pantheon Books, 1985.

Goldberg, Robert, and Gerald Jay Goldberg. *Anchors: Brokaw, Jennings, Rather and the Evening News*. Secaucus, NJ: Carol Publishing Group, 1990.

Goodell, Gregory. *Independent Feature Film Production: A Complete Guide from Concept through Distribution*. New York: St. Martin's Press, 1982.

Gradus, Ben. *Directing the Television Commercial*. Mamaroneck, NY: Hastings House, 1981.

Grenade, Charles, Jr., and Margaret G. Butt. *The American Film Institute Guide to College Courses in Film and Television*. Princeton, NJ: Peterson's Guides, Annual.

Hilliard, Robert L. *Radio Broadcasting: An Introduction to the Sound Medium*. White Plains, NY: Longman Publishing Group, 1985.

———. *Writing for Television and Radio*. (5th ed.) Belmont, CA: Wadsworth Publications, 1991.

Katahn, T.L. *Reading for a Living: How to be a Professional Story Analyst for Film & Television*. Blue Arrow Books, 1990.

Kuralt, Charles. *A Life on the Road*. New York: G.P. Putnam's Sons, 1990.

Leonard, Bill. *In the Storm of the Eye: A Lifetime at CBS*. New York: G.P. Putnam's Sons, 1987.

Levinson, Richard, and William Link. *Off Camera: Conversations with the Makers of Prime-Time Television*. New York: Plume, 1986.

———. *Stay Tuned: An Inside Look at the Making of Prime Time Television*. New York: St. Martin's Press, 1981.

Lichter, S. Robert, et al. *The Media Elite: America's New Powerbrokers*. Mamaroneck, NY: Hastings House, 1990.

MacRae, Donald I. *Television Production: An Introduction*. New York: Routledge Chapman & Hall, 1982.

McCabe, Peter. *Bad News at Black Rock: The Sell-out of CBS News*. New York: Arbor House, 1987.

McNeil, Alex. *Total Television: A Comprehensive Guide to Programming from 1948 to the Present*. (2nd ed.) New York: Penguin Books, 1984.

Matusow, Barbara. *The Evening Stars: The Making of the Network News Anchor*. Boston: Houghton Mifflin Co., 1983.

Osgood, Charles. *The Osgood Files*. New York: Putnam Publishing Group, 1991.

Pearlman, Donn. *Breaking into Broadcasting: Getting a Good Job in Radio or TV—Out Front or Behind the Scenes*. Chicago: Bonus Books, 1986.

Reed, Maxine K., and Robert M. Reed. *Career Opportunities in TV, Cable and Video*. (3rd ed.) New York: Facts on File, 1990.

Roman, James W. *Cablemania: The Cable Television Sourcebook*. Englewood Cliffs, NJ: Prentice-Hall, 1983.

Root, Wells, *Writing the Script: A Practical Guide for Films and Television*. New York: Holt Rinehart & Winston, 1980.

Rowlands, Avril. *The Production Assistant in TV and Video*. Stoneham, MA: Focal Press, 1987.

Sanders, Marlene, and Marcia Rock. *Waiting for Prime Time: The Women of TV News*. Urbana, IL: University of Illinois Press, 1988.

Shanks, Bob. *The Primal Screen: How to Write, Sell & Produce Movies for Television: With Compete Script of Drop-Out Father*. New York: Norton, 1986.

Shannon, Robert L. *Break into Broadcasting*. New York: Carlton Press, 1990.

Shook, Frederick. *Television Field Production & Reporting*. White Plains, NY: Longman, 1988.

Shook, Frederick, and Dan Lattimore. *The Broadcast News Process*. Englewood, CO: Morton Publishing Company, 1987.

Silver, David. *How to Pitch and Sell Your TV Script*. Cincinnati: Writer's Digest Books, 1990.

Smith, Betsy Covington. *Breakthrough: Women in Television*. New York: Walter & Co., 1981.

Smith, F. Leslie. *Perspective on Radio and Television: Telecommunications in the United States*. (2nd ed.) New York: Harper & Row, 1985.

Smith, Perry M. *How CNN Fought the War: A View from the Inside*. New York: Carol Publishing Group, 1991.

Smith, Sally Bedell. *In All His Glory: The Life of William S. Paley—The Legendary Tycoon and His Brilliant Circle.* New York: Simon and Schuster, 1990.

Stucker, Steve. *How to Get a Job in Radio: Proven Techniques to Save Time, Money & Get You on the Airwaves.* Albuquerque, NM: Stucker Publications, 1990.

Terrace, Vincent. *The Complete Encyclopedia of Television Programs, 1947–1985.* New York: Zoetrope, 1986.

Trotta, Liz. *Fighting for Air: In the Trenches with Television News.* New York: Simon and Schuster, 1991.

Video Tape Editing. Stoneham, MA: Focal Press, 1989.

Whitfield, Stephen E., and Gene Roddenberry. *The Making of Star Trek.* (Illus.) New York: Ballantine, 1986.

PAMPHLETS

Careers in Broadcast News. A single free copy (with stamped self-addressed 6" x 9" envelope) is available from Radio Television News Directors Association, 1717 DeSales Street, N.W., Washington, DC 20006.

Careers in Cable. $3.50 per copy. Write to the National Cable Television Association, 1724 Massachusetts Avenue, N.W., Washington, DC 20036.

Careers in Radio. $3.50 per copy prepaid. Write to the Publications Department, National Association of Broadcasters, 1771 N Street, N.W., Washington, DC 20036.

Careers in Television. $3.50 per copy prepaid. Write to the Publications Department, National Association of Broadcasters, 1771 N Street, N.W., Washington, DC 20036.

Women on the Job: Careers in the Electronic Media. A single free copy is available from American Women in Radio and Television, Inc., 1101 Connecticut Avenue, N.W., Washington, DC 20036, or from the Women's Bureau, U.S. Department of Labor, 200 Constitution Avenue, N.W., Washington, DC 20010.

INDEX